CAN PEACE RESEARCH MAKE PEACE?

Can Peace Research Make Peace?
Lessons in Academic Diplomacy

TIMO KIVIMÄKI
University of Helsinki, Finland
and
East Asian Peace Program, Uppsala University, Sweden

Routledge
Taylor & Francis Group

LONDON AND NEW YORK

First published 2012 by Ashgate Publishing

Published 2016 by Routledge
2 Park Square, Milton Park, Abingdon, Oxon OX14 4RN
711 Third Avenue, New York, NY 10017, USA

First issued in paperback 2017

Routledge is an imprint of the Taylor & Francis Group, an informa business

British Library Cataloguing in Publication Data
Kivimäki, Timo.
  Can peace research make peace? : lessons in academic diplomacy.
  1. Peace--Research. 2. Conflict management--Philosophy.
  3. Ethnic conflict--Indonesia--Kalimantan Barat.
  4. Conflict management--Indonesia--Kalimantan Barat.
  I. Title
  327.1'72'072-dc23

Library of Congress Cataloging-in-Publication Data
Kivimäki, Timo.
  Can peace research make peace? : lessons in academic diplomacy / by Timo Kivimäki.
    p. cm. -- (International relations monographs)
  Includes bibliographical references and index.
  ISBN 978-1-4094-5202-7 (hardback) 1. Peace--Research. I. Title.
  JZ5534.K59 2012
  303.6'6--dc23

                                                                    2012018435

ISBN 13: 978-1-138-11552-1 (pbk)
ISBN 13: 978-1-4094-5202-7 (hbk)

Contents

List of Figures and Tables

Figures

Tables

Preface

Indonesia's West Kalimantan province has suffered from communal conflict, and at the turn of the millennium the province became infamous for two massive cannibalistic riots. Although the large-scale violence has not continued, there have been smaller incidents with several people killed every year, and the conflict's disputes have not been solved. Since 2001 I have led a peace studies network in East Asia, with vigorous local activities in West Kalimantan. This network has been placed on the platform of the ASEM (Asia–Europe Meeting) Education Hub (and previously on the EU–Asia Link program) and it has been working in the conflict areas of West Kalimantan offering teaching on conflict resolution and peace studies in several MA classes at the local Tanjungpura University. One of the classes has been targeted at the very same ethnic leaders who mobilized the mass riots and later tried to make peace with each other. On December 15, 2008, this class stepped out of its educational setting and transferred itself into a peace process under the auspices of the vice president of Indonesia. This transition could offer a model of how purely academic work can serve the purpose of capacity-building for peace and actual pre-negotiation for a peace process. It also offers the inspiration and the main research question for this book. Could experiences in West Kalimantan point to a more general strategy of practical peace research?

The present book is essentially a product of this experience of capacity-building in conflict management in West Kalimantan. Activity aimed at contributing to peace aided me in the diagnosis of the conflict in West Kalimantan. At the same time, my knowledge of the path to conflict in West Kalimantan was constantly tested by practice; whenever blocking some paths to conflicts failed to reduce violence, the diagnosis had to be revised. At the same time whenever something seemed to "work for peace," it also gave some empirical support to our understanding of the dynamics of conflict.

While teaching the stakeholders of the West Kalimantan conflict ways in which other parties in various conflicts in the world have managed to help reduce violence, I learnt a lot from the "students." These specialists related my lessons of comparative conflict studies to the conditions in which they themselves were experts. This is why this study cannot start without a big thanks to the police, military, ethnic leaders and civil bureaucracy of the province and districts of West Kalimantan. The two *bupatis* (heads of districts) of Bengkayang and Sambas, Mr. Jakobus Luna and Mr. Burhanuddin A. Rasyid, deserve special thanks for their analyses of the two main conflicts. To Mr. Burhanuddin I also owe my nickname in West Kalimantan, Pak Long, which was quickly picked up by the local and provincial media. In addition to the two *bupatis*, I would like to express my gratitude to the leader of the Malay association of Sambas, Mr. H. Darwis; the

Madurese leaders Mr. H. Rupaat and Haji Umar Ali (leaders of Gamisma); the leader of Dayak community in Bengkayang, Dr. Yustinus Suherman Acap (the hero of the Bengkayang peace process); and the chairman of West Kalimantan's Inter-Religious Communication Forum, Prof. Rector Haitami Salim. I am especially grateful to the two police chiefs of West Kalimantan, Brig. Gen. Iwan Pandjiwinata and Brig. Gen. Erwin T.P.L. Tobing, who in addition to teaching me about the conflict in the province were open-minded enough to allow me to offer my comparative conflict studies perspectives in police classes in the main conflict districts of Singkawang, Sambas, Landak, Bengkayang, and Pontianak. These police chiefs were not consumed by a paranoia that might have forced them to play safe and end the suspicious activity of a foreigner like me. The above-mentioned people were my primary teachers in addition to being the main drivers of peaceful development in West Kalimantan.

In addition to province-level administration, I have been privileged to be able to collaborate with the office of the vice president of Indonesia, from which I was able to learn a lot. The political deputy of the vice president, Professor Djohermansyah Djohan, and the Head of European Affairs of the vice president's office, Mr. Santos Winarso deserve special thanks.

The team of the Universitas Tanjungpura (UNTAN), under the leadership of Prof. Syarif I. Alqadrie, oversaw my operations in West Kalimantan. I would not have been able to learn much about West Kalimantan without the patient guidance of Prof. Alqadrie and Mr. Erdi Abidin, who in a more academic manner were my main teachers of the specific details about the province. The amazing contacts that Professor Alqadrie had among the stakeholders of West Kalimantan, and the respect in which they held him, were the starting point of my studies in West Kalimantan. The stakeholder classes would not have been possible without the contacts, authority and organization of Prof. Alqadrie and Mr. Erdi Abidin. A foreigner could never have started any of that, no matter how many ideas and theories he might have had for West Kalimantan.

My ten years of education in West Kalimantan were funded by the European Commission's Asia Link program, the Finnish Foreign Ministry, the Finnish Embassy in Jakarta, the International Media Support (Copenhagen) and the Asia–Europe Foundation. I am also very grateful to these organizations for their great work for peace that has, as a side product, introduced me to the interesting complexities of the conflict in West Kalimantan. My research on West Kalimantan was funded by the Uppsala University's Program on East Asian Peace. The text of this book was edited by Mr. Jonathan Price, and the language editing was sponsored by the Finnish Foreign Ministry. I am grateful for this, and I know that my readers will be even more so.

In addition to the organization and leadership of local operations in the capacity-building program the UNTAN team was also in the most concrete manner my teacher on West Kalimantan. Over hundreds of hours they patiently tried to explain me, while we were driving to Sambas, Landak, or Bengkayang, while we were planning events, or while we were relaxing after long working days, how the provincial administration worked, how the ethnic organizations were structured, how the central administration managed the province and many other things that have been invaluable for my understanding of West Kalimantan and conflict. I am very grateful for this.

I am also most grateful to my translator, Mr. Segu Atio, who later joined my program as a lecturer, for his tireless and patient explanations regarding community relations, educational system, position and history of the ethnic Chinese community. Isak Suhadi, Ahmad Hanafi, and many others from the UNTAN Team deserve my gratitude for invaluable advice and services to the capacity-building program.

It is clear that my introduction to the problems of West Kalimantan was heavily dependent on the roles of Prof. Alqadrie and Mr. Erdi Abidin. This has to be kept in mind when reading my analysis. I will not blame anyone for the limitations of my own understanding let alone my misunderstandings of the province, but I do realize that my access to information and discussions was selected by the limitations of my main contact points in the university. Prof. Alqadrie is of the royal family of the Pontianak Malay Sultanate, and Mr. Erdi is also Malay. I tried to supplement my contacts by using the "snowball method" of meeting people my informants suggested. Furthermore, I occasionally moved around in the province by relying on the help of almost randomly selected activists. Furthermore, my good Acehnese friend, from my activities helping to prepare the Aceh Peace process, Mr. Delsy Ronnie, worked in West Kalimantan for a number of years, introducing me to many Madurese activists and internally displaced persons to whom I would not have been introduced by my regular hosts from UNTAN. While I want to express my sincere gratitude to these "alternative hosts" I should also, in the name of sincerity, warn my readers of the fact that the balance of my data collection must have been influenced by the royal, Malay identity of my main mentor in West Kalimantan, Prof. Alqadrie.

I am also grateful to the eminent scholars, especially Dr. Gerry van Klinken, and Dr. Isak Svensson, whose publications and comments have offered me so much scholarly inspiration—and occasionally also harsh criticism of my work and my approaches in West Kalimantan. Van Klinken also participated in the capacity-building project.

I would like my readers to see my work as a contribution from a process that has utilized a dialogue between comparative-conflict expertise and area-specialist perspectives. In this process my own contribution has been on the comparative side, while the local stakeholders and local intellectuals, as well as these semi-local international names, have offered the element of local expertise. Thus this book attempts to be informed by local perspectives while mainly contributing to theorizing on what different, pragmatic people could do to reduce violence in conflict areas such as West Kalimantan.

While my intention in this book is to identify as many of the opportunities that exist to help peace, it is unavoidable that my investigation tends to focus on those processes that I have myself been part of. This is partly because those are the ones I know most intimately, but also because these processes are the result of my identification of what can be done. The fact that I talk more about initiatives I know most about should not be interpreted as disrespect towards those initiatives that other scholars have taken, but to which I give less space in this book. Thus the final word before the introduction of the objectives of the study will be an apology. The work of many scholars, activists, and other intellectuals has been undoubtedly valuable and worth noting, even if I have not specifically taken it into account.

Timo Kivimäki, 2012

Chapter 1

Introduction

Aims and Objectives

West Kalimantan, a province of over four million people, is among the four poorest provinces of Indonesia. In Jakarta West Kalimantan is seen as one of the proofs of Indonesia's multiculturalism since its heterogeneous population has never explicitly challenged their Indonesian national identity.

The large territory of this sparsely populated province has often been considered a convenient destination for the relocation of people from the overpopulated islands of Java, Sumatra and Madura. Originally West Kalimantan, or at least its leadership, was eager to cherish its existing heterogeneity and even expand it with transmigrants from the population-dense provinces on the islands of Java and Madura. In addition to the populations that are sometimes considered "migrant" there are approximately 34% Dayaks and the approximately 34% of Malays who consider themselves local and the indigenous people of West Kalimantan. While the indigenousness of the Dayak people is undisputed in West Kalimantan, the status of the Malays is debated (Davidson 2007: 242). Of course, the entire concept of indigenousness in Indonesia is debated. Former President Sukarno claimed that almost all Indonesians are indigenous to Indonesia while local indigenousness is irrelevant. For others, indigenousness is even more local, so that Sambas Malays should not be considered indigenous in Pontianak. A local professor, Syarif I. Alqadrie, has suggested that an Indonesian could become "local" in West Kalimantan after 25 years' residence. All this is, of course, constituted in interpretations.

The common characteristic of the conflicts in West Kalimantan has so far been the theme of "localness," and the rights that belong either to all Indonesians in the province or only to the "local" communities. This way the conflict in West Kalimantan belongs to the large category of ethnic/community intra-state conflicts that Fearon and Laitin (2011) call sons-of-soil conflicts.

West Kalimantan has never given much trouble to the central administration; its conflicts have focused on intra-provincial issues and they have never been seen as something challenging the unity of Indonesia. Yet the conflict challenges that West Kalimantan has experienced are common to most areas of Indonesia. What are the rights of locals in developing their local rule and what are the rights of people who become framed as something less than locals? These questions are central for West Kalimantan as well as for the rest of Indonesia, and for many other countries too. According to Fearon and Laitin (2011), one-third of the world's ethnic intra-state conflicts (since the early 1990s, more than a quarter of all intra-state conflicts) deal with the question of the rights of "local" communities in relation to communities that "locals" consider migrant communities from other areas of the country. In this sense, the problem West Kalimantan experiences with conflict is general, and lessons from the West Kalimantan experiences are crucial not only for Indonesia but for many if not most developing countries, and for many developed countries as well. The problem of accommodating the coexistence of people who see themselves as locals and people the locals see as visitors, migrants or non-indigenous is not uncommon in the world. However, the problems of West Kalimantan ought to be solved for the province's own sake, too.

This book looks at the community conflict the province is suffering and tries to approach it from a practical, problem-solving point of view. I reserve the term "conflict" in this book to refer to violent, destructive disputes between any armed parties, and talk about non-violent disputes simply as non-violent disputes. This practice allows discussion on constructive disputes (Kriesberg 1998) and yet it complies with the general negative connotation of conflicts in conflict-prevention literature. When the police or militias kill civilians who are defended by armed fighters (Malay, Dayak or Madurese militias, for example), as in the Sambas and Bengkayang riots, we can consider these situations conflicts, while if they kill individuals with no armed protectors, this should be called something else (terrorism, democide, or one-sided violence, for example). My definition of a conflict does not make a distinction between conflicts where the state is a party and violence where state is not involved as a conflicting party, as is the practice in most of the conflict dataset projects, such as the PRIO and Uppsala data projects, which define conflict as "a contested incompatibility that concerns government and/or territory where the use of armed force between two parties, of which at least one is the government of a state, results in at least 25 battle-related deaths" (Gleditsch et al. 2002).

This book tries to mobilize the scholarly findings and the theoretical perspectives of peace research for the benefit of West Kalimantan while also opening the experiences of that region to general theory of peace and conflict. A pragmatic approach to theory and knowledge will be developed, and this pragmatism will then be used to match the analysis of sources of conflict and efforts to build peace in West Kalimantan. In this matching process, the diagnosis of conflict informs the development of prescriptions to peace-makers, while experiences of success and failure in conflict prevention advise the diagnostic process. True understanding of the conflict, in this pragmatic setting, means epistemic preparedness to act for peace. This is why the book—instead of attempting to predict something or seeking for the determinants of the conflict, or understanding it as a product of its historical context—puts together the analysis of conflict (Chapter 3) and the experiences of its prevention (Chapter 4). To identify the ways to redirect developments into a more peaceful direction requires a pragmatic understanding of the conflict, which is then tested by experiences of conflict prevention. Pragmatic knowledge is the prerequisite for successful conflict prevention, while the success of any peace action verifies the pragmatic understanding that underlies it.

A simple analogy of a path with several junctures where different actors can choose different directions will be adopted. In this analogy the diagnosis will be focused on the junctures where the path to the conflict can continue, or where it can be blocked or redirected to more peaceful directions. The way in which West Kalimantan resorted to violence is analyzed in order to avoid that path, and other possible paths to conflict. Because I have myself been involved in conflict-prevention capacity-building and the actual initiation of a peace process in West Kalimantan, the interaction between peace action and analysis of the conflict path is very apparent. Conclusions on the nature of the path to conflict are in a very concrete way drawn from the experiences of "what works and what does not" in the prevention of conflicts.

Peace research in this book is defined as scholarship that takes a negative normative stand on political violence and relates the interest of knowledge production to this stand (Galtung 1969). Peace research, thus, is academic investigation that produces knowledge that helps to prevent political violence. On the other hand, the perspective of peace research is structural or collective rather than agent-centric. Peace refers to a state of affairs where political violence is minimal for all actors under scrutiny. This way peace research differs from the actor-centered *security studies*, where the focus is the safety from political violence of one actor under scrutiny. It is not analytically possible to advocate for the destruction of a village and its people in the name of peace, whilst it is possible to destroy an enemy village in the name of security.[1]

This book focuses on the prevention of political violence that intentionally injures and kills, rather than opening up to more positive concepts of peace and structural concepts of violence (Galtung and Höivik 1971). Using various kinds of peace-focused approaches to research, my own approach to scholarship, truth, knowledge, and explanation/understanding will be explicated in Chapter 2 of this book.

My analysis of the opportunities for scholars in peace-making utilizes the ideas of John Burton (1990), Peter Wallensteen (2009), and Herbert C. Kelman (1973, 1997) on conflict problem-solving. Borrowing from the analysis by Peter Wallensteen (2009) of his own work in the resolution of the Bouganville Rebellion, I named peace action by academics *academic diplomacy*. However, my definition of academic diplomacy is broader. Wallensteen's analysis of his academic diplomacy in the resolution of the Bouganville Rebellion starts from the record of a phone call where he is being invited to advise on dispute resolution

---

1 Security studies can contribute to the objectives of peace studies, but they do not need to as their concern is the security of an actor they focus on. Galtung (1972) saw security studies and peace research as almost oppositional terms, while Buzan and Hansen (2009) see peace research as a theme of security studies. I find the difference of perspectives of the two rather fundamental as often they direct action into two opposite directions.

in Papua New Guinea. Kelman and Burton, on the other hand, are mostly focused on dispute resolution among intellectuals that has an indirect influence on conflict. Typically, these intellectuals are their students and thus it is easy for them to get an entry point for discussions. But academic diplomacy has a lot of opportunities already before the phone rings and one is being invited to assist a peace process. Getting conflicting parties to the negotiation table often requires much more than just an announcement of when a lecture on peace processes starts. If one tries to help conflict prevention among the conflicting parties before their leaders have found it possible to launch a peace process and before they have decided to invite outsiders to facilitate their peace processes, the main practical task is to find framings and entry points that provide justifications for the conflicting parties to participate in conflict-prevention activities. Academic peace work in West Kalimantan has been mostly focused on the process before the ethnic leaders were ready to sit down and talk. Furthermore, while the centre of attention in conflicts that Kelman, Burton, and Wallensteen have facilitated has been the resolution of the disputes that motivate conflict, motivations can be of secondary importance in some other conflicts. In West Kalimantan, for example, opportunities and antagonistic identities play a more crucial role than explicit disputes, and thus academic diplomacy has to extend far beyond dispute resolution workshops. This is what is addressed in this book. The aim is to reveal the menu of options for academic peace diplomacy, and for that the existing peace research literature is just a beginning.

Conflict in West Kalimantan

Since 1950 in West Kalimantan there have been thirteen conflicts between Dayak and Madurese communities, one between Dayak and Chinese communities, one between Malay and Chinese communities, and two between Sambas Malay (and Dayak) and Madurese communities. The most serious of them are listed in Table 1.1.

Table 1.1   Main Conflicts in West Kalimantan

---

1. Conflict between Chinese and Dayaks after the takeover of Suharto, 1966–67.
2. Conflict between Madurese and Dayaks, 1967–68.
3. Conflict between Dayaks and Madurese, 1996–67 in the Inner Valley, Sanggau Ledo (Bengkayang district).
4. Conflict between Malays/Dayaks and Madurese, 1999, first in the Sambas district, with Dayak involvement, then in the town of Sambas, without Dayaks.

The number of fatalities from the conflicts in 1967 (between Dayaks and Chinese) and in 1967–68 (between Dayaks and the Madurese) have often been estimated at a few thousand (Davidson 2008: 12), primarily in the northern coastal and inner valley areas of the current Sambas district. Casualties from the riots in 1996–97 have been estimated from one to a few thousand, primarily in areas of the current Bengkayang district (then sub-district). Jamie Davidson (2007: 230) estimates the number of fatalities at 500–1,700 people while Dini Djalal estimates the number of casualties at a few thousand, basing his estimate on the accounts by Christian Church leaders (Djalal 1997). A Report by the National Development Planning Agency (Bappenas), UN Development Program (UNDP) and the Gadjah Madah University's Peace and Conflict Research Institute (Bappenas, PSPK-UGM and UNDP 2006: 143) puts the body count at 1,700 casualties.

The estimate for the Sambas riots in 1999 from the recent newspaper article (Harsono et al. 2009) on the "Pontianak Appeal" by 77 leading specialists in West Kalimantan issues was "at least 3000." Most other estimates are lower, however, ranging from the official 200 to a couple of thousand. Prasojo (2009: 1) estimates 1,000 casualties (but a typo has changed this estimate to one million). Susan Sim, who was on the scene right after the riots, guesses 1,000 battle deaths (*Strait Times*, March 28, 1999). Rizal Sukma, however, relying on official estimates, puts the number of fatalities at 150 (Sukma 2005: 4). The extremely violent way in which the killings were committed was intended to cause terror, and as a result of the last riot in 1999 almost 100,000 people, mainly of Madurese ethnic origin, were forced to escape from the district.[2]

A more detailed presentation of the conflict incidents is useful for the analysis of the nature of the conflict and the opportunities for its prevention. Borrowing from and modifying and updating the careful media analysis of violent incidents by Prasojo (2009) and Davidson (2008: 89–90) I present in Table 1.2 a fuller list of the main incidents.

The battle sites of the two main conflicts (in 1996–97 and 1999) can be found on Maps 1.1a and b. Map 1.1a locates the province as one of the many recent conflict provinces of Indonesia, while Map 1.1b locates the main areas of violence within the province.

---

2 According to the Internal Displacement Monitoring Center 2009, the number of displaced Madurese was 78,000 people (while in Central Kalimantan the number was more than double that). However, the 77 intellectuals writing "the Pontianak Appeal" (Harsono et al. 2009) talk about more than 100,000 Madurese internally displaced people (IDPs).

Table 1.2 Cases of Community Conflict in West Kalimantan since the 1950s

Time and place	Trigger (as it has been presented in the media)	Conflicting parties	National political context	Severity
Conflict 1: 1950, Samalantan	Fight between Dayak and Madurese individuals.	Dayak "local community" and Madurese "migrant community" in Samalantan.	New independence and new democracy.	Low.
Conflict 2: 1952, Coastal Sambas/Bengkayang	Theft of a fishing device by a Madurese from a Dayak.	First Dayak and Madurese youngsters, then entire local communities.	New democracy.	Low.
Conflict 3: 1967, Toho town in Pontianak district	Killing of a Dayak district leader by a Madurese youngster.	Dayak and Madurese communities.	Leadership transition plus consolidation of an authoritarian new order.	Mass conflict (high).
Conflict 4: 1967, Bengkayang	Killing of a Dayak traditional leader, framed by the military for the murder of a member of the ethnic Chinese community.	Dayak and Chinese communities.	Leadership transition plus consolidation of an authoritarian new order.	Mass conflict.
Conflict 5: 1968, Sungai Pinyuh	Killing of a Dayak district leader in Sungai Pinyuh by a Madurese as a result of a land-ownership registration issue.	Dayak and Madurese communities.	Leadership transition plus consolidation of an authoritarian new order.	Mass conflict.
Conflict 6: 1976, Sungai Pinyuh	Killing of a Dayak by a Madurese, as a result of a dispute over grazing of Madurese livestock.	Dayak and Madurese communities.	Authoritarian order.	Low.

Time and place	Trigger (as it has been presented in the media)	Conflicting parties	National political context	Severity
Conflict 7: 1977, Singkawang	Killing of a Dayak police officer by a Madurese as a consequence of a prohibition on the killer to date a Dayak girl, who was a relative of the victim.	Dayak and Madurese communities.	Authoritarian order.	Low: 5 fatalities (Davidson 2008: 89).
Conflict 8: 1979, Singkawang	A debt case, where a Dayak owed a Madurese. Led to a killing.	Dayak and Madurese communities.	Authoritarian order.	Low.
Conflict 9: 1979, Salamantan, Sambas (now Bengkayang)	Stabbing of a Dayak man by a Madurese, after a row regarding grazing for cattle.	Dayak and Madurese communities.	Authoritarian order.	Low.
Conflict 10: 1982, Pa' Kuching	A dispute about grazing by a Madurese on land owned by a Dayak. Led to the killing of the Dayak by the Madurese.	Dayak and Madurese communities.	Authoritarian order.	Intermediate level.
Conflict 11: 1983, Sungai Enau (Pontianak)	Land dispute that led to a killing of a Dayak by a Madurese.	Dayak and Madurese communities.	Authoritarian order.	Low.
Conflict 12: 1993, Pontianak	Religious issues led to a Madurese group burning a Christian church and a Catholic kindergarten (used by Dayaks).	Dayak and Madurese communities.	Authoritarian order.	Low.
Conflict 13: 1994, Ketapang	A Madurese stabbed a Dayak.	Dayak and Madurese communities.	Authoritarian order.	Low.

Time and place	Trigger (as it has been presented in the media)	Conflicting parties	National political context	Severity
Conflict 14: 1996–97, first in Ledo and Sanggau Ledo, then in Bengkayang, Sintang, Pontianak, Landak.*	Stabbing of two Dayaks by two young Madurese men. A dispute over an accused molestation of a girl, a relative of the victims.**	Dayak and Madurese communities.	Leadership transition plus transition from authoritarian centralist order to democratic de-centralist.	Mass violence.
Conflict 15: 1999, first in Sambas, then also in Bengkayang, Landak, Singkawang City and Pontianak district.	A Madurese passenger refused to pay a Malay conductor for a bus fare. Madurese burglary.	Sambas Malay (later Dayak) versus Madurese.	Leadership transition plus transition from authoritarian centralist order to democratic de-centralist.	Mass violence.
Conflict 16: 2001, Pontianak	Disagreements between Malay and Madurese traders. Violent election campaigning.	Madurese versus Malay.	Democracy in Indonesia plus socialization to democracy in West Kalimantan.	Moderate: 40 fatalities, (Davidson 2008: 7).
Conflict 17: 2010, Singkawang	Statement of a Chinese Mayor that insulted Malay. Chinese cultural statue.	Chinese Mayor + Chinese community vs. Malays + non-Chinese.	Democracy.	Low. Mass rioting with material losses, but no fatalities.

Notes: * Prasojo (2009) considers the events of 1996 and 1997 to be two separate conflicts. However, since the place and the dispute in the two episodes were the same, it probably makes more sense to consider the latter incident as the continuation of the former, in one conflict. At the same time, the latter event spread out to much larger areas; ** The claim of the girl's Dayak relatives is that she was harassed by two young Madurese men, while Madurese sources claim that there was no force involved in the encounter between the Madurese youngsters and the girl. I do not know which view is more truthful.

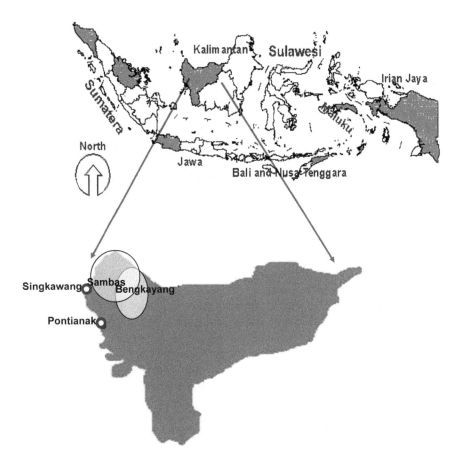

Figure 1.1   West Kalimantan in Indonesia (top) and Conflict Areas of West Kalimantan (bottom)

The conflict between the Dayaks and the Chinese still affects the society and the conflict situation in the province. The Chinese of the province are still wary of the "local communities" (AJ 2001, RR 2001, TT 2001)—the Dayaks and Malays—and this still affects the ethnic relations and balance of power in the province. However, the main influence of the conflict of 1967 is in the fact that it set a precedent for the pattern of ethnic conflict and ethnic cleansing in the province. This was the first case in which an ethnic minority was expelled from an area, and this pattern has continued in the two latest large-scale conflicts, between the Sambas Malay community and the Madurese and between the Bengkayang Dayak and the Madurese (Davidson 2008).

Otherwise, the two latest massive conflicts create the background for the tension and conflict in the area that still exists today. Many issues disputed then have still not been settled: The issue of Madurese rights to return to Sambas and Bengkayang is unsettled, the fate of the Madurese lands in these areas is unsettled, and the issue of who is and isn't local in West Kalimantan is unsettled, let alone the implications of that (Cornelis 2009). The recurrence of conflict on the very same issues is, therefore, possible. It is mainly the two last massive conflicts that influence the current occasional clashes and killings of the Madurese who try to visit or return to Sambas or Bengkayang (Tobing 2010). However, political and economic competition, crime, political statements and many other (sometimes very trivial) things sometimes spark conflict that easily aligns along ethnic and community lines (van Klinken 2007). The ways in which the two main conflicts were conducted has stigmatized the two indigenous ethnic groups and labeled whole groups for something a small amount of people did (Ali 2005, Bernardinus 2006). The two main conflict episodes, for example, both involved cannibalism. This has unfairly labeled some ethnic communities, while the false generalization has been also simultaneously useful, creating fear of offenders in these communities. At the same time it has of course been harmful for the community in its brutalization of the image of largely peaceful people.

Historically, conflict in West Kalimantan tends to emerge and re-emerge in a cyclical manner. According to Prof. Alqadrie's observations, conditions conducive to violence tend to reappear in West Kalimantan at thirty-year intervals: in the 1900s, 1930s, mid-1960s and mid/late 1990s (Alqadrie 2002).

Alqadrie's conflict cycles seem to coincide with Indonesian leadership generations: West Kalimantan seems to be violent whenever one generation is about to become too old to rule, and a new one feels confident about challenging the old one. Confusion about succession in a system that has weak institutions creates gainful opportunities and fuels conflict (Fearon 1995). Until recently Indonesia has lacked institutionalized mechanisms of leadership transition. This is why some scholars see transitions and other "critical junctures" as prone to ethnic violence in Indonesia (Bertrand 2004).

The latest violence was related to the fall of Suharto, and to the rapid Indonesian democratization that coincided with a radical decentralization program. Despite the fact that Suharto fell only in 1998, the expectation of his fall as well as the tension and competition related to it had already started early in 1996 (Eklöf 1999). Also decentralization, in the sense of practical expansion of the power of local people at the expense of the central administration in local affairs,[3] started as a practice where the local ethnic groups gained more representation in the leadership of the districts of West Kalimantan, much earlier than when it was formalized in law in 1999 (van Klinken 2007). By the time the first decentralization law had been accepted in parliament, five out of the seven posts of the district heads were in the hands of members of the local Dayak ethnic group (Davidson 2008: 119). Customary sanctions were used against business ventures as early as June 1997

---

3   This is the definition of the concept of decentralization used in this study.

(Davidson 2008: 121), and the competition for political offices had started as early as 1994 (van Klinken 2007).

The previous period of violence coincided with the transition to the new order from the rule of the first president, Sukarno (1964–67). Before that, in the 1930s, violence in West Kalimantan took place simultaneously with anti-colonial radicalization and the rise of the Sukarno generation in Indonesia. Clearly, the national realities of elite politics seem to influence the conflict pattern in West Kalimantan.

All the main periods of conflict in West Kalimantan are also periods when conflicts are more intensive in many other parts of Indonesia as well. The rise of the anti-colonialist generation sparked a longer period of violence in many parts of Indonesia, while the transitions from Sukarno to Suharto generated shorter but very intensive episodes of conflict in many parts of the country, including West Kalimantan. The transition to decentralization and democracy was violent in Poso, Ambon, North Maluku, Aceh, Papua and in Central Kalimantan, in addition to West Kalimantan.

It has been learned from comparative conflict analysis that low levels of per capita income lower the threshold of violence (Collier and Hoeffler 2004). In fact this is one of the most consistent generalizations in the study of intra-state conflicts. This could be one of the reasons why West Kalimantan, unlike many areas, was violent during the time when conflict was more common throughout Indonesia, but when still the vast majority of Indonesian provinces remained peaceful. Papua and East Timor, two other Indonesian provinces (East Timor was still a de facto province of Indonesia) among the four poorest provinces in Indonesia, were also in flames during the transition to democracy and decentralization.

The shape of the front lines of conflict also testifies to the linkages between national and provincial West Kalimantan conflict realities. When the Indonesia of the 1960s was pursuing those loyal to communist China who threatened the power of the new right-wing dictator, Suharto, West Kalimantan experienced violent riots against the ethnic Chinese (Davidson 2008, Feith 1968). Again, when Indonesia was engaged in one of world's most ambitious decentralization processes in the mid-1990s, West Kalimantan experienced two violent conflicts between "local races" and "migrant races." While the main legal instruments of decentralization were from 1999, 2001, and 2004, the practice of decentralization had already started in West Kalimantan in the mid-1990s with the expansion of local participation in local administration. Unlike in East Kalimantan, which remained calm, in West Kalimantan the power of the Javanese elite collapsed in the 1990s and they were gradually replaced by officials from local ethnicities soon after the beginning of the 1990s (Bouvier and Smith 2006, De Jonge and Nooteboom 2006).

Because of this apparent sensitivity towards national developments, explanations of the conflict in West Kalimantan should not disregard greater, national-level conflict tendencies. I will make occasional references to the similarities and differences between the conflict in West Kalimantan and the other conflict areas in my analysis of the different aspects of the local conflict. For the practical objectives of this study, it is important to keep in mind the opportunities to influence West Kalimantan on the national level. However, the main focus of this study will be on the provincial level. This is because local activities are more important for the creation of resilience in West Kalimantan and for the ability to avoid involvement in antagonistic divisions elsewhere. Furthermore, the fact that transitions within the context of democracy do not tend to be as dramatic as those within a national context of authoritarianism might suggest that the national context in Indonesia no longer provides as conducive an environment for conflict in West Kalimantan.

How Did the Two Main Conflicts Begin and Proceed?

In addition to an overview of the general conflict situation in West Kalimantan, it is useful for the reader at this stage to be introduced to the chronology of the two main conflicts that condition current conflict realities in West Kalimantan. This will be done here before the tools of analysis are introduced, even if that exposes this chapter to the shallowness of the analysis. On the level of observable behavior any story of how the conflicts started and how they proceeded would make little sense. Description of who did what and how would not help my understanding unless I managed to achieve a "thicker" description of the meanings of actions, agents, and contexts. Yet, before a deeper analysis of what created the path to conflict it is necessary to describe the situation on the shallow level of behavior and observable consequences.

In the 1990s the districts of Bengkayang and Sambas were both part of the same Sambas district. The visible provocation for the conflict of 1996–97, in Bengkayang, took place in December 1996, during a music festival in the sub-district of Ledo. According to a Dayak eye-witness (Dede 2006), two young men from a nearby village in the sub-district of Sanggau Ledo harassed or tried to kidnap a local girl, but were stopped by her two uncles. An anonymous Madurese source (Sedau 3 2006) claims that the encounter between the Dayak girl and the Madurese men did not involve anything involuntary on the girl's part, but that the protection of her reputation was based on the racist conviction of the uncles that she should not see Madurese men. It is not possible for this study to investigate whether my Dayak or my Madurese informant is right. This first incident of violence on December 27, 1996 quickly led to another on December 29, when the perpetrators took some of their friends from Sanggau Ledo to the village of Tanjung in Ledo to a pop concert. There they found the uncles in the early hours of the next day and stabbed them in revenge for the uncles' rude treatment of them (Dede 2006).

To understand the initial moves in the conflict, it is not only significant that the two perpetrators were from another village; their ancestors were also from another island, Madura. It is also significant that the girl was a local Dayak celebrity, known to most in the village of Ledo. Thus the perpetrators represented "threatening outsiders" while the victim of harassment symbolized "localness." It was easy for local men to show their loyalty to Dayakness, and to the idea of indigenous rights, by defending this celebrity. The *Asia Times* (February 20, 1997) described the campaign by the Dayaks in its headline as "Fight to the death for tribal rights."

At the same time, defending the honor of a woman in this culture of hypermasculinity (Nilan 2009), is an opportunity for men to display their "heroism" and "masculinity." Violence was not a bad instrument for this, given the local cultural context of hegemonic hypermasculinity.[4] In fact it seems that quite a number of the provoking incidents in conflicts of West Kalimantan involve accusations of sexual assaults, while many Dayak and Malay descriptions of the arrogance of the Madurese also make reference to the perception that the Madurese men do not "allow" "locals" to marry "their" women (interviews with Leo 2007 in Bengkayang and a village head in Tanjung Keracut 2003).

All this took place in the context of harsh political and economic competition between the Dayaks and the Madurese, competition in which many local Dayaks felt the Madurese were using criminal means and were succeeding too well (Andoth 2006, Dede 2006). Thus, in this case, for the Dayak men who ended up punishing the two young Madurese men and their communities who had protected these Madurese perpetrators, violence could have served many purposes.

For the Madurese perpetrators, equality was at stake. Madurese people are often believed to be good lovers, in fact better than most Indonesians. The attempt was often made to use the myth of sexual superiority to balance the inferiority of the Madurese in a culture affected by the indigenousness discourse. On an individual level some Madurese wanted to show that they should not have to be shy of their ethnic origin when dealing with the opposite sex—unless the assumption was that they were generally less than equal to the local people. Despite the culture and the pattern of avoiding ethnically mixed marriages (Bouvier, de Jonge and Smith 2006), making advances towards local girls, even a local celebrity, was considered a good strategy to demonstrate the equality (or even superiority) of the Madurese vis-à-vis the local Dayaks.

The uncles were stabbed with a traditional Madurese knife (Dede 2006), suggesting perhaps that the violent act of these Madurese perpetrators was more than an individual act. Perhaps it was to demonstrate that the Madurese demand for equality was backed up by violence if necessary, regardless of the ancient Dayak tradition against blood-letting. In interviews with Dayak informants it became clear that despite the violent history of the Dayaks the norm against blood-letting was considered sacred (Luna 2006): "Spilling of the blood of any Dayak is an embarrassment for all Dayaks" (Benediktus 2007). According to one

---

4 "Hegemonic masculinity" describes a normative or "ideal" type of masculinity occurring in specific times and places (Connell 2002). When hypermasculine identities are hegemonic, power-greedy, heroic, and violent conceptions of masculinity rule, and men who deviate from this ideal are not considered to be really true men at all.

Dayak student, spilling blood of a Dayak is followed by an "automatic reaction of mobilization" (Hilarinus 2009).

This hinted at a communal significance that these individual actions had for both sides, which was possibly one of the reasons why a community rising followed very rapidly after the initial action. The lack of confidence in the police settling this issue was another reason. First a gang of Dayak youths from Ledo and Sanggau Ledo started to form. A revenge action was then quickly planned against the perpetrators. The mob went to the local police station and demanded that the police should punish the Madurese perpetrators. According to a police official involved in the event, the police did not want to risk a lynching of the perpetrators and thus they did not let the crowd know that they had already arrested the perpetrators (interview of a Ledo police official by the author, March 22, 2006). Madurese youths also organized their mobs for violence against the Dayaks, but very soon an asymmetry was reflected in the pattern of violence, which after the first days of January was mainly by the Dayak mobs against any Madurese who had not managed to escape from Bengkayang. The military and especially the Air Force's local base managed to rescue many fleeing Madurese families, who were then transported with trucks first to Singkawang, and many further to Pontianak (Acap 2006). Violence did not spread all the way to the coast, but was very extensive in Bengkayang (then still part of Sambas) and northern Landak districts (Prasojo 2009).

The conflict stopped for a while in January 1997, but then a case of a Madurese burglar stirred up tensions again (interview of an official of Sanggau Ledo, Yon Gedean 2006). Again the story goes that the perpetrator had violated a woman he had found in the house, and again the masculine obligation to defend women emerged as a justification for Dayak violence. As a result of the incident, a Madurese village established a defense group to guard the village against a Dayak revenge attack (Liswan 2005). As this revenge did not come, the group ended up burning a few Dayak houses out of frustration. This prompted a Dayak reaction, which eventually meant that almost every Madurese individual was killed or expelled from the part of Sambas that now is the district of Bengkayang (Acap 2006).

After the conflict many Madurese had to find new homes in some new areas of the current Sambas district. However, the pressure of newcomers was felt in Sambas, where a situation of competition between the newcomers and the local Malay population was becoming more intense (anonymous official, Tanjung Keracut, Sambas, October 4, 2003).

The starting point of the Sambas riots in 1999 is not as clear-cut as that of the Bengkayang violence. In different villages people speak about very different triggers. Most Sambas Malays interviewed for this study (interviews of officials and a Malay youth leader in Azam village in Tanjung Keracut, October 2003) tell stories about increasing crime and theft, and then a situation where a Sambas "neighborhood watch" managed to catch a Madurese burglar and beat him up. Some stories tell that the neighborhood watch consisted of Dayak individuals who were a minority in Sambas, while other stories tell about a Malay reaction (both interpretations were presented in ASEM seminars on conflict prevention).

However, the most commonly heard story often mentions the Madurese terror in Parit Setia, Jawai sub-district, that started as revenge for an incident, on January 18, 1999, where a drunken Madurese hooligan was beaten by a Malay gang. According to Davidson (2008: 129), the revenge was organized by a criminal gang-leader friend and the parents of the beaten Madurese man. Both the mugging of the Madurese man and the reaction were met with relative inaction from the police. It seems clear that this inaction was definitely used as a justification, and it indeed seemed to motivate both the triggering event as well as the violent reaction by the Madurese mob (Abdurrahman 2006, Davidson 2008: 129). In the reaction a gang of about 200 Madurese men and some women armed with knives and sickles stormed Parit Setia, killing three Malay men and wounding many, including the grandfather of one of my informants, Abdurrahman (Abdurrahman 2006, Davidson 2008: 129).

Since the police did not act after the raid on Parit Setia, hardly making any arrests (after a month they had arrested just one person), this incident together with the police inaction led to a mobilization of the Malays by ethnic leaders and village officials. The Communication Forum of Malay Youth (FKPM), which later, in 2008, joined the peace-making of the West Kalimantan Ethnic Communication Forum, was formed in January–February 1999 to confront the Madurese terror. The movement to defend the Malays against Madurese terror quickly spread, spearheaded by the FKPM, but also taking in other Muslim organizations as well as criminal networks, to virtually the entire coastal, Malay-dominated, Sambas district. This organization of resistance against another Muslim group, the Madurese, was made easier by the fact that the raid on Parit Setia had taken place on January 19, 1999, during Idul Fitri (Eidul-Fitr), the Muslim holiday ending the fasting month, Ramadan. Despite the image of the Madurese as Muslim fanatics, the attack on Idul Fitri convinced some of the organizers of the force against the Madurese that the "Madurese were not really Muslim" (Abdurrahman 2006). According to Hermanto Juleng (2003a, 2003b), this perception was much boosted by the local media.

While the Parit Setia incident pushed the Malay militants to mobilization, it did not yet push them to action. The trigger of action in Sambas has also been debated, and it seems that for different areas the representative incident was different.[5] The most common representative event took place in a bus. The transportation business in many parts of West Kalimantan was dominated by the Madurese (Thoha 2005), and arguments about who was allowed to run busses and ferries were common. However, even if the theatre of the event was symbolic for a more general dispute, the event was simply about a Madurese bus passenger who had refused to pay a

---

5   This observation is based on my interviews and comparisons of the studies of my informants, especially with a village head and youth leader in Tanjung Keracut (interview on October 4, 2003). A detailed account can be found in Davidson (2008: 128–34).

Malay conductor in the Tebas village of Pusaka. It is not known why the passenger refused his payment, and whether the Madurese ownership of many of the bus lines had anything to do with it. In any case all this happened on February 21, 1999. He was thrown off the bus with the help of other Malay passengers in a way which he considered rude (Abdurrahman 2006). As a result the Madurese passenger stabbed the conductor in the stomach and arm at the end of the latter's working day. This happened in Bujang and the victim was brought to a hospital in the town/city of Pemangkat while a large crowd was watching. Early next morning a small mob of Malays burned down seventeen Madurese houses in Pemangkat and killed two Madurese people in Tebas and one in Pemangkat (Davidson 2008: 132).

The FKPM was involved from the beginning in taking the riot to the entire coastal region of Sambas (the current Sambas district). Davidson (2008: 144–5) and many other anonymous informants speculate about the role that the Malay "crown prince" (the late Raden "Wimpi" Winata Kusumah) of the traditional Sambas "royal family" played in the mobilization, by his funding of and lending authority to the project. In Jawai, fighting that had been first ignited by the raid on Parit Setia continued between the Malays of Parit Setia and the Madurese-controlled Rambaya villages (Abdurrahman 2006). However, rioting quickly spread to distant villages in the coastal Sambas and the number of casualties, almost exclusively Madurese, rose very quickly.

Since many of the Madurese "civilians" took shelter in police stations and military compounds, the Malay mobs targeted their action directly at these police and military establishments (Davidson 2008: 132). Another murder of a Dayak man, assumed to have been conducted by a Madurese criminal, outside Pemangkat on March 16, 1999, finally triggered the full escalation of the conflict into a communal war. Cooperation between Malay and Dayak "anti-Madurese" activists quickly brought the campaign further to the Dayak dominated areas, where some of the Madurese families had returned after the riots of 1996–97 (Andoth 2006, interview with an anonymous official of Sanggau Ledo, who had participated in this cooperation, Hermanto Juleng 2003a, 2003b). According to Davidson, within 24 hours over 300 Madurese houses were burned. The all-out communal conflict lasted for about six weeks (Davidson 2008: 133).

In addition to the events in Pemangkat and Parit Setia, many other events were described as crucial triggers. It should be realized that the stereotypical picture of the Madurese in Sambas was that they were doing economically well because of theft and other economic crimes as well as the Madurese control of the criminal networks and corruption of the police (interview of a youth leader in Tanjung Keracut, October 2003). Furthermore, the individual events involving theft or argument about private transportation exemplified representative cases of the conflicts that the Madurese and Sambas Malays had failed to negotiate verbally. Thus demonstrative action in such cases served the purpose of creating a precedent and constructing a practice on issues that were seen as important problems between the two ethnic groups.

The Sambas violence managed to change the voter demographics before the general elections, and allegedly it also managed to secure some publicly mandated business transactions that had been threatened by the expansion of the Madurese economic role in Sambas (Sugandi 2006). More importantly, perhaps, it could be seen as a response to the fact that violent Dayak mobs had managed to influence the outcome of political processes for their benefit in two districts (Sanggau and Pontianak) by means of destructive demonstration (Davidson 2008: 135). Furthermore it might be relevant that the conflict took place in the aftermath of a serious Indonesian economic crisis and change in the political leadership and the political system. Yet it seems that the popular participation in the conflict was mobilized by very similar patterns as in Bengkayang.

The pure narratives of the conflict events do not reveal much about the conflict causes, and now after the surface level and the approximate timeline of conflict have been established, it is time to develop a theoretical framework by paying systematic attention to the junctures in the path of conflict.

Sources and Structure

The main sources of this book are the discussions among and interviews with the main conflict stakeholders, ethnic leaders, ethnic fighters, political activists, police and military officials, local bureaucrats and eye-witnesses of the conflict. Many of the discussions took place during the preparation of lectures, seminars and workshop on conflict prevention that I have given in the province since 2001. I have cited or referred to about 100 of these discussions and interviews, but this list is just the tip of an iceberg. Ideas presented in this book draw more indirectly from at least ten times greater number of meetings with fighters, mobilizers of fighters, politicians and businessmen who benefited or lost because of the conflicts, activists advocating the cause of parties of the conflict as well as activists working for the ending of hostilities, witnesses to conflict episodes, heroes of the peace efforts after and during the conflict, people involved in post-conflict peace-building, and analysts and experts that tried to make sense of the conflicts.

In addition to private meetings, another great source for this book has been discussions in the class of stakeholders, ethnic leaders, local bureaucrats, military and police officials, and so on. It is clear that there are issues that people do not reveal in collective discussions. Furthermore, there are also issues where the presence of others leads informants to different kind of manipulative communication (it is clear that also private discussions involved a lot of manipulation). While restricting, this manipulation also sometimes revealed some of the meanings behind communicative violence in conflicts, and, thus, manipulative communication as such was an important source for making sense of the seemingly senseless violence. Furthermore, there are also issues conflict stakeholders develop only in interaction with other stakeholders. During the decade from 2001 to 2010, I gave altogether about 500 hours of seminar and lectures.

Due to my contacts with the Indonesian vice president's office as well as my local contacts with respected Malay figures, I have probably had unusually easy access to the ethnic leaders and provincial officials, and I have tried to use this access to contribute a more useful understanding of how the provincial elite thinks to the existing literature on the conflict in West Kalimantan. Various kinds of leaders do not always know everything about the conflicts that surround them. Even less do they talk openly and frankly about them. Yet, even efforts to manipulate me give me information about how these leaders see the politics of conflict. Manipulation has informed me of how different leaders want to be perceived from the outside, and how they want others to see the problems of West Kalimantan. In order to interpret this manipulation I have simply had to understand the roles they see me in: as a collaborator of an international peace-maker (President Martti Ahtisaari), a contact of Indonesia's vice president's office, and a friend of the relative of the Malay king of Pontianak. I do not believe in participatory observation that assumes neutrality for the observer. Instead, I think I will always have to consider how my informants perceive me, what kind of a role they attach to me, and thus, how they manipulate me, in order to interpret the communication game I participate in. I think that only from this conscious partisan position I can learn from the dynamics of conflict.

I have structured my study in the following manner. This introduction has first presented the objectives of the study, then introduced the conflict, and then introduced the two main conflict episodes. It has also explained the sources of the analysis.

Chapter 2 will present the approach of the study. It starts with the issue of what knowledge, understanding and explanations can be expected to contribute to peace. Then I will proceed to the differences between explanations that focus on objective and social phenomena. This distinction will help my argument, which utilizes some of the traditional generalizations in a more constructivist, pragmatist environment. I will then build a theoretical analytical framework to be used in my empirical analysis by reviewing the literature of peace research and Indonesian/ Kalimantan studies for useful ideas. After the review of empirical generalizations in peace research, I review the literature on West Kalimantan and try to see what the existing research has already done and what I can still contribute to it. From the literature of previous research I identify three junctures on the path to conflict that my research could influence: the emergence of antagonism, the emergence of the conflict motive, and the emergence of the opportunities for violence. These three junctures on the path to conflict I will then analyse by using my pragmatic approach and the lessons from conflict research and research on West Kalimantan.

The main empirical analysis on the roots of West Kalimantan violence will be undertaken in Chapter 3, which first tries to make sense of the emergence of antagonism in West Kalimantan, between "migrant" and "local" groups. Then it tries to answer the question of why anyone wanted conflict in West Kalimantan, trying to penetrate the meanings that reveal the motivations for conflict behavior. Finally in this diagnostic part, I will explain why violence was so easy in West

Kalimantan. On the one hand, I had to explore material factors, such as the ratio of police to citizens, while, on the other, I had to go deep into the normative structures of West Kalimantan societies to understand how violence was made possible by justifying it with associations to common accepted moral principles.

Chapter 4, on what can be done to prevent conflict in West Kalimantan, follows the conflict diagnosis. Since antagonism, motives and opportunities explain conflict, conflict prevention will have to focus on the prevention of antagonism, conflict motives and conflict opportunities. These are the topics of Chapter 4. While analyzing what can be done in general, this part also takes a thorough look at what has been done to prevent conflict in West Kalimantan and how that activity relates to the motives, opportunities and agent structures of the West Kalimantan conflict. In this analysis I will give priority to the analysis of the impact of the academic peace diplomacy that I myself led in the province, under the auspices of the vice president's office of Indonesia.

Chapter 2

What Kind of Junctures on the Path to Conflict Should Peace Research be Focused on?

Pragmatic Knowledge, Understanding and Explanation of Paths to Conflicts

The head of the Sambas regency, Ir. H. Burhanuddin A. Rasyid, is one of the people most intimately acquainted with the conflict in Sambas. He was brought to power by one of the main mobilizers of the Sambas Malay riot, the Communication Forum of Malay Youth (FKPM). According to him, the cultural characteristics of the Madurese are the root cause of West Kalimantan violence. "The cultural patterns of the Madurese are not compatible with those of the local population. They tend to have difficulty in assimilating to the local tradition. This is what is at the root of the conflict here."[1]

Another expert with detailed knowledge of the Sambas conflict is Haji Ali (2005), head of Gamisma, a religious cultural organization of the Madurese in Singkawang/Sambas area. He concludes the opposite. Haji Ali says that ethnic stereotypes are at the core of the conflict. Without them the actions of individual Madurese would not have been seen as the actions of "the Madurese" as a collective agent: "The future should bring an end to the discrimination against the Madurese. This would be the way to peace."

Five decades of experience and observation that no scholar could match have led to two opposite conclusions: the knowledge of at least one of these experts has led to a fundamentally wrong conclusion. More generally the very fact that people in conflict areas, with all their opportunities to observe the conflict, tend to be unable to predict, or find strategies for the prevention of, conflict suggests that I need to be careful with my method of evidence collection, as well as with my treatment of it in my conceptual and theoretical frameworks. Observation and "facts" alone do not lead to knowledge, understanding or explanations usable for conflict prevention. Somehow theory is needed to find and process relevant data and put the peace actor on top of the complex structures and processes of the West Kalimantan conflicts. For this we need an approach that does not seek for truth as correspondence between claims and reality, but truths that prove their validity by being practical.

On the one hand, this means that I am looking for truths and explanations that help adapt to the realities of conflict and peace. Pragmatic peace research

---

1 Interview by the author with the Head of Sambas Regency, Ir. H. Burhanuddin A. Rasyidon October 3, 2003.

could claim with William James (1909: 14) that "consciousness is teleological in nature: that the understanding of all mental activity and its products must include reference to the agent's purposes and interests." Erich Fromm's (1941) and Richard Rorty's (1991) activist theory of knowledge has the same pragmatist understanding of the relationship between will and knowledge. Fromm claims that any relationship between thought and reality is characterized by continuous intentional purposive activity on the part of the mind rather than passive sensory receptivity. I agree with this view.

If the conflict reality produces many surprises to the peace actors who have knowledge and understanding that peace research has produced, scholarship has failed. A concept or theory should be evaluated by how effectively it helps put the peace actor "on top of things," as opposed to how accurately it describes objective reality. True beliefs are "those that prove useful to the believer" (Margolis 2005).

Together with such classical pragmatist as Charles Sanders Peirce (Shook and Margolis 2005) and William James (1909) I recognize the law-like causal forces that drive objective realities. Regardless of our consciousness about shooting and dying, and the meaning we give them, for example, a bullet that goes through someone's heart will cause a death. Thus I will have to go after these material junctures on the path to conflict to reveal their causal regularities and mechanisms, so that peace actors can predict and adjust their action to them.

But our knowledge also creates realities. Most of the realities that constitute peace and conflict in West Kalimantan are social: They are created in the knowledge of people and in the social practices that reflect and reproduce this knowledge (Wendt 1998, 1999). Pragmatic knowledge of peace and conflict-related issues constructs realities practical for peace (Rorty 1991). This is where Rorty's thinking is different from that of the classical pragmatists. Rorty's (and I would claim Fromm's) pragmatism operates in a constructivist setting, where knowledge is pragmatic when it creates practical realities, not only when it adapts to externally given objective realities in a practical manner.

If our knowledge, for example, operates with concepts of primordially antagonistic ethnicity and we aim at integrating societies, our knowledge and scholarship constitute a social reality that are harmful for our practical missions. This way revealing impractical epistemic orientations and creating pragmatic social realities are alternative opportunities for pragmatic peace research. Strategies of conflict prevention can be found by interfering with the material junctures in the path to conflict, such as the power of the police, or the unavailability of weapons. However, given that human action is purposive and creates its own meanings and interpretations of the "strategic context" of the action, pragmatic knowledge is also useful for giving peace-actors understanding to re-articulate the meanings of violent action. Pragmatic understanding for deconstruction and reconstruction of the "strategic context" of violence means that knowledge and understanding can help peace-actors to manipulate the interpretations of conflict actors so that new non-violent symbolic outcomes and actions can be created to replace violence as a means to create outcomes that symbolically serve the interests of conflicting parties. I will shortly analyze opportunities peace research has for interfering in the material and ideational junctures in the path to conflict.

Pragmatic Peace Research on Material Conditions of Peace and War

Pragmatic peace research on material causal junctures on the path to conflicts has two main missions. First it must reveal the correlative regularity (the tendency of one condition appearing together with another conceptually separate condition) between causes and effects (Hempel 1965, Hume 1777). Second, to explain the mechanism by which the cause generates the effect is the main task of a social scientific explanation (Elster 1989, Rios 2004).

Once the correlative associations between causes and effects are known, and the mechanism in which these regularities operate is understood, the peace researcher has the tools to block or redirect objective junctures on the causal path to conflicts. If the lack of law enforcement resources, for example, is systematically associated with conflict, and we can clearly see how this lack pushes ethnic groups in West Kalimantan to self-defence and to an arms race, we have the epistemic tools for manipulating the conflict path by advocating for greater policing resources. Changing the conflict by offering knowledge to those with power ("political/social engineering") is the most elementary form of intellectual influence (academic diplomacy) for peace. This is also what classical (objectivist) pragmatists started with: if we can identify regularities, we can manipulate them in accordance with our interests. For some other objectivists (or mechanical materialists), such as Talcott Parsons, this type of knowledge production is the main task of social science (Parsons 1946). The classical pragmatist social science can certainly accept this assertion, while the applications of pragmatism today tend to find other uses for social sciences, too. Yet, the engineering task of conflict studies is one that needs to be taken seriously, especially when dealing with degenerate (Van Parijs 1981) or inflexible (Harsanyi 1961) conflict behavior, which simply reflects external objective realities, rather than being driven by free will, flexible interests and rational reflection.

Peace research has been focused on how negotiations should be organized for them to be successful; on how facilitators, mediators or arbitrators should act to be constructive; and on what kind of post-conflict peace-building would be needed for the sustainability of peace (see for example, Fisher and Ury 1981). This knowledge is like the knowledge of an engineer who is designing a bridge over a river: practical solutions are sought by means of systematically studying the experience of similar situations. Here the foundation of the role of peace research is the power of practical knowledge of the diagnosis of conflict (the path) and the knowledge of useful strategies to prevent it (the blockade, or the diversion).

Knowledge and methodologies specific to some instruments in the prevention of conflict have been developed as peace research is used increasingly in conflict prevention. Classical security theory dealt mainly with police and military measures of conflict prevention.[2] Later, John W. Burton (1990) de-militarized the field of conflict prevention by outlining possibilities in policy planning for the prevention of conflict. To distinguish this from the military and police means of conflict prevention, Burton renamed his ideas as "conflict *provention*", which referred to the non-military, and general policy-planning means for the promotion of peace.

Various instruments of conflict prevention have been developed by academics and practitioners in partnership. Peace and Conflict Impact Assessment (PCIA) methodology has arisen and been used for conflict-sensitive development cooperation programming (Austin 2003, Bush 1998, DFID 2002, FES 2004, Kivimäki and Pasch 2009). Methodologies for dialogue,[3] such as Open Space (Owen 2008) and the World Café (Brown and Isaacs 2005) have been developed as practical tools for the facilitation of a dialogue between civil society and local and general experts in conflict areas.

Peace-research practices can also affect the objective conditions of conflict societies. Through interviewing people for research purposes, and through teaching classes of stakeholders, scholars often evolve a network of contacts that could be used for peace and negotiation. While official actors often cannot approach both sides of the conflict, peace researchers normally need to do this to get a complete picture of the conflict. In the case of official actors, meeting a rebel or an enemy would also signal something that an interview in a research context would not. The idea of problem-solving workshops as part of a teaching curriculum among semi-influentials is an example of this development. John Burton (1990) and Herbert Kelman (1997) claim that both in their publications and in their practice academic teachers can match stakeholder communities in a way that helps to create meaningful linkages between the gate-keepers of conflict.

The activity of Mr. Juha Christensen—a Finnish businessman who turned out to be crucial in the pre-negotiation for peace in Aceh—in matching the conflicting parties and the mediator in the Aceh peace process testifies that businessmen like Mr. Christensen can be crucial to the initiation of peace processes (Husain 2007). While in principle people from any professional group could be helpful in the informal creation of links of communication between conflicting parties, peace researchers, due to their need to understand both sides, are exceptionally suited to this. Yet, one should not lose sight of opportunities by thinking that only scholars can contribute to the initiation of peace processes. The example of Mr. Christensen testifies to this.

---

2   See, for example, the various theories of deterring conflict behavior by game theorists like Thomas Schelling (1980).

3   See, for example, the publication sponsored by the Canadian International Development Agency (CIDA) and the Government of Canada, International IDEA, the Organization of American States (OAS), the General Secretariat of the OAS (GS/OAS), and the United Nations Development Program, *Democratic Dialogue: A Handbook for Practitioners* by Bettye Pruitt and Philip Thomas (2007).

Furthermore, Fisher and Ury (1981) show how such workshops could help brainstorm solutions to the disputes between these gate-keepers. West Kalimantan has shown that workshops can be initiated not only with the semi-influentials but with the main actors in the conflict too. Educational events can turn into actual peace negotiation, as has been the case in West Kalimantan.

The presence of scholars can also be helpful in the creation of transparency in the conflict area. This can work against violence and the abuse of power, as both are politically costly if various constituencies learn about them. In the Aceh conflict the reduction of human rights violations on both sides, but especially by the Indonesian military, after April 2005 was an important precondition for the success of the peace process. This was possible, at least in part, because of the fact that human rights violations were made visible and could be verified by the aid workers who had come to Aceh after the tsunami of December 26, 2004 (Kivimäki 2007). Transparency, however, naturally can be created by almost any kind of critical presence in conflict areas, and thus this is not something special for peace researchers.

Pragmatic Peace Research on Ideational Conditions of Peace and War

Many of the junctures in the path to conflict are created by knowledge of the social situation. Realities that push people to conflicts can be generated[4] in social interaction, and in the creation of norms and meanings and social realities. Relative deprivation as a discrepancy between expected and actual level of entitlement, can be constituted[5] in narratives that explain what Dayaks are entitled to and how the reality of their situation is. Similarly, the blocking of paths to conflict does not need to be activity that reduces some objective discrepancies between expectations and reality, but demonstrations of the fruitlessness of influential (hegemonic) interpretations.

If we understand that the Javanese migrants in Papua are substitute targets for the central government, we could design strategies that block their use as such (Kivimäki 2006). If the media reveals the "humaneness" of the Javanese in Papua (say, by exposing the lives of Javanese children in Papua), they no longer convey as abstract substitute targets for the central government, as the rebels will see them as people with similar problems to their own. But before this kind of peace journalism is possible one needs to be aware of the symbolic functions of violence. This can only be revealed by peace research.

Killing as means of enacting one's masculinity could be made an obsolete strategy if we can offer young men alternative means of enacting their masculinity, or alternative masculine identities. Again such strategies could be possible only if

---

4   For generative causality, see Smith 2003.

5   For constitutive causality, see Kratochwil 1989, Onuf 1989, Ruggie 1998. For constitution and causality as separate things, see Wendt 1998.

the meanings of conflict behavior are revealed.[6] Alternatively, if conflict behavior is a way to demonstrate one's ability to defend a future family against threats, a research focus on the realities of capitalism (=capitalist modernization) could show young men that the real ability to defend one's family lies in one's ability to generate wealth for them. The idea of demonstrating functional masculine abilities through violence has to be shown to be a case of "false consciousness" and impractical epistemic orientation. This way violence could be replaced by non-violent alternatives as ways of demonstrating something that is in the interest of young men.

If manipulation of the meanings of conflict behavior offers ways to conflict prevention, pragmatic peace research will have to use the core ideas of symbolic interactionalism (Blumer 1962), which in social science means revealing the meanings related to it, to the degree that it is possible to see the relationship between the action as means to intended consequences. Only these kinds of explanations offer symbolic strategies for conflict prevention. Peace research can have a role in challenging social constructions, socially impractical knowledge and socially constructed truths that we should not consider as true (truths that socially rational people would not consider true). Following the critical social science tradition, here the main objective of scholars could be to challenge the perception that these truths (such as the difference between indigenous and non-indigenous races) are natural by showing how conceptions of politically relevant collective entities change over time (Booth 1991, 1995, Wyn Jones 1999). The denaturalization of these constructs will help peace actors to broaden the range of strategies from which they can choose. Furthermore, peace researchers can reveal social constructs that serve partisan purposes, but which, in a social structure, work against the common good of peace and stability.

In addition to challenging impractical "truths," research can also actively create social realities. Yet, scholars should be careful as sometimes these realities can also be detrimental to peace. Habermas (1971) has suggested that positivist social science encourages people to treat their actions as something caused by conditions. This naturally reduces their options. I will show how the theories of the Institute of Dayakology Research and Development in West Kalimantan created the reality of an "automatic Dayak reaction to violations of their indigenous rights."

Sometimes, however, academic constructions of realities can genuinely help peace. The concept of the "positive no," the idea that it is positive for the relationship to say no to a situation that one considers intolerable, helps to legitimize verbal disputes in cultures where the lack of conceptual distinction between disputes and conflicts prevents the airing of grievances. This openness to problems and the resulting willingness to tackle grievances could be essential for peace.

---

6 For peace research theorizing on the cultural meaning-giving that associates masculinity with weapons and violence, see for example Jacobs, Jacobson and Marchbank 2000 and Myrttinen 2003.

Concepts like "positive peace" (Galtung 1971), "structural violence" (Galtung and Höivik 1971), "securitization" (Wæver 1995) and "human security" (UNDP 1994) all participate in a construction of global realities that is intended to be helpful for peace. These concepts are not intended to be truthful in the traditional sense. Similar local realities that academic diplomacy can create will be analyzed in Chapter 4 of this book, in conjunction to the so-called Pontianak Appeal and to the Ethnic Communication Forum.

In addition to directly changing the conflict setting with words, scholarly influence could be manifested as socialization changing problematic conflict attitudes. The various ways in which scholarly work and teaching can socialize the "humanness" of the enemy, or can re-humanize enemies to each other, have been tackled by one of the leaders of the conflict theory, Herbert C. Kelman, who sees the dehumanization of the enemy as one of the results of the conflict process. As a result of this dehumanization one of the normative obstacles to conflict disappears, as the perception is that fighters are no longer dealing with people but instead with something less than human (Kelman 1973). Perceptual division between ethnicities serves dehumanization, as it makes it possible for fighters to perceive the other as something different from oneself. Thus socialization to a humane, non-discriminatory, anti-racist language and culture would be a great challenge to all in West Kalimantan. Instead of just revealing naturalized social constructs of ethnicity that are detrimental to peace, scholars can also participate in the uprooting of those constructs and the socialization of less antagonistic perceptions.

Scholarly (and journalistic) practices can also do something to change the social constructions of war societies. In political conflicts actors often need legitimacy, support and acceptance. In addition to violence being harmful for this, conflicting parties often want to associate peace with themselves and war with their enemies. In order to do this, they have to give statements that show their commitment to peace. In some cases these statements have become something to which conflicting parties then become committed. Even if promises were made just to please political constituencies, publicity about them can create a situation where conflicting parties get "entrapped" in their own promises and on the path to peace (Mitchell 2000, Salancik 1977, Staw 1981). Scholarly and media publicity of promises and commitments can be part of this entrapment to peace.

What Kinds of Junctures Should Peace and Conflict Studies be Focused on?

Instead of re-inventing the wheel, it makes sense to look at what peace and conflict studies have already established on the junctures that are most critical on the path to conflict. Here I will first look at the scholarship on conflicts in general and then move on to the analysis of conflict specifically in West Kalimantan.

General Peace and Conflict Studies and Junctures on the Path to Conflict

A policy-relevant analysis of conflict often pays attention to certain junctures on the path to conflict. Traditional security studies focuses on capabilities that induce possible conflicting parties to threaten each other and secure themselves. The capacities under most intensive scrutiny have been those of states. The mainstream research on international conflicts[7] tends to regard states as the main actors. Also, in realist,[8] liberalist (Goldsmith 2006, 2007) and constructivist (Acharya 2009) Southeast Asian scholarship, emphasis is on the special role of the public sector in conflicts and their resolution. The experience of conflict resolution in Aceh, where civil society actors took the lead in conflict resolution, proves that ignoring the opportunities of civil society actors would be a serious mistake (Kivimäki 2007, Kivimäki and Gorman 2008). Pragmatic peace research will need to explain the West Kalimantan conflict by looking at how the government and society-led mechanisms for containing the potential and capability for violence failed, thus causing conflict. The focus on societal forces is especially important, since the conflict pattern in West Kalimantan is communal and therefore does not directly involve the government.

In classical realist security studies and international relations theory, brute power is seen as the source of military opportunities. Thus, for classical realists, junctures of a material nature, related to the opportunities to attack and defend, are the crucial junctures that need to be focused on in conflict prevention (Morgenthau 1946/2006).

Structural realists also focus on the opportunity side of conflict prevention, but see opportunities arising out of structural power/capacity conditions, rather than seeing opportunities just as a consequence of the individual capacity of an actor. Thus for structural realists, conflict prevention should focus on the second type of structural juncture, which relates to opportunities for violence (Waltz 1979).

When looking at ways to block these opportunities for violence, the realist tradition of classical security studies focuses mostly on the opportunities governments have both to wage war and to prevent their opponents' opportunities for violence. The realist obsession with states and governments as the only actors with opportunities for violence and conflict prevention is not restricted to international politics, but stands also as an explanation of both international wars and intra-state wars.[9]

For our pragmatic analysis, capabilities and opportunities are important elements that seek to find ways to block or reroute conflict developments. If it were possible for leaders to incapacitate actors in the conflict and render them

---

7   For exceptions, see, for example, Taliaferro 2001, 2006.

8   This aspect is covered well in the realist accounts of security in Southeast Asia as well as in his review of other realist accounts by Jürgen Rüland. See, for example, Hoadley and Rüland 2006.

9   See, for example, Posen 1993.

unable to commit violence against each other, that would reduce the levels of violence in the society. Thus, the issue of capacities and opportunities for violence will be under focus as one category among the necessary conditions for conflict in Kalimantan.

However, in order to identify all the opportunities, I will, instead of just looking at material power capabilities, also study immaterial capacities and opportunities, such as the ability to navigate around norms and emotions that normally prevent people from causing violence. Undoubtedly, some contingent realists have been paying attention to historical constructs and subjective perceptions, instead of seeing everything as objective and material.[10] To some extent, the role of cultural, or socially-constructed, capacitating factors that offer opportunities for violence has been theorized by Anne McAdam, Sidney Tarrow and Charles Tilly (2001). This kind of an explicit focus on the facilitating constructs is needed, instead of just considering subjective elements and perceptions as exceptions to the otherwise purely material world of capacities. Instead of only looking at material junctures of the first two types, one needs to seek understanding of the discursive strategies, and partisan and naturalized social constructs that offer conflicting parties violent opportunities in order to block their opportunities.

The power of non-material capacities and opportunities is considerable also in West Kalimantan: weapons alone did not make war in West Kalimantan possible. In fact, most of the killings were carried out using agricultural tools or knives and torches. People were mentally made capable of violence by myths and rituals that made them forget or ignore the normative obstacles to violence, while spells and the influence of the spiritual realm tackled those emotional obstacles related to the fear and repulsion of conflict. However, the realities that traditional security studies deal with, for example the lack of police resources, also played an important role.

Opportunity structure in West Kalimantan was also affected by the ways in which violent acts enabled people to articulate interpretations of the order that existed between locals and migrant communities. Not only did violently and criminally ignoring the local norms constitute criminal and violent behavior, it was also an articulation and demonstration of a reality where local norms do not matter. The relationship between this demonstration and the reality can be understood by imagining what would have resulted if Dayaks and Malays had not reacted to this demonstrative behavior by some Madurese youth. If local norms were not enforced, or if new norms were not negotiated, behavior that ignored the local norms would have created the de facto situation where local norms did not exist. Thus the language of demonstrative argumentation and the opportunities to replace demonstrative communication with explicit negotiation between "locals" and "migrants" are options pragmatic peace research should take very seriously. The question here is: Why was it possible for rogue Madurese to demonstrate an order where local norms do not exist, and why was it possible for some Dayaks and Malays to demonstrate a reality of "guests" and "visitors" by asking the guests

---

10   See, for example, Brooks 1997.

to leave[11] (eventually by burning their houses or killing them)? Why were there no obstacles to this demonstrative behavior and why were there no opportunities for the explicit airing of opinions on how the relationship between the rights and obligations of the Dayaks, Malays and the Madurese was to be organized?

Security studies have taken the interests of conflicting parties for granted. National interests that motivated actors have been regarded as something natural and thus not requiring scrutiny (Morgenthau 1946/2006). However, if I want to identify all the possibilities of conflict prevention, I also need to look into motives that explain conflict. Traditional peace research with a conflict-resolution emphasis refuses to take the motives of conflicting parties for granted and pays primary attention to the issues that motivate conflict. One of the leading peace research journals is called the *Journal of Conflict Resolution*, which implies an emphasis on resolving the disputes that motivate conflicts. Similarly, classical peace research theories on conflict management, such as the theory of relative deprivation (Gurr 1970) or the theory of greed-based conflict (Collier and Hoeffler 2001), tend to base their main explanation of the sources of conflict on the motivations related to conflict and on various alternative terms of peace. According to Runciman (1966: 248–52), relative deprivation is a subjective assessment of a group of people that their actual receipts in social exchange are not near enough their deserved receipt, and this assessment becomes a motive for political violence. Relative deprivation often occurs, for example, when a group of people lack something they desire, which they see as feasible (maybe they have had it before) to have, and which they see other people having. According to others, relative deprivation is a situation where there is an intolerable gap between expected need satisfaction and actual need satisfaction; a discrepancy between deserved and actual enjoyment of goods and conditions of life (see for example Davies 1962, Gurr 1970, Gurr and Duvall 1973, Gurr and Lichbach 1986).

Greed-based theories, at the same time emphasize the role of opportunistic gains, such as access to natural resources or money from the overseas diaspora in the motivation of conflict behaviour (Collier and Hoeffler 2001).

If conflicting objectives can be negotiated it is possible for the conflicting parties to avoid violence without having to seriously compromise their original objectives. Furthermore, an understanding of motives would help avoid developments that create strong interests (grievance motivations) or incentives (greed motivations) for violence. This is why it is, of course, practical for peace actors to pay serious attention to the motives (incentives and grievances) in the search for opportunities to prevent conflicts.

---

11   It should perhaps be mentioned that the idea of asking someone who has violated the local norms to leave the village, district or province is not totally exceptional in the Indonesian context. Many cases where lynching and mob violence has been a result of a moral outrage, the victim has been beaten and then asked to leave (Welsh 2008: 84–6). This way expulsion is not only a way to communicate that someone has always been a "visitor," but can be read also as a signal saying that someone no longer belongs to the community.

More recent peace research with an emphasis on conflict transformation has also paid attention to the structures that give rise to violent disputes, instead of only focusing on the disputes themselves.[12] As conflict resolution and conflict transformation approaches both add to the variety of junctures necessary for conflict development and could potentially be manipulated to prevent conflict, I will adopt these approaches, too, and focus both on opportunities for violence and on the motives that explain conflict.

In the Weberian tradition, which sees society as consisting of purposive agents, the focus is often limited to these two elements on which security studies and conflict resolution focus: motives and opportunities. On the one hand, to understand and explain human behavior, I have to know the desires of the actor—what does he or she want to achieve by carrying out the observed actions? On the other hand, I need to be aware of the constraints within which he or she operates: which alternative courses of action does the person have and what sorts of consequences do these produce?[13] All this appeals to pragmatists, too. Blocking paths to conflicts must also mean removing opportunities for violence, while rerouting paths to conflict must mean, for pragmatists, the search for opportunities to allow conflicting parties to satisfy their goals without violence. Here, conflict resolution could be seen as the most concrete form of rerouting conflict developments so that the end result is an agreement instead of violence.

In the Weberian tradition, however, the existence of conflicting parties is taken for granted: conflicting parties are natural. Yet, empirical research seems to suggest to us that, as collective agents, conflicting parties emerge and disappear and their existence is very much based on how people and their interactions construct antagonistic agencies.[14] In a way, as John Paul Lederach (2003) says, all conflicts between collective agents are identity conflicts, as they always involve the process of identification of who "we" are, those whose motives and opportunities count, and who "they" are, those whom we hate and want to fight against. Some post-structuralists go much further and suggest that, instead of identity being one of the elements in all conflicts, identity and policies of security form a mutually constitutive pair: identity defines the action of agents of security, while at the same time action and policies define the identity of such actors (Hansen 2006). While taking seriously the interaction between identity and action, my pragmatic analysis gives more autonomy to the idea of interests and free will: identity does not determine these even if it affects them, but instead our will participates in defining our identity. Rather than taking the post-structuralist path, I find it more practical to see the emergence of antagonistic collective identities as a necessary juncture on the path to conflict, and thus studying this emergence allows us opportunities to divert the conflict path. Leaving the emergence of a conflict agency outside of the focus, and taking the agency as given, would produce an insufficient explanation,

---

12   See, for example, Lederach 1995, Väyrynen 1999.

13   Elster 1989: 13.

14   See, for example, Fisher 1990, Rieber 1991, Stein 1996.

and, more seriously, fail to identify all of the junctures that can be influenced to prevent conflict in West Kalimantan.

While agency is a necessary independent variable in the explanation of conflict, it is naturally related to the identity-related motives of conflict. The construction of collective identity is always motivated by something. For example, while the motives of the Dayak population during peace were often related to the economic needs of personal survival, with the emergence of a collective agency of local people as an agent antagonistic to the existence of the "newcomers",[15] local motives emerged: the need to preserve local traditions, the importance of local representation. These identities and motives play an important role in the explanation of the conflict. Thus, in identifying clusters along the path to conflict, I have to pay attention to the emergence of antagonistic identities, in addition to the motives of agents that seem to be natural.

Therefore, while looking at opportunities for interventions that could reduce violence, I need to avoid theoretical parochialism and the ideal of parsimonious explanations. This is because I am not looking for the strongest explanatory variables, but instead for all elements that contribute to conflict and which thus need to be tackled. Instead of seeking the best theory, I have to accept some sense of flexibility and even eclecticism. I need to look for all opportunities, not just those that theorists of one theoretical approach emphasize. Thus I need to take seriously all three main junctures that conflict theory focuses on, and which could offer opportunities for conflict interventions. I need to investigate:

1. What created the antagonistic agency?
2. What caused the emergence of the motive for violence?
3. Why did obstacles and hindrances to violence fail to prevent conflict?

Studies on West Kalimantan and Junctures on the Path to Conflict

The study of West Kalimantan is dominated by anthropological, historical, hermeneutical and constructivist studies with deep insights into the culture and life of West Kalimantan. While most of these studies refer to and draw from a selection of comparative conflict studies literature, their ambition is not to utilize peace research and comparative conflict studies in a more comprehensive manner, let alone to contribute to it with generalizations. In fact none of the main scholars in the field of study of West Kalimantan have their scholarly origin in peace research. Instead, most studies contribute to the understanding of the conflict in West Kalimantan by offering theories grounded in empirical observation, a deep

---

15   In Kalimantan, the concept of a "newcomer" is problematic, since many of the Madurese, who were considered newcomers, had actually lived in the province for decades, often for generations. Also the concept of "migrant" is problematic, as this is mostly used for fellow Indonesians. Even though the Madurese population originated from the island of Madura, they were nevertheless Indonesians –and thus not really migrants.

understanding of the society and culture of West Kalimantan and an interpretation that links with an idiosyncratic anthropological and sociological tradition. My strategy for contributing to this literature is to try to offer a more thorough and comprehensive grounding of the study of West Kalimantan conflicts in the literature of peace research.

The way in which Davidson classifies the existing theories of Indonesian conflicts underlines the uniqueness of my approach. Davidson (2008: 4–9) classifies the existing theories on the basis of the period these theories draw their explanations into three categories:

1. theories that see the explanation of Indonesian conflicts in the post-Suharto scramble;
2. theories that explain recent conflicts by referring to the structures and dynamics of the New Order period in Indonesia (1966–98); and
3. theories that seek explanations from colonial history.

Peculiarly, Davidson does not identify any theories that seek explanation to recent conflicts and problems of national integration from the genesis of the nation. It may be that the critical attitude that Indonesian scholars felt it necessary to adopt towards the authoritarian rule of Suharto has prevented critique of the father of the nation (the first president, Sukarno), who was ousted by Suharto.

While I naturally see the point in seeking explanations to problems from historical constructs in the present social reality, the idea of trying to reduce the source of conflict to historical events is unacceptable for a pragmatist. While we can change history by re-interpreting historical events and developments, we cannot change the events as such, and thus a pragmatic analysis that aims at finding epistemic tools for changing belligerent realities into peaceful ones cannot settle for historical explanations. My explanations have to be such that they do not end in history, but in the future. The proof of my theories will be practice: If my prescriptions only produce surprises when put into practice my analysis has failed. This is why in this book I relate my diagnosis (Chapter 3) directly to the experience and potential of conflict prevention (Chapter 4). This is my test of the analysis that goes into the diagnosis.

Despite the differences in theoretical objectives, it is possible and indeed necessary for this study to mobilize the existing research for my own analysis by structuring the main arguments of the existing analysis of conflict in West Kalimantan by looking at the relationship these arguments have with the three questions:

1. "What created antagonistic agency?"
2. "What motivated violence?"
3. "Why did obstacles to conflict—such as morality, fear and the police—fail to prevent violence?"

The original indigenous Dayak and Malay analysis of the conflict explains it by means of some kind of a primordial model of the antagonism. This analysis points to the fundamental, irreconcilable differences in the cultures of Madura and Kalimantan: Madurese culture simply did not belong in Kalimantan, and since there were Madurese people on the island, the very presence of them caused antagonism and conflict (Awang 2003, Burhanuddin 2003).[16] The stereotypical portrayals of the Madurese culture and the cultures of the Dayaks and the Malays will be utilized in the empirical chapters of this study. However, while the perception of the Madurese as incompatible with other cultures of West Kalimantan is clearly a part of the antagonization process, the main question is: What has caused this perception? In a pragmatic analysis, it is useless for me to settle for primordial explanations, unless I really think forced ethnic cleansing is a viable solution. I need to understand why the Madurese were perceived in the way they were by Dayak and Malay conflict actors.

A constructivist version of this explanation emphasizes the primordial perception as a source of conflict. Hélène Bouvier, Huub de Jonge and Glenn Smith (2006), and Smith (1997) see this perception as part of the explanation of the antagonism, or at least as the justification for not working for an improvement of the relationship between the communities: if the perceived cause of conflict is the primordial characteristics of one of the parties, the solution can only be the dispelling or destroying of this group. However, the constructivist approach to the primordial interpretations can help me unpack and deconstruct the primordial views by means of critical peace research that denaturalizes the naturalized ethnic identities. By re-linking behavioral patterns to objectives, and structural and institutional constraints, it will be possible to explain Madurese, Dayak and Malay behavior on the basis of something other than rigid "qualities of an ethnic group." By trying to find the "meaning" of violent conflict behavior, it will be possible to see Madurese/Dayak/Malay violence as meaningful, even if destructive, communication: saying things with a murder as Daniel Horowitz puts it (Horowitz 2003).

Existing research on the mobilization of Dayak and emergence of Malay political identity in the conflicts of the 1990s (Davidson 2007, 2008) offers an alternative to the primordial explanations of conflict agency. Davidson's accounts of the rise of the self-sufficient and more assertive Dayak political identity and the reaction to this identity (and the Malay reaction to the successfulness of assertive behavior in political competition) among Malay leaders explains the collective behavior of Dayaks and Malays much better than any primordial accounts of what Dayaks and Malays are like.[17]

---

16   An interesting review of these theories can be found in Munawar 2003.

17   Van Klinken (2007: 63–8) challenges the view in which identity is crucial to the explanation of Dayak and especially Malay behavior during the conflicts of the 1990s, but he surely does not suggest that primordial accounts would explain this behavior better.

Yet, there is very little research on West Kalimantan Madurese identity (Sugandi 2006 being one of the main exceptions), something which would certainly be needed to counter the fatalist primordial explanation. In this book I will not dig deep into the history or ethnography of the West Kalimantan Madurese societies, but I will try, with the help of my extensive discussions with Madurese leaders, businessmen, activists and students, to understand the violent behavior of the Madurese thugs, and the occasional communally motivated defense and hiding of these criminals as something that rises out of the resurgence of the collective Madurese feeling of being pushed around by the local order. The feeling of being discriminated against by the local tradition created a basic communal identitive consciousness that led to solidarity even towards the Madurese thieves and thugs. When rebelling against the local traditional order of the Dayaks, the Madurese thugs represented "us" for the Madurese of West Kalimantan. I think understanding of this element in the agency structure of West Kalimantan conflict is something that has been lacking from the existing literature.

Existing explanations merge the motive with the explanation of the antagonism and often place the explanation into the context of the de facto decentralization. The main legal instruments of decentralization in Indonesia were the law on decentralization in 1999, the two laws on the special autonomy of Aceh and Papua of 2001, and the revision of the 1999 law in 2004. Yet, the practice of decentralization had already started in West Kalimantan in the mid-1990s with the expansion of local participation in local administration. While, traditionally, top administrative posts had been occupied by Javanese military men with little if any connection to the province, many districts and sub-districts started receiving heads from the local communities as early as in 1994 (van Klinken 2007: 56). Assertiveness against other ethnicities was a tool in a competition that emerged in the economic and political fields. De Jonge and Nooteboom (2006), as well as Bouvier and Smith (2006), point to the fact that the elite of Suharto's authoritarian government were primarily Javanese. While in East Kalimantan, where conflicts did not erupt, this dominance of the Javanese was sustained, in West Kalimantan the collapse of the Javanese dominance created a space of political power that various non-Javanese politicians had an interest in exploiting. Marginalizing the Madurese as something related to progress in democratization or decentralization could help "local" politicians limit the competition from the Madurese. This was a common perception of the motives of some of the indigenous violence.[18] Violent assertiveness had proven useful for the Dayak mobs who supported their candidates against Malay candidates in the selection of district heads in Pontinak

---

18   Bouvier and Smith 2006. This is also a simple version of one of the central arguments of van Klinken (2007) related to the connection between the decentralization and conflict. Van Klinken points out that the conflict had started in 1995 in Sintang, where the Dayak people revolted against the fact that their ethnic candidate failed to win the position of Head of District. In this rioting, the argument marginalized other candidates as people who did not belong to the ethnicity of the majority of people.

and Sanggau districts. Davidson (2008: 135) suggests this was one of the motives for the elevation of the profile of the Malay identity and organization. Standing up against the Madurese could elevate the political bargaining leverage of the Malays in West Kalimantan.

The same logic of competition by means of antagonism was used in the economic sphere, especially by middle-class people seeking public subsidies or business licenses (van Klinken 2008). Bambang Hendarta Sutapurwana (2003) suggests that competition for public privileges related to the orange-farming business was an important hidden motive for the conflict in Sambas. In the orange-farming business, the central monopoly had collapsed at the beginning of the 1990s (as a result of corrupt developments involving one of the sons of President Suharto, Mr. Bamgang Triatmojo), and it had caused tremendous distress among local people involved in the business (Davidson 2008: 128). Also, according to Bambang Hendarta Sutapurwana (2003), an antagonism between indigenous Sambas Malays and the "migrant" Madurese was mobilized by competition that was motivated by the lucrative orange-farming business in Sambas (and Tebes).

Unlike in much of the conflict research that is based on participatory observation, the existing literature on West Kalimantan avoids one common mistake. Instead of seeing the ethnic identities and their polarization as a product of fear and grievances only, West Kalimantan literature also clearly identifies the greedy sources of antagonistic identities. Unlike Bertrand (2004: 4), who claims that "Ethnic identities become politicized and the potential for mobilization is heightened when groups feel threatened by the structure and principles embedded in political institutions," Van Klinken, Davidson and others recognize that ethnic antagonism was also part of a power strategy with which it was possible for Dayak and Malay organizations to claim power. What one could possibly add is that, in the creation of Madurese unity and opposition to the local norms, greed of course played an important part as well. Understanding the competitive context of the formation of antagonistic identities will bring us a long way in the study of how violence could be denied its usefulness in competition and how non-violent means of competition and conflict resolution mechanisms could be introduced to divert the path to antagonism and conflict.

What the existing analysis seems to fail to explain in the emergence of antagonism was the fact that the main focus of Malay and Dayak aggression was not the traditional Madurese but the youth who no longer "felt Madurese." Many of the Madurese victims of this aggression, and the perpetrators of the initial criminal "Madurese" aggression, mentioned that they did not consider themselves Madurese, and that they had lost their contact with the island of Madura (TB 2001). De Jonge and Nooteboom (2006) note that the "Madurese migrants" of the bellicose West Kalimantan were not newcomers, as was the case of the Madurese of the peaceful East Kalimantan, and that many of the young Madurese of West Kalimantan had lost their Madureseness. If there was ethnic-based antagonization why did it happen between groups that emphasized their ethnicity as very important (Malay and Dayak) and a group that did not consider belonging to any ethnicity (youngsters that outsiders then considered Madurese)? My own analysis suggests that the reason for this was related to the "grammar of conflict." The main antagonism emerged between people who considered local indigenous rights important (Malay and Dayak politicians and businessmen who wanted to benefit from indigenous privileges) and people who wanted to promote an order that did not grant primacy to customary law, *adat*, and indigenous rights (young Madurese bullies). The first moves in the conflict were not emphasizing ethnic allegiance, but instead were constructing a reality of the irrelevance of local indigenousness. Only the reaction to these initial moves was ethnic, emphasizing ethnicity and indigenous rights.

Moving on to the motives for violence, benefits that the public sector derived from business and politics have already been mentioned as a motive that existing research has highlighted in explaining the violence. George Aditjondro (2001) suggests that many of the motives of conflict in Indonesia are related to gainful motives, and internal divisions of the military. In West Kalimantan the division part is clearly demonstrated by the violent competition between the police and the army after their separation as two distinct institutions. However, the tracing of the process to conflict episodes clearly seems to suggest that violence in West Kalimantan was more related to the absence than the extensive presence of the national securocracy. Unlike in Papua and Aceh (let alone East Timor) where the army and the police have been parties to the conflict, in West Kalimantan military and police presence seems to correlate with lower levels of violence. However, greed-related motives among local leaders seem to have more empirical support in West Kalimantan. Van Klinken sees at the heart of the explanation the greedy motives of local elites who anticipated benefiting from the lands, businesses and criminal networks of the Madurese who were to be expelled from the district (van Klinken 2007). Yulia Sugandi (2006) suggests that general and local elections also played a role in motivating the exclusion of the Madurese from Sambas and Bengkayang.

Related to the greed-based motives of the local elites is an explanation by Jamie S. Davidson, which links the nation-level and local-level explanations into a path-dependent historical explanation of the conflict. Despite the fact that Sambas Malays who initiated the 1999 conflict had no previous history of hostilities with the Madurese, Davidson suggests that the process logic of West Kalimantan conflicts started in Suharto's manipulative counterinsurgency. Three elements of that history lived as crucial causes of conflict in the latter half of the 1990s. Firstly, the precedence of ethnic cleansing (in 1967, the group that was expelled was the Chinese) created a sense of feasibility to the future ideas of winning inter-ethnic competitions by expelling entire ethnic communities. Secondly, once the Chinese were expelled from inner areas of Sambas in 1967, competition for lands between the Dayaks and the Madurese started and created a permanent setting of competition between the Madurese and the Dayak. Thirdly, the organizations of Dayak vigilantes (Laskar Pangsuma, for example) and the social network that was mobilized in the establishment of such organizations lived on and continued as a source of power in West Kalimantan politics. While Davidson's careful analysis of the path-dependency in West Kalimantan offers explanations to what made violent options look more feasible (the 1967 precedent) and what created the opportunities for violent actions is valuable for pragmatic analysis on what kind of opportunities should be blocked and what kind of alternative precedents could be emphasized, an analysis that tries to reduce the entire logic of conflict into its preceding moments leaves very little for peace agents to manipulate. As mentioned earlier, it is not possible to change historical events and developments. Yet, in general, the existing research on the gainful motives underneath conflict behavior points to the directions where rules would most need clarity and where explicit negotiation between communities would be most needed in order to transform the violent competition into a verbal dispute.

Grievances have also been suggested as motives for at least Dayak violence. Discriminating and centralizing capitalist modernization has had fundamental effects on the lives of the Dayak population (Peluso 2006), and this, according to Bamba (2000), is a root cause of the dissatisfaction and frustration of the indigenous Dayaks. Bamba's explanation is undoubtedly part of the Dayak construction of the conflict. It seeks legitimacy for the ethnic cleansing by the Dayak mobs in Bengkayang, as it argues for the naturality of the Dayak reaction. Bamba's powerful reconstruction and explication of the Dayak rationale is built on an idea of natural indigenous rights, which is then compared to the reality of Dayak economic and political conditions. The disparity between the naturalized idea of indigenous rights and the reality of modernization is then used as the source of frustration in the explanation of Dayak violence, much as the theory of relative deprivation is used to explain frustration-sourced violence.

However, as van Klinken (2006, 2007, 2008) has shown, this explanation suffers from the fact that most of the leading figures of Dayak and Malay violence were not really deprived people. Instead, they were often people who had greatly benefited from modernization, business and the modern prospects of decentralization. What van Klinken overlooks, though, is that elites of almost any conflict are not the ones with grievances, and yet they do need the constituents with a genuine grievance to legitimize their cause and to mobilize their soldiers. As one violent actor from another conflict told me, collective grievances motivate but the ones who have resources are the ones that can act: "I did not get involved in fighting because I was poor, but because I am one of a people who are poor [here the reference is to the collective group this informant considers to represent]. The fact that I am not poor and uneducated means that I have certain political responsibilities toward the poor people [in my group]" (anonymous informant, interviewed by the author in Jakarta, February 2000). By pinpointing the material grievances that provoke violent motives, the existing research goes a long way to pragmatic conclusions on what are the economic and political structures that need revision in order for the violence to disappear.

In addition to the analysis of objective grievances and sources of greed, some of the existing analysis of West Kalimantan pays attention to the buildup of expectation that better explains the perceived relative deprivation of the "local" communities in West Kalimantan. Davidson (2007) explain the international discursive roots of "indigenism" among West Kalimantan Dayaks, as well as the birth of the civil-society organizations of the "locals," which all helped to create a heightened expectation of what rightfully belongs to the "locals" (see also Davidson and Henley 2007). With understanding of the ideational sources of the perceived relative deprivation it will be possible for pragmatic research either to take the perceived grievances seriously and analyze the possibilities of social engineering that addresses them, or to deconstruct the foundations of the ideas constituting the discrepancy between the expected/demanded receipt and reality.

However, the current explanations have not fully tackled the macro-level issues that are important if one wants to derive generalizable pragmatic lessons from the West Kalimantan experience. The role of the economic crisis cannot have been totally unimportant, especially in the explanation of the economic motives of the Sambas conflict in 1999. Economic fluctuations, relative deprivation, the changes in economic opportunities, do not portray prominently in his explanation of conflict in West Kalimantan and elsewhere in Indonesia. This is why their role will be briefly analyzed in the section on conflict motives in this book.

Also, the expectations of regime change must also have been related to the motives of the conflicting parties in both the Bengkayang and Sambas conflicts. While Bertrand's (2004) book on Indonesian conflicts focuses on these expectations in the "critical junctures" of Indonesia, his analysis of the critical junctures emphasizes fears and grievances, which are obviously part of the big picture of conflict. However, critical junctures involve a lot of opportunities and greed. The expected fall of the economic and political empire of Suharto must have given rise to competition and movement to the vacuum of economic power. While Bertrand understands the necessity of seeing the big picture, his view is not in line with the recent discoveries in comparative conflict studies as his explanation emphasizes the grievance side, while the current conflict research seems to be more convinced of the relevance of the greed side of conflict motives. The greed side is well covered by Davidson and others, but these scholars are more interested in sub-national micro-processes, pushing aside macro-processes by pointing to exceptions that should be covered by macro-level explanations. If many other areas in Indonesia did not collapse into conflict, as a result of a transition or an economic collapse, or the power transition, this does not constitute evidence for a claim that there is no relevance in these macro-level developments (as seems to be the expectation in Davidson 2008: 7–8). Conflict causes and sources are always probabilistic and thus random examples of differences do not prove the absence of national or international level determinants or generalities. If, for example, violence in Indonesia is much more common during the times of transitions, this is a reason for a study of the impact of such macro-level changes as power transitions on conflicts in the peripheries.

Alqadrie's (2003) observation that conflicts in West Kalimantan tend to reappear every 30 years (Alqadrie 2003), which also seems to be the length of the Indonesian generational leadership cycle during the authoritarian times, could suggest that the impact of regime change on conflict and violence in West Kalimantan is substantial. At the same time, explanations that Davidson calls the post-Suharto scramble (van Klinken, Bertrand, Huxley, Aditjondro) might exaggerate the role of just one transitional change in conflict motives in West Kalimantan and elsewhere in Indonesia.

To bring in the national context into perspective, one should use something solid to measure the conflict trends in Indonesia and compare them to those in West Kalimantan. For peace research that measurement has to be the number of conflict fatalities. Lives lost to conflict are the concrete core problem for a peace researcher, while it would be difficult to see any reasons to value one person's life more than someone else's. Thus battle deaths appear to constitute an optimal tool for an analysis that could reveal whether West Kalimantan conflicts are an exception in the Indonesian context, thus rendering national-level explanations useless, or whether West Kalimantan represents the national pattern, which then is likely to be affected by nation-level explanations. If we only look at battle deaths of conflicts involving the state, and where both sides are armed (both conditions are suspected in the case of West Kalimantan), we can use the data provided by the Peace Research Institute Oslo and the Uppsala Conflict Data Program (Lacina and Gleditsch 2005[19]). The numbers of fatalities looks low, but this is due to the fact

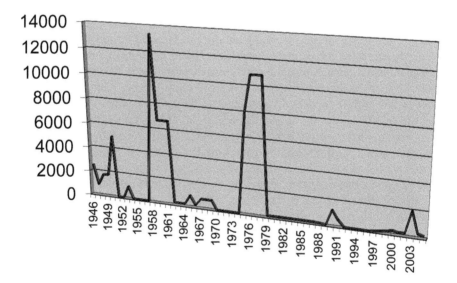

Figure 2.1   Battle Deaths in Indonesian Conflicts

19   The latest update, from 2009, of the data is available at www.prio.no/CSCW/ Datasets/Armed-Conflict/Battle-Deaths.

that most media reports count indirect fatalities as conflict fatalities. In the graph in Figure 2.1, only direct fatalities are counted. Furthermore, the PRIO/Uppsala data is often criticized as conservative in its estimates. Yet, since it practices the same conservatism and coding criteria for each conflict, this graph does present an accurate estimate of the profile of battle deaths over time.

The graph in Figure 2.1 seems to suggest that West Kalimantan was exceptional during the main periods of violence, 1966–68 and 1996–99, as the rest of Indonesia was relatively peaceful. The thesis of the post-Suharto scramble is made almost ridiculous in the light of this graph as the time soon after the downfall of Suharto does not seem exceptionally violent. However, as we remember, the definition of "conflict" in this graph is too narrow for such a conclusion. West Kalimantan conflicts were partly killings of unarmed parties, and in any case the state did not take part as a conflicting party.

I have complemented the graph based on the PRIO data with some sources on Indonesian one-sided violence, and non-state wars (Figure 2.2). The data on one-sided violence since 1989 is from Kreutz (2006), HSRP (2006), and Eck and Hultman (2007) while the data on non-state war since 1989 is from Harbom and Wallensteen (2009), and Gleditsch, Wallensteen, Eriksson, Sollenberg and Strand (2002). The data on earlier one-sided conflict is estimated by using arithmetic averages of several low estimates, most importantly Rummel (1994), Cribb (2001) and Kiernan (2007).

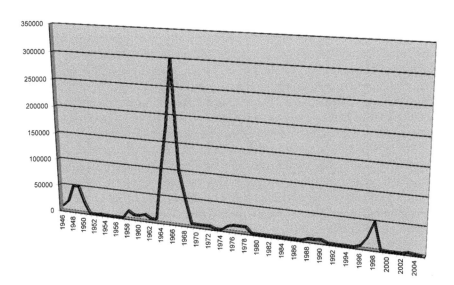

Figure 2.2   Fatalities of Political Violence in Indonesia

In a comparison of all political violence between the whole of Indonesia and West Kalimantan we can clearly see that the three periods of transition are all very conflict-prone both in Indonesia as a whole and in West Kalimantan. Thus national trends should not be undermined.

Furthermore, despite the noise made on conflicts after democratization and the liberation of the media, the reality of the Indonesian conflict is that while the transition and the economic crisis were bloody, the period was in no way exceptional, and thus explanations over-emphasizing the role of the otherwise exceptional period of democratization cannot be encouraged by this overview of Indonesian fatalities of political violence. This is why, in this study, I will give due attention to the two transformations that took place at the latter half of the 1990s, the economic crisis and the slow transition to greater regional autonomy.

However, the main problem in existing research into the motives for violence seems to be the fact that analytical explanations fail to explain Madurese violence as part of the same conflict as Malay and Dayak violence. This is partly because most of the main theorists of West Kalimantan conflict do not seem to consider the Madurese violence as part of the conflict. This is true both of van Klinken and Davidson. Even though the latter never explicitly admits it, Davidson's explanations always focus on the motives and opportunities of the Dayaks and the Malays, but never the Madurese. Van Klinken (2008: 35) is more open about this, claiming that conflicts in West Kalimantan are best described as "one-sided pogroms against an immigrant minority, namely the Madurese." Yet, violence in West Kalimantan is clearly interactive, communicative and characterized by a mutual fear, and in that sense leaving one side out of the explanation is simply a mistake. One cannot fruitfully study communication, interaction or a system of mutual fear without looking at the interaction from both sides.

The motives of the Madurese have traditionally been associated with the violent Madurese culture. In the more scholarly analyses no motives are sought for the Madurese violence. Primordial explanations have very little pragmatic value: if motives are predestined by the objective characteristics of a race, there is little room for constructive conflict resolution. But the lack of current scholarly research into the Madurese motives for violence leaves us with very little in terms of an analysis of the conflict motives of the first phase of the conflict.

In my analysis the dispute between indigenous ethnic groups and "migrant people" is related to the interpretations on the role of ethnicity in politics. Here motives are related to the opportunities that the language of conflict in West Kalimantan offers. In West Kalimantan, it is possible to argue about terms of inter-community interaction by means of violence. There was a Madurese motive to construct, by means of violent opposition to local customs, a situation where only Indonesian law, and not the local customs of the Dayak or Malay indigenous people, had relevance in everyday life. In this setting the logical opposite violent construction is one in which an extreme difference is created between indigenous and non-indigenous groups: by asking (and then forcing) the Madurese to leave, the Dayak and later Malay mobs were not only rejecting the equality of indigenous and non-indigenous groups, but they were constructing the agency of "visitors" (=Madurese) and hosts (=Dayaks/Malays) into the political and economic scene. In the Indonesian context lynching and mob violence often imply this demand that its targets will have to leave (Welsh 2008: 484–6). In this sense, while articulating an interpretation about the positions of the Madurese, violence also serves the purpose of sending people of that ethnicity away.

Existing research into the conflict in West Kalimantan has not emphasized the emergence of antagonism or the appearance of conflict motives in its explanation of the conflict. Rather, it has mainly focused on the opportunities for violence and the failure of the obstacles that should have kept violent economic and political competition in check. Many scholars seem to associate these opportunities with the chaotic process of decentralization (Brown 2001, van Klinken 2007). Huub de Jonge and Gerben Nooteboom (2006) furthermore emphasize the fact that the primacy of the authoritarian elite, the Javanese pro-Suharto circles, had lost their stronghold by the time of the beginning of the conflict in Bengkayang. In the absence of institutional procedures and rules of political competition, space was made also for violent competition, in both the economic and political spheres. According to van Klinken all this was already visible in February 1994, when Dayak youngsters started rioting after failing to get their own (Dayak) candidate selected for the leadership of the district of Sintang (2007: 55–6). Clearly the lack of regulation of political competition contributed to the Sintang riots, which were not yet directed against the Madurese, and which did not result in massive casualties.

Jamie S. Davidson (2003, 2008) adds to this explanation by showing that political imagination did not restrict political opportunities for violence. West Kalimantan in general and Sambas district in particular had already in 1967 experienced a situation that had shown that indigenous people can expel a non-indigenous population by means of violence, if their economic or political interests so demand. During the anti-Communist cleansing of 1966–67, Davidson claims that the Indonesian military incited Dayak anger at the Chinese population, whom the military suspected of Communist sympathies, and once this anger was provoked there, the Suharto administration did nothing to stop massive violence by Dayak mobs against the Chinese people in northern West Kalimantan. As a result rural areas of Sambas (and current Bangkayang) were cleansed of ethnic Chinese. While this happened 30 years before the next major incidence of mass violence, the experience of 1967 provided a model for the resolution of interests of political competition: indigenous people were able to "throw out" "visitors," and thus this model was used also in Bengkayang in 1997, and in Sambas in 1999. I do not see any reason to challenge the main argument of Davidson about the significance of the experience of "throwing the visitors out" in the creation of the sense of "feasibility" of such an option in the future. Instead, I will build on that in my analysis of the creation of relative deprivation among the Dayaks and the Sambas Malays. Yet, I feel that the picture was much more complex, and thus there is no reason to summarize the sources of conflict in a way that highlights this factor more than many other crucial factors.

Violence was also seen as an opportunity in another manner. According to Nancy Lee Peluso (2008, Peluso and Watts 2001) and Yulia Sugandi (2006) violence was used to consolidate ethnic solidarity. Instead of strong motives or great antagonism, opportunities for doing many things with violence—competition, getting rid of competitors, and consolidating group identity—were the main explanations of violence in West Kalimantan.

While my own analysis seems to confirm this conclusion, I will suggest one modification to this theory by Peluso and Sugandi. I think that the main identity-related opportunity that explains violence in West Kalimantan is not collective but individual. It is related to the individual's opportunity to prove his commitment to a religious group or a community. Instead of violence as such consolidating ethnic identity, it seems to be possible in West Kalimantan for individuals to prove their commitment to a community by using violence. Welsh (2008) suggests that violence, in her analysis mob violence in Indonesia, is intended as something "enforcing moral purity" in a community. This seems very likely. But in so many cases it is clear not just that violence is focused on its target, but that its function is also related to the violent actor himself. It is intended to show the moral purity of the violent actor. Many of the fighters I have interviewed made their decision to join violent action once there was an opportunity to show by means of violence their belonging to a group. Punishing an ethnic community whose members have violated a girl of one's own ethnic community is an opportunity to show not only that one is a loyal member of the community, but also that one is a man who does what a man is supposed to do: defend a girl. The relationship between masculine identities and violence in Indonesia has been studied in some of the studies at the crossroads of gender studies and peace research (Nilan 2009, Wilson 2006). In this scholarship the problem of the relationship between hegemonic masculinities and violence has been analyzed in a much more detailed manner than is possible here. However, the approach has not been pragmatic in the sense that the investigation would be tuned to discovering opportunities to change the position of what these scholars call aggressive masculinity in the definition of "men." Nilan and Wilson portray identity discourses as something with causal powers, but they do not mainly focus on how violence is used to enact manhood and how this violent strategy could be made unavailable.

Christians or Muslims sometimes use violence against a group that is associated with an act of violence against a church or a mosque. Sometimes their real interest is not in the punishment of the group, but in showing that although they have been slack with prayers, they are still good Christians or Muslims. Here the crucial factor is that the "language of conflict" allows opportunities for violent demonstrations of belongingness and the "rules of grammar" allow for the demonstration of one's belonging by means of violence. Brutality is not a way to tarnish the image of one's group or a way to risk common economic development (as it perhaps should be), but instead it is a way to show loyalty and belongingness.

Chapter 3
Junctures on the Path to Conflict

Antagonism

In the media, fighting in West Kalimantan has been characterized as ethnic, while many scholars prefer to call these conflicts communal (Alqadrie 2002). The latter characterization clearly describes the sides in the conflict better, since fighting tended to stay within community boundaries rather than the hatred of the Sambas Malays spreading from Sambas to Ketapang or other districts or provinces of Kalimantan.

Yet, it seems that the "successful" ethnic cleansing in Sambas in 1999 by the Malays encouraged the Dayaks in Central Kalimantan in 2001 (International Crisis Group 2001), while the expelling of the Madurese in Bengkayang in 1997 could have had an encouraging effect on the Sambas Malays in 1999. Similarly, the cleansing of the Chinese in 1967 by the Dayaks encouraged the Dayaks to cleanse the Madurese too (1967–68) (Davidson 2008). Thus antagonization also spread beyond ethnic boundaries, with Dayak hatred of the Chinese encouraging Dayak hatred of the Madurese, Dayak hatred of the Madurese encouraging Malay hatred of the Madurese, and Malay hatred of the Madurese encouraging Dayak hatred of the Madurese in Central Kalimantan.

In some other cases, antagonization spread to other communities of the same ethnicity. According to people interviewed for this study—for example, in the Dayak-Madurese conflict of 1996–97—coastal areas south of Singkawang in Sunyai Pinjuh were affected by the antagonization of the relations between the Madures and the Dayaks, despite the fact that local communities of Dayaks and Madurese had managed to avoid Dayak-Madurese antagonism before the conflict. Before the conflict, Islamic Madurese people used to use their cars to help Catholic Dayaks get to church on Sundays. At the beginning of the conflict, the local Dayaks defended and hid the local Madurese (interviews with anonymous informants). Inter-community antagonization took place also in Sanggau Ledo during the conflict of 1996–97. Many of the Dayak instigators and agitators of conflict in the sub-district of Ledo came from the sub-district of the Sanggau Ledo area and were unknown to the locals (Dede 2006). The fact that the violence of 1996–97 took place simultaneously in so many different communities also suggests that there were ethnic loyalties beyond people's own communities. Nevertheless, loyalties in conflict situations were still primarily communal.

Community identities and loyalties can be positive in suitable issue areas. Their existence does not, as such, explain the emergence of antagonistic conflicting parties. On the contrary, the suppression of ethnic identities and the discrimination towards individuals on grounds of their ethnic association are often seen as being related to ethno-political violence (Gurr 1994). However, it seems that the problem with community identities and loyalties in West Kalimantan was related to the fact that they were relevant in relation to issues of security: people relied on community groups, rather than the state, for their security. Thus I need to specify the nature of the community identity and loyalty that I see as negative, or as a contribution to conflict. Communal security identity, for example, clearly seems to be this kind of a negative community identity.[1] According to Poulton and Youssouf (1998), when security becomes factionalized along ethnic lines in a society, the sheer security priority of ethnic groups leads them to oppose each other's prosperity. The better-off the other communities are the more efficient they are in mobilizing militias. Ethnic/community security identity leads to negative interdependence. Here otherwise benign defensive action creates a structural setting that favors offensive behavior. When each group tries to defend its own people without paying attention to the common security, each group's security will be negatively affected by the strength of other groups. This way purely defensive behavior easily becomes threatening, and violent.[2]

Poulton's and Youssouf's case study is about northern Mali, but the logic fits into the structural setting of West Kalimantan. The background of the negative community loyalty in West Kalimantan was that the modern official administrative structures failed to help people achieve prosperity and security, and as a result, people sought help from their families and communities.

Fighting was also avoided in many villages and in some sub-districts in Sambas as well as in Bengkayang—even though the Madurese people eventually had to escape from those villages and sub-districts. Actually, community divisions were generally also very pronounced in these areas. But due to the relatively small number of Madurese there, community thinking did not begin to travel along defense issue lines. The majority communities did not feel threatened by the Madurese, while the Madurese's communal strength could not protect them from the much stronger majority ethnic communities. The main bulk of violence took place in areas where the migrant community was rather large and its influence on the economy was significant (Boni 2009). In the main conflict areas it is easy to see a polarization of the security situation between the locals and the migrants, whereas wherever the migrant population has not presented a security challenge to the local majorities, conflicts have not occurred, or they have had a significantly lower intensity (Andoth 2006, TK 2003).

In the main conflict areas, security and order were regulated in the most clearly ethnic manner, and ethnic/communal thinking penetrated into all issue areas of politics. In Ledo, in December 1996 and January 1997, the communities of two stabbed uncles sought revenge by resorting to their communities, even though

---

1   For the contribution of such an identity to a communal security dilemma, where one's security means the other's insecurity, see for example, Poulton and Youssouf 1998.

2   Fearon 1995, Lake and Rothchild 1997, 97–131.

they also demanded action from the police (Dede 2006). In February 1997, after the alleged molesting of a Dayak woman by a Madurese burglar, the perpetrator's village formed an ethnic-based self-defense force, rather than seeking protection from the police. Yet, once the asymmetry of forces became too evident, the Madurese victims of Dayak violence did seek protection from the public sector, but from the air force, rather than from the police (Acap 2006, Sedau 3 2006). The same happened in Sambas in 1999, where the individuals who had been punished by Malay people in Parit Setia sought security and revenge from the community of the Madurese after failing to get help from the legal system (Davidson 2008: 129).

The situation is not entirely different now. In the first meetings of the Ethnic Communication Forum of West Kalimantan, the leaders of Sambas, Singkawang and Bengkayang communities accepted in 2008 the idea that the ethnic leadership in every case should support working through the police, and should accept the primacy of the role of the police in settling crime issues that involve individuals from different communities. However, when the forum expanded to Landak in 2009, it became clear that the police was still not trusted enough for the Landak ethnic leaders to declare that they would not organize for the defense of members of their own communities in case members of their communities were mistreated by individuals from other communities.[3]

However, progress is taking place, and ethnic defense identity is losing ground. In 2003, in my discussions in Sanggau Ledo, for example, public officials considered Dayak communal customary law and order supreme in all issue areas, including those of law enforcement, security and criminal law (AT 2006). Then, even the police admitted that their security role was subordinate to the role of ethnic defense arrangements. Still, some years ago it was not possible to discuss the possibility of ethnic leaders publicly declaring that disputes between members of ethnic groups should be submitted to the police. However, this very declaration was made by the inaugural meeting of the West Kalimantan Ethnic Communication Forum in Pasir Panjang, on December 15, 2008. This meeting, however, still excluded Landak.

While communal defense identities are dangerous, they do not, as such, create antagonism. In fact, if one community dominates the social order, the risk of a communal security dilemma is minimal.[4] In such situations, alternative sources of security and law in the minority communities are not accepted, except for the small

---

3 When referring to discussions and decisions of the West Kalimantan Ethnic Communication Forum, or its district-level meetings, I will not give references as the information is based on my own observations. I acted as the secretary of the first meetings, until the forum in its third province-level meeting, selected a secretary.

4 A security dilemma is a situation where the search for security among some potentially conflicting parties automatically reduces the level of security among other potentially conflicting parties. Such a security dilemma often leads to an arms race and socially irrational outcomes, where a level of security is achieved at a cost that is higher than if the security dilemma did not exist.

community neighborhood-watch type of arrangements. However, when tension between ethnic communities grows, it is unlikely that the majority community's law-enforcement and criminal code will treat other communities kindly. Harsh, exclusive local laws and law enforcement easily provoke a counter-reaction and create confusion in the normative order. As a result, different ethnic communities try to enforce different sets of norms (Fearon 1995, Lake and Rothchild 1997). This was clearly the case in Bengkayang in 1996, as the Madurese community increasingly started to isolate itself and organize its own safety and protection from Dayak criminal punishment (Sedau 1, 2006). In February 1997, even the minority defense force tried to show its might by behaving in an oppressive manner. A Madurese mob, who had been established to protect the community from revenge action after a Madurese burglar had assaulted a woman, became frustrated by the fact that no Dayak reaction followed. Since their anticipated fight did not occur, some members of the mob decided to burn some Dayak houses in order to provoke such a fight (Acap 2008, Andoth 2006). This was the beginning of the next phase of the Bengkayang riots, which eventually threw out almost all Madurese people from the district (then sub-district).

While at this stage one cannot say for sure why the tension rose in Bengkayang and Sambas at the end of the 1990s, it can be established that an agent structure in which security and law enforcement are entrusted to many intermingling ethnic groups is one that is very vulnerable to antagonisms, as Fearon (1995), and Lake and Rothchild (1997: 97–131) have found out by using comparative data. When crime becomes a community issue, every single member of the potentially hostile communities can spark an escalation of community antagonism by committing crimes that the other community finds it impossible to accept.

Crime as the trigger of community tension has been the main pattern in West Kalimantan. If we look at the 17 cases of communal violence in Chapter 1 of this book, we can see that in 14 cases the trigger of conflict was inter-ethnic crime. In 12 of the 14 clear cases of escalation from crime, the perpetrator was a Madurese individual. In one case it was Dayak, and in another it is likely that the Indonesian army framed a Chinese man as the perpetrator of their own crime.

In the cases of Sambas and Bengkayang (and in Central Kalimantan, before riots there) several Madurese did their best to communalize their criminal behavior. A Javanese doctor interviewed by a Western reporter (Peter Kerr, *Jakarta Post* July 19, 2001) suggested that most trauma injuries treated by his hospital, apart from traffic accidents, were caused by traditional Madurese knives. Even many of the Madurese interviewed for this study confirmed the persisting Dayak and Malay view that most of the Malay/Dayak–Madurese conflicts are triggered by a Madurese injuring or killing a Dayak or Malay. However, according to them, these incidents should not trigger community hatred, since they are merely matters of two or more individuals who just happen to be from different ethnic origins (Abdullah 2006, Ali 2005, JM1 2001, Sabran 2006, Thoha 2005).

A Malay informant (Abdurrahman 2006) who participated in the mobilization of a mob in the Sambas conflict expressed the difficulty of treating Madurese crimes as individual issues as he reluctantly admitted that a majority of Madurese were not criminals: "but still, the crimes were Madurese crimes, not individual ones." Even in the face of the fact that goods stolen by Madurese did not end up as "common Madurese property," but as individual property, he could not consider the incidents as anything but collective Madurese misdeeds. This is precisely because of the communal nature of security: Madurese individuals were protected and hidden from the police by other Madurese individuals, who referred to communal Madurese solidarity. Thus, every individual incident affected collective community relations.

Later, in Chapter 4, I will reveal another reason why inter-ethnic crimes became framed as communal: if crime can be used as an opportunity for the articulation of an order without dominant local customs, the community of the perpetrator is likely to sympathize with the crime, while the community of the victim is likely to attribute the crime to all those benefiting from the rule that was articulated by crime (i.e., the rule according to which local customs are not binding or meaningful).

The system of communal loyalties in security issues was (and to some extent still is) naturalized within a framework that saw members of communities as fundamentally different due to the "ethnic characteristics" of each individual within the ethnic community (Burhanuddin 2003, Luna 2006). People in West Kalimantan generally consider that the conception of security is fundamentally different between communities. These security identities are then naturalized in stereotypes of the nature of people in different communities. According to the district head (Bupati) of Bengkayang, the district (then sub-district) where the Kalimantan violence of 1997–98 took place, "The explanation of conflict in Bengkayang (Sanggau Ledo) is cultural. The Madurese are spoiled by nature. They have no discipline. We cannot help that" (Luna 2006). Furthermore, Madurese were perceived as poorly educated, entrepreneurial and arrogant.

Many Malays and Dayaks interviewed felt that the Madurese had proved their unwillingness to integrate by settling in all-Madurese villages (Abdurrahman 2006, Andoth 2006). This was seen as a proof of the characteristic Madurese arrogance. To some extent, the isolation of the Madurese was a myth. Observations made of the scenes of ethnic cleansing in Sambas, for example, prove that many of the Madurese houses were actually burned and destroyed in the middle of Malay areas. More systematic investigations by a Malay scholar in Pontianak, Ngusmanto G.M. (interview 2003), also prove that Madurese interaction with other communities is more extensive than often portrayed by the conflicting parties. However, in conflict areas during the time of tension, they probably did isolate themselves and defend and hide their own individuals, who, in the eyes of the Dayak customary law (often also in the eyes of the positive law), were seen as criminal. While this was perceived as emanating from the objective natural characteristics of the Madurese, opportunities for attempting to integrate the Madurese into a common normative system of which the Madurese community could have felt ownership were lost.

The most problematic stereotypical image of the Madurese is related to the perceived Madurese tendency to violence and crime. Madurese were known to carry their sickles (traditional Madurese knives) openly, and thus it was often believed that they did that for criminal purposes (Alqadrie 2003, International Crisis Group 2001). Emphasizing physical power was also probably part of the Madurese way of claiming space in the primarily Malay or Dayak societies. However, for an outsider the differences between Malay, Dayak and Madurese practices were not noticeable. Very often one can also see Dayaks and Malays carrying their tools for cutting grass, and if one had not been exposed to the dominant framing of ethnicities in the province, one could see these as threatening weapons. According to many Madurese informants, their knives were also used as tools and not for violence (Sedau 1, 2006). However, these knives were allegedly treated differently by the police than the weapons/tools of the Dayaks and Malays. The evidence of Madurese crime is not conclusive. While one hospital claimed that Madurese knife-wounds were common in their first-aid department, according to police statistics of some Sambas areas, the rate of crime rose after the "ethnic cleansing" had taken place (Sugandi 2003).

At the same time Dayaks were often perceived by Malays and Madurese as backward, primitive and stupid (interview material), while the Malays were often seen as lazy, cowardly and incompetent (Bouvier, de Jonge and Smith 2006, Smith 1997). Needless to say, these perceptions were often very far from the truth. Yet, the perception of Dayak stupidity and Malay laziness could have contributed to the unwillingness of some Madurese to commit themselves to a common normative order. Often, the question was not so much one about unwillingness to accept certain norms in principle as it was about a sense of superiority caused by assessments of individuals from the other communities based on pejorative stereotypes: stupid Dayaks and lazy Malays did not deserve a fair treatment. According to a youth leader in Tanjung Keracut (TKK 2003), "the Madurese considered us 'krupuk' and gave us no respect." A "krupuk" is a prawn cracker, but when it is a characterization of a person, it means almost the same as a "doormat" would mean in the English language. A person who is "krupuk" is "easy to break" (like a cracker), and thus the submission by the "krupuk" is based on something slightly more violent than in the comparable English expression "doormat."

While communalization of security created a vulnerable agency structure where crime easily leads to conflict, this did not, in itself, create antagonism between communities, and neither did the pejorative community stereotypes that naturalized the securitization of community relations. What, then, created the tension in this volatile communal structure of agents? The communal agent structure itself did not create roles and positions that would have easily clashed. The final problem was not that there was a community division that was shared by all, but instead that the conflicting parties perceived agency differently, and that each of these constructions of agency served the interests of the community differently.

The main dividing lines in West Kalimantan conflicts were related to (a) the discourse on the rights of local people as opposed to "non-locals" or "newcomers" (who actually were not new in the area) versus (b) the discourse on the rights of all

Indonesians. In the first discourse, agency in West Kalimantan was structured in two groups with different rights. In the latter discourse, agency consisted mainly of individual Indonesians with equal rights. This, it seems, was the situation that created the antagonism and the polarization of the agent structure both in the 1960s and in the 1990s. The discourse on localness was latent during the times of peace, but it was expressed, framing Dayak and Malay common agency (as indigenous populations), during the conflict episodes. Jamie Davidson has explained the international discursive sources—the debate on the "Fourth World", the awakening of the Native Americans, the birth of the International Working Group on Indigenous Affairs (IWGIA) and the debate on Cultural Survival—for the conception of local rights in his analysis of the rise of Dayak indigenousness (Davidson 2007, Henley and Davidson 2007: 6). According to him, a discourse of "indigenism" that was born out of the frustration of marginalized indigenous people was taken—by the foundation named Pancur Kasih, the Dayak Solidarity Fund, and the Institute of Dayakology Research and Development (IDRD)—to address the marginalization of Dayaks in their own areas, and to develop self-sufficient organization and governance among Dayaks (Bamba 2003, Davidson 2007: 226–30). However, indigenous rights were also used, against the original purposes of at least some of the Dayak activists, for the justification of superior rights of indigenous people in comparison to "migrant communities," and to justify violence against migrant communities in the name of rights customary to the Dayaks (IDRD 1999). The appeal of the scholarly "Dayakologists" gave scientific credibility to the claim for indigenous rights, while these rights were then interpreted in the villages in a varying manner (Acap 2006). An unfortunate epistemic attitude was born out of this scientific discourse, treating Dayak violence in the riots of the 1996–97 as an objective effect of the causal powers brought about by the violations of the Dayak's *adat* rights. This discursive source of conflict will be treated in more detail in the discussion on what made violence possible from the point of view of its legitimacy.

At the same time, the Madurese clung to the nationalist discourse on the rights of all Indonesians (Ali 2005, Rupaat 2005). This was understandable because of the usefulness of the national framing for their local position of power. The indigenous discourse did not offer the Madurese an equal position, while the nationalist discourse did. In a situation where "migrant" races are assumed to be subject to local constructions, it is understandable that those who see themselves as equal Indonesians do have a problem with adopting and assimilating into the local identity and the local system of customs (Nagian 2003).

However, the Madurese articulation of the centralist framings made them a perfect displaced target for the frustration and aggression that Dayaks and Malays felt against the central state. For decades, people from ethnicities that were alien from the center had been dictating their affairs, despite their local majority position. Against the history of Jakartan centralist dominance in West Kalimantan, it was understandable that the local communities felt a fascination with the ideas of decentralization and local rights (Bamba 2003). However, instead of being capable of explicitly negotiating the rules of inter-ethnic coexistence, and instead of being able to resist the power of the center (Jakarta), the Madurese were seen as a community which represented the center to the locals and to whom the new framing of local rights was demonstrated (Nagian 2003).

The dynamics in which the Madurese became "displaced" targets of the local communities is related partly to the agency structure, and partly to the motives of communities and the opportunities that the West Kalimantan culture of conflict offers for the articulation of interpretations of agency. The fact that agency was constructed in two different ways created part of the problem. On the one hand, agency was constructed as one national community of equals; on the other hand, it was constructed as two communities, local and guest, within a hierarchical structure. This was the problem that explains the first step in the emergence of antagonism between communities in West Kalimantan. However, the fact that different identity constructs served communities differently is a matter of conflict motives: It was in the interests of the Madurese to demonstrate the meaningless of local rules, while it was in the interests of the Malay and Dayak communities to reconstruct the authority of the local rules by punishing the "visitors" for their rejection of the local rules. Finally, the fact that there was an opportunity to argue for the national identity by violently ignoring the local rules and that there was an opportunity to emphasize the local rules by throwing its challengers out was a matter of conflict opportunities. Thus, these dynamics are something I will return to in the following chapter on conflict motives and conflict opportunities.

In the emergence of antagonism between the Madurese and the Malays and Dayaks, one peculiar fact is that other migrant groups, such as the Javanese or the multinational corporations, were never perceived with as much resentment as the Madurese. According to many people, other ethnic groups tended to mix with others and were thus more accepted than the Madurese.[5] From the point of view of especially Dayak grievances, these groups were as much to blame for the loss of Dayak lands and for the marginalization of the Dayak population in West Kalimantan. The Madurese, however, were probably an easier target, and thus they became the scapegoats, or, as Horowitz puts it, "displaced targets" (Horowitz 2003: 135–46) of Dayak misfortune. Target displacement is very typical for conflicts between "locals" and "migrant communities," as in most cases the "migrants" substitute the central government as the target of aggression (Fearon and Laitin 2011). The fact that the Javanese have not, with a few exceptions, been the target of Dayak and Sambas Malay aggression has been for a more unusual feature of the conflict in West Kalimantan, and can possibly be explained with the power political logic of target displacement. Targeting migrants instead of the central administration is already a target replacement strategy that avoids choosing

---

5   It is interesting to note that the hesitancy of various ethnic minorities to integrate can be perceived as a problem also in other areas in Indonesia (Chinese on Nias, Bataks in the Dairi regency, Javanese in Bali and Acehnese in Medan, for example). Local rights can apparently be claimed only by integrating with locals.

too strong targets, the central administration. However, in Indonesia, the majority ethnicity, the Javanese, could still have been too dangerous a target for the Dayaks and the Malays. Trying to hit the Javanese would have certainly sparked an angrier reaction from the central state. This could be part of the reason why the Madurese became the substitute target.

The local population often rejects the claim that the Madurese were a displaced target, and that they had any problems with the central administration (Abdurrahman 2006, Andoth 2006, Bernardinus 2006). However, the nature of target displacement is such that the people who replace their real target with an easier one do not admit to or recognize the replacement. Otherwise, target replacement would obviously not make much sense: it would be unlikely for conflict actors to fully understand and accept the fact that the objects of their aggressions did not really have much to do with their frustration. Yet, there are signals that suggest that the Madurese symbolized the state, and the state symbolized the Madurese community.

In some instances, in the language of the local rights activists and indigenous combatants, the two were almost used interchangeably. One Malay activist (Abdurrahman 2006) in the 1999 Sambas riot, for example, said that one of the crucial triggers for the Sambas riots was the insulting statement made by General Wiranto, then commander of the Indonesian Defense Forces. "Wiranto was in West Kalimatan considered as Madurese ... [and the insult was the suggestion that] Dayaks and Sambas Malays were cannibals." If a statement made by a top Javanese general from Jakarta is seen as an insult from the Madurese, then there definitely seems to be some interchangeability between the Madurese and the state in "indigenous discourse." When the Malay activist avenged himself upon the local Madurese for the insult made by the (Javanese) head of the Indonesian military, the local Madurese became, in a very concrete manner, a scapegoat for the state and a displaced target for the anger and frustration that the local West Kalimantan Malays felt towards the central state. Yet, West Kalimantan Dayaks and Malays are careful to emphasize that they do not hate the Javanese, and that they are not against the central state.[6] When I asked Bonggas Bernardinus (2006), a traditional Dayak leader who had a leading role in conflict activities in Sanggau Ledo, whether the fact that Sanggau Ledo is led by Dayak *adat* and that Indonesian law is irrelevant in the sub-district meant that, in a way, Sanggau Ledo had separated from Indonesia, he was clearly offended and flatly rejected my suggestion: "We have never fought Indonesian troops." Of course, even this is not entirely true, as the Dayak militias, undoubtedly including Mr. Bonggas

---

6 However, a public servant from the Sanggau district who served in Sanggau Ledo during the conflict suggests that the risk of conflict between Dayaks and several smaller ethnic groups, including Javanese, is a real danger in the near future. According to the Dayak traditional leader, Suherman Acap, there was an inter-ethnic case of the murder of a Dayak person by a Javanese criminal in the region. This incident nearly caused a violent ethnic reaction.

Bernardinus, also fought the Indonesian troops during the Bengkayang conflict in 1997 (Davidson 2008: 102).

When the killing started, the situation was confusing. On the one hand, community traditions and rituals played an important role, and thus one would think that the agent structure was as plural as the ethnic structure. But actually, as never seen in times of peace, Sambas Malays, for example, resorted to many of the traditional ways of the Dayak, and the brotherhood of the Malay and Dayak indigenous camps was emphasized to the extreme (Burhanuddin 2003). In interviews, the two largest ethnicities were often, even during peaceful times, described as "brothers" due to their alleged common origin in Southern China (interviews by the author 2001–06) and due to their interaction, intermarriages, and so forth. According to some, Sambas Malays were simply Dayaks who had converted to Islam (Davidson 2007: 242, note 5), while others reject this perception.[7]

At the same time, the "visitor status" of the Madurese in the minds of the Dayaks and the Sambas Malays was not obvious in the beginning. According to the head of one of the villages in Telok Ramat, which was eventually hit by large-scale violence, the Madurese were "almost considered as local" before the escalation of the conflict (TK 2003). However, violence mobilized the divide between the indigenous and the "guests". Also, the district head of Sambas felt that "at first the Madurese were treated as brothers, but the conflict changed everything" (Burhanuddin 2003).

The confusion also ignited the Chinese community in Sambas, as they were desperate to articulate a communal framing which could prevent a division between the indigenous and the non-indigenous. Within such a framework, the Chinese would not be seen as enemies of the stronger indigenous communities. Two Chinese informants from the Sambas district, for example, were afraid of being classified with the Madurese as non-indigenous people, and thus enemies of the Malays and Dayaks. To prevent this, and to frame the agent structure as communal, they both gave material support to the anti-Madurese campaigns of their Malay neighbors (AJ 2001, LBH 2001). With this maneuver they clearly demonstrated that the Madurese were a common enemy for the indigenous Malays and the Chinese, and that the conflict was due to the objective community/ethnic characteristics of the Madurese and not caused by their status as non-indigenous to West Kalimantan. The practice of helping the Malay mobs against the Madurese was common among many Chinese in Kalimantan (Atio 2005, Welles 2006).

Furthermore, in the conflict of Bengkayang, migrant populations that were not Madurese made it easier for the indigenous Dayaks to identify their ethnic

---

7   A strong argument against Davidson's interpretation in current West Kalimantan is the strong emerging organization of Muslim Dayaks (Sahyudin 2004). The truth about the origin of Malays and Dayaks, and the question of whether Sambas Malays really are just converted Dayaks, is not important for the analysis of agencies in Sambas: obviously, collective identities are perceptions rather than objective, material realities.

affiliation as separate from the Madurese by marking their ethnicity in their houses. According to Human Rights Watch, "To safeguard themselves against attacks during the conflict, non-Madurese residents scrawled 'Melayu' [Malay] or 'Jawa' [Javanese] on their homes, and Chinese hung a strip of red cloth on their doors" (1997: 4).

Articulation of the indigenous rights framework required that non-indigenous people like the Madurese be treated as guests. The terminology of the discourse was interesting and explained some of its contradictions. Indigenous races did not use the term "migrant" for the Madurese, because "migrant" would have referred to a foreigner, a non-Indonesian, and the Madurese were Indonesians. To speak of their "Indonesianness" would have been impossible, since in the discourse on "Indonesianness," the "national rights of all citizens" was the main challenging discourse for the "indigenousness discourse." The term that the discourse on indigenousness uses for the Madurese is closer to the term "newcomer"; except that, since many of the Madurese had not come recently to West Kalimantan, the word did not have the connotation of recentness, but simply referred to the Madurese as "comers" (Abdurrahman 2006). Yet the timing of their arrival was essential, too, since the Dayak and the Malays had also arrived in Kalimantan; they were not locals, as were the people who had always stayed there. However, instead of explicating the claim of indigenousness and negotiating it, indigenousness was "negotiated" through action and demonstration. This resulted in an antagonism in community relations.

During and after the conflict the "local" interpretation has been that without total assimilation a "non-local" culture cannot gain equal rights, and will have to accept an inferior position as visitors. The answers of an MA student group from Siantan (close to Pontianak) in a student assignment on indigenousness illustrate the expectation well. The students write about three ethnic groups: the Bugis, who have assimilated to the local Malay tradition and assumed equal rights, the Chinese, who have not assimilated, but who have accepted a lower political status, and the Madurese, who are the problem. According to the students, "The Bugis have lived in the area for a long time and have assimilated with local Malay people through inter-ethnic marriages." This way the Bugis have become local. However, the Madurese are resisted because of their refusal to assimilate. According to the students of Siantan, "The Madurese people have lived here for quite a long time. However, they tend to live in their own group and keep a distance from others. They are strongly attached to the rules and culture of the Madurese society. They also tend to listen to the religious leaders from their own ethnic group. The Madurese people's anomic attitude can be seen from the fact that they tend to obey the rules of their own group. As a result, there is a gap between the Madurese and the local people."

While the Chinese in Siantan are also resistant to assimilation, they are so far tolerated as they do not even seek total equality. According to the students, "The other group that tends to live exclusively are the Chinese. However, they are relatively moderate in their relationship with other ethnic groups. Unlike the

Madurese who have an 'offensive' character due to their culture of *carok* [deadly duel to defend honor], the Chinese are relatively more defensive. They concentrate more on the economic sector." However, whenever the Chinese seek political equality and local rights, as has been the case in Singkawang and Pontianak, they are resisted by the "local" ethnic groups. This has been clear in the strong resentment of the Malay community towards the Singkawang Mayor, who is ethnic Chinese (conflict 17 in the list of conflicts in Chapter 1), as well as in the political competition in Pontianak City, where the Chinese population represents one of the largest voter groups.

In summary the division of people into locals and newcomers had four major implications for the Madurese "visitor community". It meant that:

1. The Madurese were supposed to adopt and accept the local culture.
2. The Madurese were expected to adopt and accept the local customary law and the local ways of enforcing local customs.
3. Unless totally assimilated,
   a. the Madurese needed to accept that in their position they could at any time be asked to leave, and
   b. the Madurese lands were not really theirs.

The main conflict implication in this way of framing the agency was that the very existence of the agency of the migrant community was put into the hands of the host community: migrants were not supposed to participate in the creation of the norms or the identity of the area, and their existence as actors in Sambas and Bengkayang could end if the hosts so decided. This created an antagonistic feeling against the Madurese community, which refused to behave as it was expected to in the position that the indigenous side envisaged for it. Thus, the indigenous side resented the way in which the Madurese "arrogantly refused to learn the local habits and culture."[8] One of the Malay community leaders explained[9] that Madurese were chased away from Sambas because they could not behave like locals: "In Rome, you live as the Romans do."[10] When I asked why even those Madurese who had been living in West Kalimantan for generations would need to change their habits instead of the Malays attempting to tolerate the Madurese habits, neither the community leader nor the chief of the regency (Bupati) understood my question. The distinction between indigenous and non-indigenous was totally naturalized in the minds of most West Kalimantan people. It was something that could not be

---

8   This was often repeated in discussions with villagers in Tanjung Keracut (Sambas), October 2003, Sanggau (Bengkayang), Sanggau Ledo (Bengkayang), Bengkayang and Jagoi Babang (Bengkayang), March 2006.

9   This was during my seminar for community leaders (except for the Madurese leaders, who had already escaped) in Sambas town.

10   The corresponding wisdom in the Indonesian language is "dimana bumi dipijak, disitu langit dijunjung." In Sambas, this saying can be heard very often.

challenged. For those who were able and willing to step out of the discourse on indigenousness, the answer was related to the naturalized images of the Madurese as a community: one could not adjust to criminal habits and culture, and since this was the characterization of the Madurese, adaptation to Madurese cultural values was not possible.

Clearly, in addition to perceiving the Madurese as a visitor-community that behaved arrogantly (given its guest status), there was also the perception that the Madurese could never become locals due to the fact that they somehow, in an objective sense, did not belong to Kalimantan. According to the head of the district (Bupati) of the other problem area, Sambas, Ir. Burhanuddin A.R., "Madurese culture does not belong here," and since it caused conflict, the Madurese had to be moved: "To cure the illness the cause of symptoms has to be removed" (Burhanuddin 2003).[11] In areas where they have been expelled, the absence of conflict is now seen as a logical consequence of the absence of the Madurese.[12] In conflict areas where Madurese still live, such as in Singkawang, the antagonistic division of people is less visible and the conflict explanations tend also to pay attention to the intolerant attitudes of the "indigenous" inhabitants (Mastro 2006, Razi 2006).

The legal practice of dividing the agent structure between locals and migrants led to a practice of treating the local customary law (*adat*) as higher than national law in most issues in most of the conflict areas. This meant that the migrant communities had to adjust to the customary rules of the Dayaks in Bengkayang, and the Malays in Sambas. In Sanggau Ledo, for example, the normative code applied to conflict situations was and still is the Dayak *adat* of that particular sub-region. In addition, law enforcement relied mainly on customary institutions, and even the sub-district administration saw the role of the modern police as supporting the return of the Dayak customary institutions to the customary law and order (Aleksius 2006s, Bernardinus 2006). In some cases, the national instruments of law and order were seen as irritants to the customary order, and one of the customary leaders described several incidents in which the army had to leave the area after they had begun to be perceived as a source of tension in the sub-district (Acap 2006).

Both the mobilization of the Dayak militias in the Sanggau Ledo riots and the peace process utilized mainly cultural institutions, while only the finances came from the modern public sector: 50% from the district and 50% from the sub-district (Acap 2006, Andoth 2006, Bernardinus 2006). Both the mobilization and the peace process used modalities that were typical of the Dayak community in that specific sub-district.

---

11   Both district leaders have, however, since softened their conflict diagnosis: today, both think that the impotency of law enforcement created a situation where individual incidents burdened community relations.

12   Discussions in March 2006 with the heads of the sub-districts (Camaat) of Jagoi Babang (Mr Aleksius), Sanggau Ledo (Franz Andoth) and Samalantan (Alfonsius Muksin).

In areas like Bengkayang, where the explanation of conflict was reduced to the cultural characteristics of the Madurese, there has not yet been any reflection on the possibility of the dominance of the local Dayak *adat* becoming a problem and a source of conflict in the relations between the local Malays (who are subject to Dayak customary law) and the majority population. Yet, recently, in the issue areas of security, the urban areas of Bengkayang especially are moving towards giving primacy to the official law-enforcement instruments. As a clear signal of de-antagonization and an effort to avoid deep divides, in spring 2010 a member of the Bengkayang Madurese community was, for the first time, allowed to participate in the West Kalimantan Ethnic Communication Forum as a representative of the Madurese community of Bengkayang.

For many Dayak and Malay areas, indigenousness also implied different ownership rights. Communal ownership of the lands was applied in many cases either in tandem with or placed higher than the formal, individual land ownership system. This is why, at the beginning, right after the conflict, Malays and Dayaks felt that the lands that were occupied by the Madurese were not really theirs, even though in many cases the Madurese owners had paid for their lands. Furthermore, it was felt that ownership of land by those who were not "sons of the land" was somehow wrong. Even in areas with no history of conflict, like Ketapang, the growing ownership of the Chinese and especially the Madurese is still often seen as a potential source of conflict (Bachtiar 2005).

It is interesting to see the fluidity of this expression of the framing of the agent structure as bipolar, divided between the indigenous and the "guest community." As time has passed, the urgency of explaining away the guilt of conflict has been reduced and the urgency of post-conflict development and peace-building has gained primacy. This has downgraded the importance of re-affirming the difference between locals and outsiders. At the same time, the importance of guaranteeing potential investors protection of their assets by the local officials has gained importance. A few years after the Sambas conflict (in 2002), the head of the Sambas district pointed out to me that most of the so-called Madurese lands, where the Madurese had been chased away, did not really belong to them according to the local conception of land ownership. In 2007 the same head of the district, however, emphasized that the legal land titles are still intact in the archives of the district—"not a single Madurese has lost his land"—and that foreign investors should thus not doubt the primacy of modern land ownership in Sambas. This development in the thinking of the leader of the district shows how the identity as actors in a developmentalist setting is creeping in and perhaps slowly bridging the gap between the Madurese and the Malay.

At the same time, the conflict situation as perceived by the Madurese was very different. Their main discursive project was the articulation of a strict national equality among citizens. The national equality of Indonesians required that the Madurese had the right to

1. an unyielding parity, and
2. an improvement of their position from a secondary position to a position in which they could claim equal ownership of politics and economy in West Kalimantan, as did the two indigenous communities.

When confronted with the discourse on indigenousness, many of the Madurese interviewed felt that, as Indonesians, they were just as indigenous as the Dayaks or the Malays (JM1, 2001). Many of them, in fact, did not really identify themselves as Madurese before the conflict of 1996–97; they were just Indonesians (JM2, 2001). In the case of the violence of 1996–97, many Madurese had indeed lived in the area for decades, some had been born in Kalimantan and only a few had any ties to the island of Madura (Sedau 1, 3, 4, 2006). Often, they did not really talk much Madurese anymore and many said that they no longer had many people around them with whom they could use the language.[13] However, many of the victims of Malay and Dayak rage in Sambas districts were refugees from the 1996–97 violence, and thus relative newcomers to Sambas, even though they had mostly been living in West Kalimantan, in the Sanggau Ledo area, all their lives.

It was not possible for the Madurese to impose their interpretation of the positive law by expecting help from the officials or the police, since neither was available in West Kalimantan in sufficient strength. Furthermore, many of the village officials supported the interpretation of the local rights framing. Thus, it was understandable that when tension intensified, the Madurese resorted to their own community members in their pursuit of equal rights and equal power. The communal pursuit of power and social position and the rejection of the localized normative orders led to the same outcome as in the case of many other migrant communities. The articulation of communal rejection of local norms was defined as "criminal action" in the minds of those who respected local norms, and the communal protection of an equal position was defined as communal protection of the Madurese criminals. Again, inability to explicitly negotiate the rules of inter-community coexistence led to demonstrative activities that, outside of the framing of the Madurese, were clearly threatening. In Sambas, almost a decade after the last Madurese had left the regency, people were still talking about conflict trauma and referred to the "Madurese communal terror" just before the massive riots (interviews).

The criminal element in the demonstration of "citizen's rights" exemplified the contradictions in the discourse of the Madurese. While rejecting the local norms and defending people the locals considered criminals, many Madurese also contradicted the national criminal law. However, the national-level framing of community relations was necessary for the "Madurese cause," and thus a communal defense outside the boundaries of national law was not good for the

---

13 Interviews in three Madurese resettlement areas, Sedau (Singkawang, March 17, 2006), Bhakti Suci and Satuan Pemikiman 2 (Pontianak), October 2003, interviews with members of Gamisma = Generasi Muda Insan Madani, a Madurese cultural organization.

creation of "national order" as opposed to the local constructs of order. However, consistency was not deemed necessary by the Madurese side either, as no effort was made to explicate the Madurese claims and negotiate them with the other communities. In addition, some young Madurese men chose to insist on their construction of reality, and instead of arguing with words they concentrated on demonstrating their national (as opposed to local) framing of order and agency by violent, criminal action.

Today, after the passage of time has lessened the tension between ethnic groups, the Madurese community leaders still frame their agency in West Kalimantan in national terms. However, they also try to regulate and tone down the antagonistic ways in which their rejection of the division of people between locals and non-locals was articulated before the main episodes of violence. The dominance of the Malay or Dayak cultures as the "local way" is still seen as discrimination.[14] Still, leading Madurese community figures that I have interviewed for this study all accept the idea that the Madurese should learn to abandon the violent ways and the carrying of knives which are typical of some Madurese (none that I have met have carried knives, though).[15] While the Madurese deserve the same position in the society as do the Dayak and Malay people, Madurese community leaders now admit that a communal defense of the Madurese position should not utilize violent means. This is, however, not because the Madurese should be polite guests, but simply because carrying knives does make situations of dispute more prone to explode into violence.

Furthermore, it seems clear that in Malay areas the Madurese community leaders now often attempt to emphasize the role of Islam in their culture in order to create a bridge between the Madurese culture and the "local" culture. The main ethnic organization for the Madurese in the Sambas/Singkawang area is Gamisma, which in its original name, Generasi Muda Islam Madura, and in its entire organizational ideology emphasizes the role of Islamic education among the Madurese (Ali 2005, Haryadi 2005, Liswan 2005, Marsat 2005, Muhammad 2005).

Despite the positive development and the de-escalation of the agent structure in West Kalimantan, there are also some worrying trends. The international tension between the Muslim civilization and Christians, especially in the West, has had its effects in Kalimantan; religious issues have become a source of division there too. Despite the fact that Malays and Dayaks still perceive each other as brothers and as people who originate from the same region, issues of religious discrimination have started to influence the relations between these two communities. The ban on the Islamic call to prayer in Bengkayang has been seen

---

14   Interviews in three Madurese resettlement areas, Sedau (Singkawang, March 17, 2006), Bhakti Suci and Satuan Pemikiman 2 (Pontianak), October 2003.

15   This was repeated by many of the Madurese community leaders, especially by Haji Ali of Gamisma (a religious cultural organization of the Madurese in the Singkawang/ Sambas area) and Thoha (2005), a Madurese businessman from Singkawang.

as discriminatory (interview of a Malay in Bengkayang town, October 2007), and the temptation among the Malays is to mobilize nationalist arguments based on a primarily Muslim Indonesia against it. The fact that such a ban is obviously unconstitutional does not help the situation, as any reference to the national law would once again pit the rationales of the "local" and the "national" against each other, thus mobilizing a local Dayak passion nurtured by decades of authoritarian national discrimination against local rights.

Since Bengkayang and Sambas never really explicitly negotiated any rules for inter-community coexistence, the positions of the Malay minority in Bengkayang and the Dayak minority in Sambas remain undefined. The approach of the area has been to avoid drawing attention to issues that could cause disagreement or break the perception of harmony and brotherhood between the two groups (Burhanuddin 2003). As a result, the explication of rules will be difficult: one must be prepared for disagreements if one wants to negotiate and explicate understandings on the inter-ethnic code of conduct in the province. The reason why it would be essential to overcome these difficulties is that conflict between the two main ethnic groups in West Kalimantan would have far more serious consequences than conflicts between big and small groups. The fact that Malays can constitute a security threat to Dayaks almost anywhere in the province and vice versa means that ethnic antagonism and communalism between these groups would instantly be securitized, and communities would instantly become meaningful for the defense of their members. As we learned from an analysis of the pattern of the distribution of violence between areas in West Kalimantan, this is explosive and needs to be avoided between the Dayaks and the Malays. The issue of the lack of a culture of direct negotiation has contributed to the difficulties in the agency structure, but it has also contributed to the difficulties in the resolution of conflicts of interests, as well as to the culture that allows opportunities for violent demonstrative argumentation. This is why this lack of explicit negotiation will have to be discussed in conjunction with its effect on the prospects of reducing motives and opportunities for violence.

Motives of Violence

The immediate incompatibility that motivated conflict violence in West Kalimantan was simple. In the two main conflicts, in 1996–97 in Bengkayang and in 1999 in Sambas, the local population wanted the Madurese community to leave the area and the Madurese refused to do this. The reason why the local communities wanted this was that the locals had been subjected to arrogance, crime and violence by the Madurese.

However, the crimes that were the first phase of the conflict also had communal motives. Crime was often committed as a means of claiming equal rights for the Madurese community. Of the 14 cases of conflict in West Kalimantan since 1950 that were clearly triggered by Madurese crime, in 8 cases one can see the crime as a peculiar way of enforcing equality between the Madurese and the local ethnicities and at least once superiority of the Madurese was attempted (the cases refer to the list in Table 1.1 in this book). In two cases, this was related to the right to date a local girl despite the resistance of her relatives. In four cases the question was related to equal rights to land, while twice the issue was a political and economic decision where equal treatment was doubted by the Madurese perpetrator.

The indigenous violence was intimately tied to the demand to expel the Madurese from the area. This demand is clearly tied to the practice of articulating an agent structure where "locals" and "visitors" are in a hierarchical structure. According to Dayak and Malay combatants interviewed for this study, the Dayak/ Malay demands became stronger during the growth of the tension between the Dayaks and the Madurese. At the beginning, all the Dayaks wanted was for the Madurese to change their violent ways. When this did not happen, they started demanding that the Madurese leave. Finally, since this did not happen, the Dayak members of the mob in which my interviewee participated felt that killing the Madurese was the only option.[16] The phases in the conflict were the same between the Malays and the Madurese a few years later in Sambas.[17] However, here the first stage of the conflict process was the increasing criminality and violence on a lower, more individual level.

The fact that the victims and the perpetrators in many of the visible conflict-triggering incidents came from two antagonistic groups is naturally part of the answer, but one murder, even between antagonistic groups, does not normally motivate the forcible eviction of an entire community, unless there are more serious motives behind the incident. Furthermore, I am not discussing an isolated incident of one crime, but instead at least a perception of a systematic campaign of criminal bullying and crime by individuals of Madurese ethnic origin. It seems that I have to follow the chain of the motives of the conflict a bit further to make sense of them.

Making conflicts intelligible by revealing the motives behind violent acts requires the exploration of two types of conditions. One the one hand, investigation can focus on conditions that make the status quo unbearable for one group of people and push them towards the use of violent means in order to make the situation bearable again (Gurr 1970). On the other hand, analysis can reveal conditions that make violence lucrative, tempting or beneficial (Collier and Hoeffler 2000b). In this vein, Raymond Tanter (1998: xii–xiii) divides political violence into grievance-motivated and gainful violence. This division also structures approaches to conflict studies.

---

16   SA 2001; this perception was confirmed by interviews with community leaders in Sambas City and combatants from Jawaii, Tebas.

17   The three-stage logic was supported by some of the people interviewed (class of community leaders from Sambas) for the project, while it was rejected by others (Abdurrahman 2006, Suratman 2006).

Horizons both for gain through violence as well as for grievances that make peaceful life unbearable are found on various levels. On the national level the difficult relationship between Jakarta and the provinces is the durable structure that seems to offer the main framework for most long-term conflict motives. On the same level, the economic crisis at the end of the 1990s seems to have offered the passing conditions that magnified the durable motives for violence. Small-scale violence has taken place even in the absence of the "magnifiers," and it still continues to happen with small numbers of casualties. However, the large-scale killings in Sambas and Bengkayang require an additional explanation relating to conditions that magnified the grievances and violent opportunities that had existed for decades. I will start with an analysis of the passing conditions of the economic crisis and then go deeper to analyze the more durable motives for conflict. After the national level, I will move on to the sub-national level, trying to find motives that are not rooted in the national level of problems.

The Asian Economic Crisis and the Motives for War in West Kalimantan

It seems that the main conflict peaks of the 1960s and 1990s took place during a period of a sharp decline in national income. Furthermore, during the latter half of the 1990s, the economic crisis treated different regions and different ethnic groups differently. Earlier development had created an expectation of prosperity, and the illusion of the feasibility of continuing economic development. Indonesians had this in view in 1996, when the economy was developing quickly. The economic crisis led to the collapse of the value of the currency, and this resulted in a situation in which individual Indonesians suddenly realized that their Chinese shopkeepers had started to demand much higher prices for products with foreign components. Since the level of education was low, it was difficult for ordinary Indonesians to understand that the Chinese shopkeepers were not suddenly demanding higher profits, but that the higher prices were related to the increased rupiah-priced expenses for the shopkeeper. This misunderstanding led to a conclusion in which the feasibility of the deserved income for Indonesians was prevented by greedy Chinese shopkeepers, and this again motivated some Indonesians to target their grievance-motivated aggression against the Chinese population. This created an exceptional situation in the whole country and this exceptionality, where the threshold of violence was lowered, affected the vulnerability of West Kalimantan to conflict violence.

However, the main ethnic target of aggression in West Kalimantan was not the same as in the rest of Indonesia. There, instead of the Chinese, it was the Madurese who felt the consequences of Dayak and Malay frustration. Also, all in all, West Kalimantan as an exporting province was not particularly hard hit by the sudden collapse of the value of the rupiah in 1997. Furthermore, the first episode of violence in Bengkayang in December 2006 took place before the economic trouble started. That episode, at least, could not have been influenced by the economic trouble, even if the latter episodes could have been.

The economic crisis could have had direct economic consequences by creating the relative deprivation that motivated the Sambas riots in 1999. However, the problems of the corrupt rules of the Indonesian economy that led Indonesia to an exceptionally severe crisis could have affected West Kalimantan even before the economic crisis. Some scholars see a link between the export-oriented orange-farming and logging businesses and the motives for conflict (Bambang 2003, Davidson 2008). Both of these business areas are corrupt and influenced by the clash of modern and traditional norms. The people suffering from the illegal marketing monopolies in the orange business are often associated with the poor Sambas Malays, while the owners of plantations are either ethnic Chinese or relatives of Suharto. The facilitators making threats and coercive arrangements to maintain the monopoly are assumed to be Madurese (interview material, see also Bambang 2003).

In the illegal logging business, the actors are also associated with ethnic groups (Yuyun 2003). The corrupt police who allow logging in return for bribes are often associated with the Malay group, even though the situation has changed dramatically since the beginning of decentralization. The businessmen who actually do the logging vary from region to region. In some regions, these activities are indeed associated with the Madurese community, while elsewhere they are associated with the Chinese or with the Javanese or Malaysian Malays.[18] Naturally, the main frustrations related to the corrupt businesses were not the result of the economic crisis, rather the other way around: corruption was, in part, the reason for the disappearance of investor confidence in Indonesian capital markets. The people whose rights these illegal activities violate are often associated with the Dayak ethnic communities, whose relationship to forests is closer than the relationship of other groups.

What happened in the 1990s as the de facto decentralization started was that the monopolistic practices moved from the center to the provinces. Competition for privileges thus also moved to the peripheries (Van Klinken 2007). Therefore, it would be possible to claim that there is a relationship between the causes of the economic crisis and the existence of the basic grievances (Aditjondro 2001, Huxley 2002). These causes must have been there already during the 1996–97 incidents of mass violence in Bengkayang.

Furthermore, before the conflict in Sambas, that fact that the perpetrators of the corrupt economic activities suddenly benefited tremendously from the collapse of the rupiah while all the others only got poorer must have underlined and magnified the irritation people felt towards these businesses.

The Sambas violence took place after the economic meltdown. This crisis affected the morale of civil servants and the police, whose basic salaries suddenly covered only part of their expenses. With the collapse of the rupiah, the purchasing

---

18   Interviews with forestry activists, scholars and Dayak people and community leaders (in Pontianak, Sambas, Sanggau and Sintang in 2000–03) clearly testify to the existence of a *perception* of this corruption.

power of the salaries of public officials was suddenly cut substantially, and this might in some cases have resulted in a reduced motivation to perform well, or created a need for the police to take side jobs for the sake of subsistence. A relatively high-ranking police official from the region who participated in one of the seminars of the Indonesian Conflict Studies Network publicly explained these pressures in his presentation. He showed a calculation of his expenses and clearly showed how his salary could not cover them after the collapse of the rupiah. On an individual level this presentation was very clear in showing the pressures for the police to create a side income from corrupt money.

In addition to the resource problems related to the economic collapse, there are problems that indirectly result from the economic crisis and the corrupt practices that preceded it. At the time of the crisis there were clear indications of intra-police and police-army infighting on issues related to the enforcement of illegal monopolies, related to the supplementary incomes of the police and the military (Aditjondro 2001). This suggests that the police and the army did indeed become increasingly involved in side jobs, even illegal ones. On September 30, 1998, after the Bengkayang riots but before the Sambas conflict, four policemen were killed when an army unit bashed into a police station with an armored vehicle after a dispute about suspicious business activities on the part of the police and the military (Dini Djalal, *Far Eastern Economic Review*, April 22, 1999). Thus, in addition to creating direct relative deprivation for the conflicting parties, it seems that the economic crisis created a relative deprivation within the forces of law enforcement, and that this created conditions conducive to conflict. Administrative reform in the military, with the separation of the police from the military that was legally formalized in April 1999, obviously made the division of illegitimate business profits even more difficult.

In addition to making law enforcement difficult, the economic crisis could have affected conflict motives by also reducing the willingness of the provincial administration to execute good governance. The loyalty of the regional administration towards Jakarta has often been based on personal benefits offered to the regional bureaucrats and military officers by the Indonesian rule in the provinces (Crouch 1978, Kingsbury 2002, Kingsbury and McCulloch 2006, Robison 1986). When the ability of the state to pay sufficient salaries and the ability of the central administration to control its provincial bureaucrats and military officials further deteriorated due to the economic crisis, the importance of the corrupting, clientelistic practices of seeking personal benefit from public offices naturally increased among the local military and civil administrations. This could also have contributed to the relative deprivation of the conflicting parties.

Furthermore, the anticipation of a top-level leadership transition motivated Jakarta to move more police resources to Jakarta, leaving fewer resources for peripheral areas like West Kalimantan. Resources were likely to have been moved to the center already before the 1996–97 Bengkayang riots, as it was during this time that the province scored the world's lowest ratio of police to civilians (Haseman 1999). This could have allowed the awakening of the collective motivation of the "migrant" Madurese community to even out the imbalance between them and those who considered themselves as indigenous: it was the time for the migrant community to demonstrate the fact that they were not just guests in the province. Furthermore, and more generally, the anticipation of change—and especially the anticipation that the stranglehold of Jakarta over the province would ease up— could have motivated ethnic groups to ensure that the anticipated changes would serve the interests of individual and collective conflict actors (van Klinken 2007). A sense of crisis and opportunity was definitely already present, according to many informants, in December 1996 when the Dayak riots started.

The Difficult Relationship between Jakarta and West Kalimantan

In general, the relationship between the center and the periphery in Indonesia is the mega-structure that conditions most of the conflict motives in West Kalimantan and in most of Indonesia. On the one hand, centralized modernization and the expansion of state power in the national peripheries, such as in West Kalimantan, create the national context within which many of the local Dayak (and Malay) grievances of West Kalimantan interact (Peluso 2006). On the other hand, the transformation and reform on the national level of the relationship between the centre and the national peripheries is the context that once provided competition and gainful motivations for conflict, and still does. This reform had economic and political implications. With the collapse of the Javanese military elite in West Kalimantan politics in the 1990s local ethnic groups had suddenly more space for local competition. According to De Jonge, Nooteboom, Bouvier and Smith, this was the main reason for inter-ethnic competition in West Kalimantan (Bouvier and Smith 2006, De Jonge and Nooteboom 2006), and this also explains why some other provinces (where the transition was less drastic as the Javanese elite held their positions better) escaped violent ethnic competition. The collapse of the national economic elite in West Kalimantan is exemplified by the collapse of the orange-farming monopoly of Suharto's son at the beginning of the 1990s. The economic transition created some grievances, but also opportunities for local business entrepreneurs (Bambang 2003). Finally, the push towards decentralization was interpreted in ethnic terms and this constituted the agency of "the migrant communities," and created grievances for the Madurese community.

In regard to a more long-term perspective on the development of communities, the Dayaks had already experienced political and economic deprivation during the period of President Suharto, 1966–98 (Bamba 2000, Peluso 2006). This period meant an expansion of administrative and economic modernization and the expansion of the power of the central state into the provinces. On the one hand this meant institutional developments that undermined the role of traditional structures of governance (Bertrand 2004). The institutional ideology of modernity during the "New Order" of President Suharto was inherently hostile to the traditional societies, such as the Dayaks, whom the central administration often saw as backward and anti-modern (Bertrand 2004: 8). The grievances related to the institutional developments were combined with the securitization (Waever 1995) of the administrative structure, with the concrete consequence that core provincial administrators had to be military officials from the center to be able to tackle the inherent security challenges that were seen as central to the nation.

In addition to political grievances, there were social, demographic and cultural problems. The local Dayak way of life has also been threatened by national population pressures. The population density, especially in Java and Madura, has caused insecurity in the food supply and tension in these central areas of the country. According to official Indonesian sources, the sustainable population level was exceeded in Java by 11 million people (Williams 1996), while the situation in Madura was even worse. In an effort to tackle the problem of overpopulation, the government launched an ambitious program for the transmigration of some of the population from the dense areas to other areas such as West Kalimantan. While most of the Madurese involved in West Kalimantan conflict were not part of official transmigration programs—in fact most of the Madurese "migrants" were spontaneous rather than government organized—the flow of people in the decades preceding the main conflicts was extensive (Davidson 2008: 91) and it must have affected the grievances of the local population, especially in areas where traditional production still required a low population density.

An analysis of the spread of conflict activities in West Kalimantan seems to justify the conclusion according to which population pressures were an important part of Kalimantan conflict grievances. The conflict areas were and still are areas with a higher population density than the highland areas, yet they have relatively similar production patterns. One could say that the conflict areas are ones where the traditional ways of life have been pressured by the influx of migrants from other parts of Indonesia. In Pontianak, population density does not pose a serious challenge (except in terms of traffic) because of the modern urban ways of production, whilst in the highlands the low level of population density means that the traditional production and use of land and forests is not threatened.

The historical distribution of migrant populations also seems to suggest that population pressures have been an issue. It seems that the years 1996 and 1997 were the peak years for official transmigration programs. In 1997 alone, it was planned that more than 350,000 people would move from Java and Madura to Kalimantan (Williams 1996). In an island with about 10 million people, an addition of 350,000 people is something quite substantial and necessarily affects the social balance. The transmigration program was canceled too late; in March 1999 in West Kalimantan (*AFP*, March 24, 1999), almost immediately after the Sambas conflict. Only days before the end of the transmigration program, intensive fighting had killed 165 people in Sambas (*AFP*, April 13, 1999).

Dayaks had been marginalized politically due to the pro-Javanese policies of President Suharto's modernist "New Order." Dayaks were mostly ruled by the Javanese, and this rule took the perception of Dayak intellectual and educational inferiority as its starting point: traditional Dayaks had to be civilized by the modern Javanese. In fact one of the early motives and justifications for transmigration was based on this thinking: according to the province's Javanese Governor, Mr. Kadarusno, in 1973 West Kalimantan needed migrants to civilize the Dayaks ("Kalbar minta dijadikan daerah Transmigrasi" *Utama*, February 27, 1973. See also Davidson and Kammen 2002: 59). Thus the Dayaks' lack of empowerment together with this pejorative attitude contributed to local grievances.

In addition to political, demographic and institutional grievances, modernization in the economy meant in West Kalimantan the erosion of traditional community land ownership (of the Dayaks, Peluso 2006). The traditional Dayak sedentary swidden (slash and burn) farming required large areas of land. Modern farming with individual land ownership was foreign to the Dayaks, and the differences in national and local land ownership concepts had been one of the main challenges to social stability in West Kalimantan for some years (Bamba 2000). Modern land ownership had already won over the traditional method in most urban areas and in areas close to major cities. In the more peripheral highland areas the threat of modern land ownership had not yet manifested itself. It was in the semi-modern Inner Valley areas of West Kalimantan that the transition had not yet taken place, but here modern land ownership was needed to guarantee land titles to newcomers as well as to companies that were assisting development projects. Thus, it is perhaps not surprising that the conflicts of 1996–99 took place in the semi-modern Inner Valley areas of Bengkayang, Northern Landak and Sambas.

Nor is it surprising that when the traditional land ownership of the Dayaks and Malays was threatened in Bengkayang and in Sambas, it was here that the discourse of indigenousness gave rise to an interpretation in which the "visitor community" of the Madurese did not really own its lands (Andoth 2006). The framing of rights in terms of a sharp distinction between locals and "newcomers" was partly motivated by the need to protect the local lands and local ways of life that required the community ownership of large land areas. Local grievances against the Madurese were linked to the fact that many of the modern infrastructure projects attracted a lot of migrant workers, including the Madurese, to the province. The Suharto-era was characterized by an enormous expansion of Madurese migrants in the province of West Kalimantan (Davidson 2008: 91). According to Davidson, though, competition for lands between Dayaks and the Madurese dated back to the expulsion of the Chinese by Dayak militias (Laskar Pangsuma) in 1967. After this expulsion, the lands of the Chinese were divided between the remaining communities rather as loots of war.

The use of forests also emphasized the conflict between the local and the national. The objective importance of forests for traditional Dayaks and the symbolic value of them for modern Dayaks were clearly a part of the grievance-related motivations of the Dayak communities. Referring to official documents, Davidson (2008: 95) shows that during the first years of the rule of President Suharto, the areal of modern national use of West Kalimantan forests increased 25-fold. During Suharto times, forestry concessions were often distributed through corrupt arrangements to non-indigenous national and even international businessmen: these were sometimes Javanese or Chinese, in some cases even Chinese or Malays from Sarawak, Malaysia, but they were often also Madurese.[19]

Later, more gainful sources emerged as the relationship between the nation and its provinces changed in the 1990s. The main reasons for these sources of violence were competition and the lack of clarity of the rules of such competition. The competition for licenses became localized, offering many opportunities to claim rights for licensed economic activities, such as logging, by mobilizing ethnic arguments and ethnic groups for private economic profit (van Klinken 2007). In many cases, the confusion relating to the rules of economic competition led to the use of ethnic mobilization to protect completely illegal private economic activities (Davidson and Henley 2007).

For example, there was a Chinese gold-miner who was married to the daughter of a local Dayak leader of a sub-district. His mining operations ignored the Indonesia's environmental regulations, and caused a loss of livelihood for the local Malay fishermen. When confronted with angry local Malays, he framed the resistance to his illegal activities ethnically and appealed to the leader of the sub-district (his father-in-law), with the consequence that the Malay mob was dispersed by a Dayak mob that felt that the Malay minority was not in a position to set rules on a business that was protected by a leader of the biggest community, the Dayaks. Yet, for the Malays the question was not one of power, but one of rules and of the protection of their livelihood (Atio 2003).

Similar stories are not unusual in economic activities that require licenses, permissions or are regulated by environmental norms, such as the logging business, fishing and mining. It seems that, in terms of the motives for contemporary conflict in West Kalimantan, the limits of clarity and enforcement of the rules of economic interaction play an important role. Without further clarity on these norms, and without better enforcement of the rules of economic interaction and competition, small-scale conflicts caused by the mobilization of ethnic mobs for the protection of illegal activities will not be possible to avoid. Furthermore, ethnic groups should agree on limits for the mobilization of ethnicity in the economy. If it were possible for the ethnic leaders to set these limits, it would be easier to avoid businessmen presenting convincing arguments to members of their ethnic groups to explain why the protection of their individual economic interests should be a matter of concern for all members of their ethnic community.

At the same time, the democratization and decentralization of the political regime suddenly opened up new opportunities for Dayak politicians and contributed to gainful motives for violence. As mentioned by Davidson (2008), Dayak competition for power was already strong during the first half of the 1990s, while the Malays were left behind until they, too, took a violent assertive approach to this competition. Mobilization of the poor and relatively deprived Dayaks has been very easy for Dayak politicians, and this has often led to friction with other

---

19   Interviews with Kalimantan forestry activists and an anonymous forestry consultant from Finland, February 1998, March and October 2003.

ethnic groups. In Sanggau Ledo, during the conflict, the Dayak customary laws and institutions were already seen as the only source of collective norms during the conflict, even though one could say that they were challenged by the presence of outsiders such as the Indonesian military and the Madurese, who refused to assimilate.

On the opportunistic side, the Dayaks as indigenous people naturally had a motive for monopolizing the local resources. Strengthening the discourse of indigenism (Davidson and Henley 2007), decentralization and local rights served their interests. The idea of decentralization and the monopoly on natural resources could have been a major factor in politicizing the Dayak and Malay ethnic groups: creating the agency of indigenous people simply served the interests of the Dayaks in Bengkayang and the Malays in Sambas (Davidson 2008).

However, the idea of indigenous rights once again clashed with the anti-racialist national principle of "unity in diversity", according to which political or economic rights cannot be based on ethnic origin. This tension between "national" and "indigenous local" was strengthened by the discrepancy between modern national and indigenous land rights conceptions—this also contributed to disputes that motivated violence. According to a study by the World Bank (Barron and Madden 2003), discrepancies between formal and informal (traditional indigenous, for instance) rules are a surprisingly common motivational source of disputes and violence all over the country.

In West Kalimantan, the confusion of local and national norms even led to interpretations that were clearly against any legal interpretation of the Indonesian laws. The idea that Dayak customary law could replace Indonesian law in areas of Dayak majority was an example of this. In a sub-district at the margins of the conflict (in the district of Sanggau), a Dayak mob interpreted decentralization by preventing people from ethnic minorities from voting in local elections (Javanese transmigrant, interviewed in Sanggau, March 29, 2003): to these people, decentralization and democracy meant that the local ethnic group exercised ethnic majority rule. Needless to say, this interpretation was also opportunistic and illegal, but it was still one that resulted in an election outcome which favored the mob.

The changing relationship between Jakarta and the Indonesian peripheries also fueled gainful political motivations for conflict. Already in 1999, competition for political office followed totally new rules, and new local opportunities had arisen in Sambas. The political affiliations of the Madurese, Chinese, Malays and Dayaks made ethnicity relevant for this opportunistic political competition. According to interview material (interviews by the author, 2000–02), former President Megawati's party PDI-P, and especially its root-party PDI, tended to be most successful among the Dayaks.[20] Many of the Madurese tended to be supporters of three Islamic parties, but most commonly the Islamic Development Party, PPP.

---

20   Again, demonstrating the stereotypical images of ethnic groups, many Malays and Madurese thought that the stupid Dayaks believed that PDI was an abbreviation of Partai Dayak Indonesia, instead of Partai Demokrasi Indonesia.

This party probably had many supporters among the Malays as well, since the former party chairman, former Vice President Hamzah Haz, was from Kalimantan (he studied in Pontianak). Otherwise, many Malays tended to be supporters of the Golkar Party, while today the spread of Malay political support is more varied.

Political motivations have been claimed for the Sambas riots due to the ethnic patterns of voting. Riots and the ethnic cleansing of the province took place before the local and national elections and, to the surprise of many, the Islamic parties often supported by the Madurese did not end up winning, but the previous ruling party, Golkar, often supported by Sambas Malays, won the provincial elections with a large margin. Some researchers even claim that they have found Golkar flags in a surprising number of the homes of the central provocateurs and mobilizers of the Sambas riots. The post-conflict situation among the Madurese communities also supports this thesis. As people without a permanent address, the internally displaced Madurese people went for a long time without an electoral district and were thus unable to vote.[21] Expelling the Madurese from Sambas served, therefore, the interests of Malay parties. Whether there indeed had been Golkar supporters with political motives, and how much these motives explain the actual violence, is impossible to know for certain. The evidence is too weak to come to far-reaching conclusions, and in any case, it is highly likely that these violent political strategies (of expelling the Madurese in order to improve election success) are not widely accepted or shared among Malays or among Golkar supporters in Sambas.

The ethnic pattern of voting seems to have changed in the 2004 elections, and after that it has been difficult to estimate which ethnic groups would be most likely to support which parties. However, party politics still has ethnic dimensions, as candidates for political offices, regardless of their party affiliations, tend to seek support for themselves by mobilizing their ethnic constituencies. The fact that the election system in local elections only has one round means that united ethnic groups tend to be more successful in elections. If, for example, a city or a district is divided between three equally large ethnic groups, it is likely that the candidate that can best mobilize and unify his or her ethnic group will win the position of head of a district or major of a city. However, if there were another election round between the two best candidates and the winner had to gain over 50% of the votes, inter-ethnic alliances—and thus ethnically inclusive political mobilization—would be encouraged. The current system, with one single election round, encourages ethnic mobilization and makes both democratization and ethnic peace difficult for Kalimantan. Voter preferences in favor of peace and inclusiveness would be needed in order to prevent the rise of conflict motives caused by ethnic exclusion, discrimination and ethnic political competition. Furthermore, the rules of political competition have to be made clearer in order to develop non-violent ways of political competition.

---

21   This, at least, was the perception of some of the donors and many of the inhabitants of those three of the camps for internally displaced Madurese which were visited for this study.

The grievances and gainful motivations of the Madurese preceding main conflict episodes are often neglected in studies of the West Kalimantan conflicts. This is true for the West Kalimantan intellectuals, who often buy into the primordial explanations of culture: if the natural characteristics of the Madurese or their culture explain their violence, then motives are unnecessary in explaining conflict behavior. But scholarship that sides with the Madurese also neglects the analysis of the Madurese motives, as it often fails to try to explain the first phase of the conflict, the rise of Madurese crime and bullying. Nevertheless, Madurese aggression was, indeed, essential to the conflict episodes in West Kalimantan; the Madurese were not only victims, but offenders as well. Many of the Malays, Dayaks and Chinese interviewed felt threatened by the Madurese tradition of openly carrying their traditional knives (sickles). The availability of traditional Madurese weapons in everyday conflict situations was also often mentioned as a major irritant. Two of the Chinese people involved in anti-Madurese operations mentioned this—the fact that Madurese debtors came to their shops with their sickles to demand loans or rescheduling of their debts—as one of the main motivations for their financial assistance to the Malay mobs in their violence (AJ 2001, LBH 2001).[22]

Many of the Madurese motives for violence were related to the long process of transition and competition between ethnic groups in the 1990s. Davidson (2008) also mentions land competition between the Madurese and Dayaks after the expulsion of the Chinese in 1967. However, most informants suggest that Madurese violence increased in the 1990s, and this must have been the result of the rise of "local" power in areas where the Dayaks had gained political and economic control after the decline of the Javanese power. The fact that there was a perceived increase in Madurese violence and communal protection of the violent perpetrators seems to be related to the communalization of security, which has resulted from confusion related to the rules and the changes in these between the state and the provinces and districts. Even before the decentralization law and before the fall of Suharto, there was an anticipation of change in the relationship between Jakarta and West Kalimantan. Yet there was no explicit discussion on how this change would affect the rules between local and migrant communities. The increased transmigration programs had increased irritation among the local populations and created pressures for framing the Madurese as the scapegoat in all of this. As the result of the rise of indigenism, local order became expressed in indigenous terms, and this was naturally harmful for the "migrant communities" (Davidson 2007). The Chinese community began expressing interpretations that put them into a framework together with the local communities (RR 2001, TT

---

22   At the same time, some Chinese shop owners also testified to harassment and the extortion of protection money from members of the other side of the Sambas conflict—the Malays—especially the Malay cultural organization, Forum Komunikasi Pemuda Malayu, FKPM, which played an important role in the mobilization of the violent Malay riots in Sambas (Welles 2006).

2001), but this was not possible for the Madurese, who had already become the target of anti-centralist sentiments.

Province-Level Grievances and Gainful Motives

While many of the grievances on the level of the province emanate from the national levels, the province-level ideological mobilization is needed for the grievances to be contrasted to an imagined, "deserved reality" that is unbearably better than the experienced reality. Furthermore, the precedence of ethnic cleansing in West Kalimantan in 1967 created a perception of feasibility for the "deserved realities." The provincial ideological climate (the spirit of indigenism) and the province's history of ethnic cleansing with grievances that are linked to the national realities together constitute the discrepancy between actual and deserved, feasible receipt. All of this was required for the sense of relative deprivation among the conflicting parties in West Kalimantan.

In West Kalimantan, the emergence of the Dayak mobilization of the global discourse of indigenousness precedes the national transition. Van Klinken (2008) mentions the establishment of the Dayak Union (Serikat Dayak) in 1919 as the starting point for the collective mobilization of the Dayaks, who somehow naturally do not satisfy van Klinken's criterion of an ethnic group (instead, van Klinken 2008 considers Dayaks a group of several ethnicities, which just imagine one ethnicity). However, this mobilization started gaining political relevance only in 1981, when a group of urban Dayak intellectuals established Pancur Kasih (YKSPK) as an NGO with a mission to resist the centralist framing of the Dayaks as backward objects of modernization. Instead, Pancur Kasih aimed at helping the Dayaks to help themselves by developing self-sufficiency in the fields of both economic and intellectual development (Davidson 2007: 226–9).

The intellectual origin of the Dayak mobilization was strengthened ten years later, when a group of students established the Institute of Dayakology Research and Development (IDRD), which then offered scientific authority for the claims for indigenous rights. With this authority, Dayak activists then first constructed the reality of indigenousness in West Kalimantan politics. Then, by referring to international scholarly and political writings on indigenousness, the institute framed the objectives of indigenous Dayaks' rights as something that could be internationally and scientifically proven as something Dayaks deserve.[23] With these acts the institute managed to create the hierarchy in the relationship between Dayaks and the Madurese, and the "deserved receipt" that Dayaks could then compare to the actual receipt. The discrepancy between the deserved and the real receipt, the relative deprivation, was created.

---

23   This interpretation is based on my discussions with some of the scholars of the Dayakology institute, especially Bamba (2003), and by reading some of the material produced by the institute, especially the journal *Kalimantan Review*.

However, this discrepancy would have remained abstract and academic, until the province had a precedent that could make the self-sufficient Dayak ownership of its own areas look feasible. Jamie Davidson emphasizes in his explanation of conflict in West Kalimantan the role of this precedent from 1967, when, due to reasons related to the Indonesian army's anti-Communist counterinsurgency, it became useful for the central administration to mobilize the Dayak community to expel Chinese communists from their territory in the aftermath of President Suharto's coup. This showed to the Dayaks that it was feasible for the Dayaks to expel an ethnic group if the interest of self-sufficient indigenousness so requires (Davidson 2008). If this was then possible vis-à-vis the Chinese it should not be impossible vis-à-vis the Madurese.

In the case of the Malays the "deserved receipt" was not mobilized by a long, intellectual mobilization of Malay civil society groups. Rather, the utility of political ethnic mobilization was demonstrated to the Malays by the Dayaks, whose assertive collective behavior gained a lot of political results at the expense of the Malays, in West Kalimantan, where coercion and assertiveness was fully rewarded by the political praxis (Davidson 2008: 133–4). Mobilization of the Malays then took place in cooperation between local officials, businessmen and civil society leaders, on the one hand (in the Malay Youth Communication Forum, Forum Kommunikasi Pemuda Malayu, FKPM) and partly by using the old structures of the Malay kingdoms. The motives for the mobilization, after the events in Parit Setia, were mainly defensive. The Malay imagination of their collective deserved receipt was affected by the Dayak example, while the success of that example in terms of ethnic cleansing and political bullying demonstrated the feasibility of an approach where the Malays "take themselves what they deserve" (Abdurrahman 2006).

For the Madurese the feeling of relative deprivation was based on the changes that took place under the provincial competition between the Malays and Dayaks after the decline of the Javanese elite in West Kalimantan. The assumption of special rights for the indigenous groups created a situation where the actual receipt, compared to the previous, was much more limited. Thus, instead of imagining the deserved receipt (as did the Dayaks), the Madurese only needed to look back in history for it. For the Madurese, what was left and what they opted for in areas where they were strong enough was a communal defense of their interests (JM1, 2001). Of course, this communal defense did not stop at defense alone, but individuals and groups also used communal power to expand Madurese might locally for their private benefit and for the protection of individual perpetrators. The majority of the licenses for river transportation as well as road transportation went to the Madurese, until they more or less gained a monopoly on transportation in many areas (Abdurrahman 2006).

The Madurese were also involved in the enforcement of illegal monopolies for other communities (such as the Chinese) and businessmen, and all this was done for the gains it produced. It was perceived legitimate in the situation where the Madurese community had become squeezed by the competing Dayak and

Malay communities. After antagonism, there was a Madurese fear of revenge; this motivated them to organize defensive mobs, which eventually became frustrated and became involved in further violence.[24]

Explanations of gainful political violence are more recent and place emphasis on the incentives for war, the "reasons for which to fight" (Collier and Hoeffler 2004, Collier, Elliot, Hegre, Hoeffler, Reynal-Querol and Sambanis 2003, Fearon 2005). One of the main empirical generalizations of the gainful explanation is related to natural resources as the incentive to compete for state power or for local office. Violent mob activity in Sintang and in Pontianak, where the assertive Dayak groups got their way in the nomination of district heads, showed the utility of this. The weakness of law and order rewarded assertive violent behavior, and according to Davidson (2008) this also encouraged Malay gainful motives for violence. Finally, the fact that decentralization in West Kalimantan, unlike in East Kalimantan, for example, meant the demise of the Javanese political elite meant that political competition among provincial groups was especially tough (Bouvier and Smith 2006, De Jonge and Nooteboom 2006).

Special sub-national characteristics of production in West Kalimantan further made the province prone to economic gainful violence. Dependence on natural resources gives an incentive for armed groups to fight for political power (Collier and Hoeffler 2000b), and makes democratization more difficult (Acemoglu and Robinson 2006). While West Kalimantan is rich in forestry resources, the degree of regulation of foreign trade in this province with an extensive border with Malaysia creates an incentive for violent competition for economic and political power. The weakness of law enforcement and the legal system in West Kalimantan escalated violent inter-ethnic economic competition, according to van Klinken (2007).

Political competition with an undeveloped culture for negotiation and one lacking political and judicial institutions of arbitration and regulation created a lot of greed-based motives for violence. This makes new political opportunities and natural resources a curse rather than a blessing for a country or an area that has not fully managed to institutionalize the regulation of political and economic competition. The curse of resources in a developing country leads to violent political struggles and to the criminalization of large segments of the economy.

Motives Related to the Conflict Process

Once the conflict process took over—after antagonism and the original motives had sparked the first acts of hostility—then it started creating its own motives for further violent action. For some scholars who favor diachronic investigations and the path-dependent logic of explanations, these motives were seen as central. For Jamie Davidson, for instance, the experience of the expulsion of the Chinese and the following competition for the Chinese lands between the Dayaks and the

---

24 This could even be sensed from interviews with some of the Madurese "self-defenders" (JM1 2001 and SN 2001).

Madurese was the genesis of the conflicts that followed (Davidson 2008: 47–90). Violence became a preferred mode of resolving political issues, and competition for land and resources. The role of violence in the processes of political developments became routine (Davidson 2008: 93, Suriansyah 2004). The intention in this section is not to follow Davidson's argument only, but instead to look broadly on the motives that conflict research treats as belonging to the process of conflict (as opposed to motives that are in conditions exogenous of the conflict).

On the individual level, the motives for Madurese, Malay and Dayak violence were often very similar to motives for ordinary criminal violence. The ongoing violence and conflict often managed to hide the individual motives and helped to frame them as collective, thus making them more acceptable. The need to prove oneself in front of one's friends was clear in many if not most of the interviews, especially with the younger combatants. Very often, young combatants wanted revenge against particular Dayaks/Malays or Madurese, but relocated their targets to any Dayaks/Malays or Madurese. Two Malay activists involved in violence (Abdurrahman 2006, Suratman 2006), for example, constantly referred to incidents in Jawaii and in Parit Setia committed against their relatives in defense of his own activities in Singkawang.

None of the people interviewed admitted to any sadistic violent motivations of their own, but the fact that they often described the motivations of their friends as sadistic suggests that sadism could also have been a factor in their own cases. Often, those with personal social status-related problems were keen on making ethnicity an issue in everyday disputes: it was often illiterate or very poor Dayaks who were the most fanatic haters of the Madurese. The interviewee YMD (2001) mentions his friend who he thought was compensating for the low social status caused by his illiteracy, by showing extreme bravery in his defense of his community against the Madurese. By emphasizing collective identities such as ethnicity as the basis of social status they could reduce the relative weight of the status indicators that were problematic to them.[25]

However, most of the violence with conflict-process-related origins also had social, collective motives. Violence sharpened the ethnic stereotypes and proved the violent racist motives to be correct. Its growth both proved to the Madurese that the Dayaks/Malays really were violently discriminating against the Madurese and legitimized the Dayak/Malay perception of the violent nature of the Madurese and their culture. According to most Sambas Malays interviewed for this study, at that stage the main motivation for Malay violence was related to the fact that the indigenous groups in Sambas simply got fed up with Madurese violence and crime. This explanation was also shared by the head (Bupati) of the district (Kabupaten) Sambas, who is also of the opinion that the repatriation of the Madurese community

---

25   This motivation for racism seems to be very general. It was found by theorists of "rank imbalance" or "status-inconsistency" in their studies of the motivations of Ku Klux Klan mobs in southern USA (Galtung 1966).

cannot take place before the "socialization of the Madurese into the norms of the locals" (Burhanuddin 2003).

A youth leader in Tanjung Keracut village explained that this violence was like the pressure on a spring (representing Malay patience). It could be pressed to a certain extent, but after that the spring was bound to bounce back (TKK 2003). According to the village head of the same village, Malay mobs burned the houses of the Madurese only to chase them away in order to stop killings by the Madurese. According to both, the escalation from burning houses to mass killings was outside anyone's control: "It was much like an accident."

The cultural motivation was mixed with political explanations, as many of the Malays involved in riots felt that the Madurese had their own corrupt ways of avoiding the police. In the perceived absence of police protection, there was a strong motivation towards ethnic/community self-defense and action to chase away those "visitors" who refused to learn the local ways (MJ 2003, TKK 2003). Even the district head (Bupati) of Sambas shared this assessment: lack of security contributed to the motivation for rioting (Burhanuddin 2003).

In addition to the lack of security forces that could have prevented the escalation of conflict, the fact that there were no mechanisms of communication between the two groups promoted the conflict process and sharpened the incompatibilities. The Malays would not have felt like a spring that had to go down when pressed if it had been possible to confront the situation before the spring bounced back. In addition, if the pressure on the spring had been stopped in time, the force of the spring would not have been as strong as it bounced back. If it had been possible to negotiate the grievances before the people ran amok, the confrontation could have been less violent.

Obstacles to and Opportunities for Violence

The question of what motivated the violence in West Kalimantan is not as relevant as that of what made it possible and so easy to carry out. This is simply because it would seem that the motivations for violence were not direct "necessary conditions," and they were not so strong in comparison with many other conflicts. The peculiarity in West Kalimantan was that stronger motives were unnecessary, since obstacles to violence were so flimsy that even weak motivations, the kind that are found in many societies, managed to cause large-scale violence. This, it seems, is based on four reasons:

1. Conflicting parties in West Kalimantan seem to find a way around the general norm against conflict. Excuses and triggers are used as a justification for revenge.
2. Conflicting parties in West Kalimantan seem to find a way around the fear and morality that most societies have in respect of brutality and violence.

3. Conflicting parties in West Kalimantan seem to find a way to use violence as means to express one's loyalty towards a community and to argue for a particular construction of order.
4. Conflicting parties in West Kalimantan seem to find a way to circumvent law enforcement.

Norms against conflict are not absent in West Kalimantan. For example, informants explain that the Sambas Malays took pride in their gentleness, which was seen as characterizing the Malay race. According to many informants the Malay will avoid a dispute; he will run away without losing his pride, rather than fight. Yet, if provoked seriously enough, he will "run amok," and this can mean unrestricted violence. Thus in that community a trigger or an excuse was needed in order to justify running amok. But the Dayaks and the Madurese also have needed excuses to move into a conflict framing. Conflict behavior in the normal setting is unacceptable in most cultures.

The observation that conflicts usually need a triggering incident (which is not the motive, but the case that is referred to when justifying conflict behavior) is originally from Ronald Fisher (1972). The fact that this triggering incident becomes something that represents the entire relationship between the conflicting parties has been discovered and studied in the context of international relations by Christer Jönsson (1979). The representative case is the one to which most informants refer after the event when explaining why the conflict came about.

Once the excuse and the trigger are there, conflict actors are still prevented from acts of violence by fear and by the norms against acts of violence that under normal conditions would make them incapable of extreme violence, even if they had worked out excuses for violence. Every conflicting party has to find its ways of circumventing both fear of and norms against violence. This is often done either by seeing oneself as unable to decide otherwise or by turning the opponents into something less than human beings (Kivimäki 2006), so that violence is not seen as violence against a fellow human being.

While the socially constructed opportunities for violence are often related to failure to block conflict paths by means of morality, in some cases social practices offer opportunities to express arguments and commitments by means of violence. Thus norms do not only fail to prevent violence, but a new reality—the construction and language of conflict can also facilitate conflict violence by offering individual fighters opportunities to be heroes of their communities or to argue for a specific set of new norms by committing brutal, violent acts.

Finally, when the mental and social obstacles to violent action have been overcome, orderly societies still normally have physical obstacles to violence in the form of the enforcement of law and order (Collier et al. 2006a). In conflicts where violence is magnified by modern weapons, access to weapons becomes an objective obstacle, while a police presence acts as an obstacle to criminal and mass violence.

Excuses and Triggers

Community conflicts in West Kalimantan were often triggered by disputes and criminal violence between individuals who just happened to belong to different ethnic communities (Haryadi 2005, Liswan 2005, Marsat 2005, Rupaat 2005).

Community criminal events became more common and their communal interpretation became more pronounced during the time of the Madurese effort to intensify their pursuit for an equal status and of the development of a more exclusive indigenous order. This happened first in the mid-1990s, in the context of an anticipation of a change in leadership and in the political system. This pattern repeated itself after the Madurese community had to escape from Bengkayang and had to settle and find their space in Sambas (Burhanuddin 2003, Darwis 2009c). A wave of crime could be seen as the first phase of the conflict episode both in Bengkayang and Sambas.

The development of the indigenousness discourse provided the original excuse for some of the Madurese youth to consider the local criminal code as alien and to distance themselves from it in the name of the community. While many Madurese felt that this was wrong (Ali 2005, Rupaat 2005), and even though many of the victims of the Madurese's violent lawlessness were Madurese (Peter Kerr, *Jakarta Post* July 19, 2001), violent individuals among the Madurese people could justify it in their minds and in their sub-communities by referring to the needs to grow space for the Madurese people in areas strictly controlled by local customs and the local indigenous ethnic order. This was due to the general critical community feeling towards the growing exclusion of the migrant populations from the legal code, which was increasingly based on the indigenous *adat*, customary law, of the largest of the indigenous groups, the Dayaks in Bengkayang and the Sambas Malays in Sambas.

Furthermore, even though not all Madurese felt it was justified for them to disregard the local normative order, many still felt that the Dayak or Sambas Malay order was alien enough to justify the protection of Madurese individuals who had broken it. Somehow, misbehavior that undermined the local order, was collectively resented as discriminatory by many Madurese, was sympathized with by a wider circle of people. Thus, there was a general excuse that, at least in a limited Madurese subculture, "justified" the first phase of the conflict episode, the wave of violent "crime," and the community protection of the "criminals."

While the exclusiveness of the local order was used as a general justification for the Madurese communal resistance, the indigenous violence in Kalimantan was almost always justified by the single crimes that the Madurese individuals committed. Human Rights Watch (1997: 3) has drawn up a list of events that were considered in Bengkayang by Dayak mobs as representative cases or triggering events for the massive conflict there in 1996. This list represented a part of the Dayak collective memory, and thus was mainly meaningful as part of the Dayak consciousness at the time of the Bengkayang conflict, rather than being a historically accurate list of blood-letting in West Kalimantan. The list includes the following cases:

1. 1968: A Dayak who was the head (*camat*) of Toho subdistrict was stabbed by a Madurese in Anjungan, near Pontianak. No serious rioting followed.
2. 1976: A Dayak was killed by a Madurese in Sei Pinyuh, north of Pontianak. No serious rioting followed.
3. 1977: A Madurese man stabbed a Dayak policeman to death in Singkawang, Sambas district. His death led to riots in Samalantan sub-district, about 180 kilometers north of Pontianak, in which more than 5 died and 72 houses were destroyed.
4. 1979: A dispute over a debt led to an attack by three Madurese men on a Dayak in Sempang Bodok in the village of Bagak, Sambas district. Two other Dayaks were almost killed by another Madurese. The attacks led to a large community clash in Samalantan, in which 15 Madurese and 5 Dayaks lost their lives, and 29 houses were burned down, half of them Madurese, half Dayak. The unofficial death toll ran into the hundreds. The clash led to a government-sponsored peace treaty between Dayaks and Madurese, and to the erection of a monument to commemorate it in Samalantan, which stands to this day.
5. 1982: A Dayak ex-policeman was killed by a Madurese in Pakucing, Samalantan sub-district, after he complained about the Madurese cutting his rice.
6. 1983: A Dayak was killed by a Madurese in Sungai Ambawang, near Pontianak. The murder led to a wider clash with an official death toll of 12, the unofficial over 50, and 100 houses destroyed.
7. 1992: The daughter of the Dayak ex-policeman who was killed in the 1982 incident was raped by a Madurese. The rape led to a minor clash between Dayak and Madurese youths. A similar fight between youths of the two groups broke out in 1993 in Pontianak.

In addition to the historical cases, more recent cases were naturally more direct triggers for Dayak and, later, Sambas Malay violence. In one instance, the trigger for the conflict was an incident in which a Madurese thief was beaten by Dayak individuals. In another, a Madurese passenger who had refused to pay a Malay bus conductor was thrown out of a bus in a way which he considered rude. In the famous case of Bengkayang violence, the first main incident of mass violence in a generation, the trigger on the Madurese side was the beating of a few Madurese youths from Sanggau Ledo who were trying their luck with a Dayak girl in Ledo. In all these cases, Madurese collective retaliation took place. In the first incident, this took the form of the burning of Dayak homes and, in the second, of physical punishment of the Malay bus conductor. In the Sanggau Ledo case, the beaten Madurese youths came back with a group of more Madurese youths and stabbed the two Dayaks that had defended the girl the Madurese boys were pursuing. In all these cases, a few days of calm, "the lull" as Horowitz (2003: 89) calls it, was followed by preparations for more severe action.

A concrete representative, well-publicized situation when the police did not protect the community seems also crucial for the triggering of a violent communal reaction. In the case of the conflict in 1996–97 in Sanggau Ledo, the police had actually taken appropriate steps to prosecute the perpetrators of offences that triggered mob action, but since the Dayak mob did not learn about this their ethnic community felt the need to take the law into its own hands (Human Rights Watch 1997). Thus the lack of sufficient law-enforcement capacity was not just an opportunity for those who wanted to use violence for their crime or revenge (I will return to that opportunity later); it was also an excuse for action.

A mobilizer of Malay revenge against Madurese perpetrators of a violent crime in Jawaii explains his trigger for resorting to violent means, by saying that after a murder in which "100–200 Madurese" participated collectively, the informant and his friends demanded action from the local subcommand of the provincial army (KOREM) and from the provincial police, but "neither moved." In the end, this student activist says, only one of the 100–200 Madurese men was arrested. This experience was then used by my informant as the justification for his own violent response (Abdurrahman 2006).

While crime in general was the excuse for action, a single visible incident was often used in an exaggerated version as the trigger; the representative case that justified the decision to move against the Madurese community. In Sanggau Ledo, the stabbing of two uncles of a Dayak girl who, according to the local community, had been harassed by the Madurese boys was the immediate trigger. Both of the uncles were hospitalized but neither suffered any permanent damage (Dede, interview on March 23, 2006). Still, the representative case of the stabbing of the uncles is still told in Sanggau Ledo (interviews in March 2006), and in this version both uncles died instantly. Another thing that the witnesses do not remember or tell was the fact that the main perpetrator of the stabbing is half-Dayak (his mother is Dayak, even though he himself identifies after his father as Madurese; Davidson 2008: 228).

Fear and the Norms

While excuses and triggers offer collective legitimacy for violence, everyday norms as well as fear still tend to prevent violent behavior. According to Randall Collins (2008), fear and morals often paralyze conflict behavior even if conflict actors have a clear target for their strong motives of aggression, and even if there is an abundance of opportunities, excuses and triggers for violence. According to Collins up to 75% of front-line soldiers never aim at their enemies because of the paralysis caused by fear and morals. In conflicts people often also seek ways to neutralize individual fear and the everyday norms against brutality. In West Kalimantan community tradition was effectively modified and abused for this purpose.

The failure of normative obstacles to conflict in West Kalimantan seems to have been related to a long-term transition in the province. If we look at the distribution of violence within the province and at the balance between modern and local normative orders in the conflict districts and in peaceful districts, we can see that the transition from traditional to modern played a role in creating conditions under which the normative obstacles of violence could fail. It seems that the conflict areas somehow fell in between the normative orders of traditional and modern society. They were not strongly influenced by the modern authority and order of the state as Pontianak was. At the same time, they were not strongly influenced by traditional authority either, nor by the normative orders of the religious communities or the traditional sultanates.

Modern cities survived due to their modern order, while the highland areas of inner West Kalimantan (from Ketapang to Kapuas Hulu) survived because of their traditional order. However, Bengkayang and Sambas could not resist conflict, because neither modern nor traditional rules really applied there. Instead, ethnic concerns were twisted and manipulated to serve the partisan interests of the conflict. The leader of the Bengkayang Dayak community, Suherman Acap, verified this fact, complaining that in the conflict areas Dayak customary law was too weak and could be manipulated to legitimize conflict. Due to the fact that people had forgotten what the Dayak customs really require from Dayak individuals, Dayak village and *benua* (a traditional administrative area consisting of about six villages, on average) leaders were able to mobilize people by using invented or "revised" customary norms (Acap 2006, 2007).

According to Syarif I. Alqadrie (discussions 2000–10) and Haji Ali (2005), Madurese leaders also manipulated both their cultural and their religious heritages for the purpose of facilitating conflict. Amulets were issued by Madurese Muslim leaders for the protection of Madurese combatants, and rituals were also utilized to increase the fighting spirit of the Madurese. Furthermore, the concept of honor killing, *Carok*, was mobilized from the Madurese customary tradition, but used in a manner that allowed for killing somebody other than the one who had committed a violation of honor. In this way, a tradition was mobilized in a distorted manner for the sake of communal revenge (Alqadrie 1987).

By referring to tradition and cultural norms, the perpetrators of violent acts tried to avoid the normative pressure against violence. The use of the traditional Madurese knife and references to the tradition of *Carok* helped combatants to circumvent community condemnation and managed to divert the responsibility for their actions from themselves to the entire community. Yet, during the first phase of the conflict, violence was mostly used for personal gains, robbery, extortion and personal revenge.

The Madurese culture was part of the strategy used to build up fear, but often the mobilization of courage also utilized religious discourses. Religious overtones were especially important in the first mass conflict, in which the opponents of the Madurese were the Christian Dayak community. Religious leaders who supported the Madurese combatants by offering services that they alleged would make the combatants invulnerable felt that the battle was at least partly motivated by the duty of advancing Islam. Sometimes the targets of conflict revealed this, as in Pontianak on January 29, 1997, when some Madurese attacked a Catholic foundation (McBeth and Cohen 2002: 26–7), and in Siantan, where the target was a Dayak Catholic NGO, the Pancur Kasih Social Work Foundation (Human Rights Watch 1997).

Some of the Madurese interviewed also argued for the defense of their community against the Christian Dayaks (and, peculiarly enough, also against the Muslim Malays) by using the Islamic rhetoric of *jihad* in relation to the defense of the Islamic community (SN 2001). According to Alqadrie (2002), Madurese combatants sometimes also used protective water charmed with "Islamic" spells. Yulia Sugandi's studies among Madurese refugees also reveal that in many cases Madurese religious leaders also facilitated Madurese fighting by offering protective amulets—often in exchange for large sums of money (Sugandi 2006). According to Alqadrie's comparative studies (2002), Madurese violence was often facilitated by the poor quality of their local religious leaders. Well-educated Madurese religious leaders did not encourage, help, protect and hide their parishes from police prosecution in conflicts, while sometimes inferior religious leaders did that. Good Madurese religious leaders have, in fact, managed to do the opposite by pointing out the immoral side of the fighting as well as the heresy involved in trusting amulets and magic (Abdullah 2006, Ali 2005, Sabran 2006).

Ancient community norms were also utilized in order to transform revenge in the minds of people into something respectable. The analysis of a *Straits Times* reporter describes this discursive strategy: "The killing of the Madurese was not for reasons of revenge, but rather the need to fulfill traditional obligations that have bound the Dayaks since time immemorial" (Susan Sim in *The Straits Times*, March 23, 1999). For the sake of the credibility of this construction, in many areas Dayak revenge was prepared by following ancient Dayak rituals. According to the Human Rights Watch report (1997) on the 1996–97 conflict, a traditional *Tariu* dance was conducted in the town of Sanggau Ledo, led by Dayak war commanders (*panglima perang*) from various villages. This dance was meant to awaken the spirits of the ancestors.

In many areas, Dayaks gathered around a red bowl filled with chicken's or pig's blood, feathers, a matchstick, and a piece of roof thatch "to signify that word of the war must fly from one village to another, even in darkness (the match) or bad weather (the thatch)" (Human Rights Watch 1997). A traditional Dayak doctor (*Dukun*) read a mantra and placed his hand on the heads of the combatants as they drank the holy blood. Instantly, they fell into a trance within which they gained the ability to detect the Madurese through their sense of smell. They also became invulnerable and fearless, and suddenly wanted to drink the blood of the Madurese (Bernardinus 2006, YMT 2001). A local Dayak pastor told a British newspaper reporter, further, that "The *kamang tariu* is the spirit which possesses the Dayaks in time of war. When it is present, it provides physical protection and immunity from thirst and fatigue ... The *kamang tariu* drinks blood, it has to be fed blood"

(Lloyd Parry 1998: 100–101). Those involved in war "did not want any of it. They did it against their will." The collective Dayak spirit made them do all the violent things in the war (Lloyd Parry 1998: 102).

The details of the rituals varied from one traditional area (*benua*) to another, also revealing that the rituals were modifications rather than authentic replications of the common ancient Dayak heritage. Furthermore, sometimes rituals from other Dayak tribes were used if they were useful for the purpose of going around norms and fear. The practice of gathering around a red bowl, for example, is actually associated with only one of the three historical Dayak social movements of Kalimantan, the Tariu movement. Two of the others had a clear target in their mobilization against the Dutch (the Nyuli movement in East and Central Kalimantan), the imperialists and the Western missionaries (the Adat Bunga movement in South Kalimantan), but the target of the Red Bowl/Tariu movement was less clear (Alqadrie 1987). Nevertheless, it could be used in mobilizing all the Dayaks of the Bengkayang and Sambas areas.

Some told of the use of drums or a gong, some talked about a high-pitched scream during the attack, while others said the ritual and the attack were both silent. Some associated the trance with the *sirih* leaf, which is the symbol of the devil's sword and was kept under a red headband against the back of the fighter's head. For some, the red headband was a symbol of the fact that the person was possessed by the spirits of ancestors.[26] For some, killing and drinking human blood end the trance, while others explained that this strengthened it. All the explanations from different sub-districts or traditional areas had the idea of a trance in common. The trance made people lose consciousness or it might even have given the ancestors control of their bodies. This was very useful for the moral legitimacy of violence: if a trance or the ancestors controlled one's actions, then one no longer needed to be morally responsible for them.

In some places, Dayaks fought in ceremonial traditional dress and red headbands and used long knives, machete-like traditional *tankitu*-swords (also called *mandau*-swords in Putussibau), *tombaks* (Dayak spears) and home-made muskets as their weapons. Fighting was led by the traditional leader, the *ketua adat*, and the bird commander, the *Panglima burung* or simply by the war commander, the *Panglima perang*, while the pre-war rituals were conducted by the bird commander (Bernardinus 2006, NY 2001).

The command structure seems to have varied from one area to another. In some areas, war leadership belonged to a war commander, a position nominated by the traditional leader—in some cases the village's traditional leader, in others the *benua*'s[27] traditional leader. In other areas, the traditional leader of the village was also directly involved in the war effort (various interviews by the author in the

---

26   When posing for the picture, Mr. Bonggas Bernardinus refused to wear his headband in order not to put my safety at risk.

27   *Benua* is a larger traditional administrative unit consisting of five to six traditional villages.

district of Bengkayang). Some mobs were described as having a flexible leadership based on the rulings of the ancient spirits that had possessed the bodies of the combatants (Lloyd Parry 1998). What is common to all of these, and important from the point of view of our research, is that the war effort was always organized along the lines of traditional authorities, possibly with modern authorities acting as facilitators in subordination to the traditional structure.

Many of the casualties were caused by mobs of young men who went from house to house. Some mobs also patrolled roads and stopped every car and bus, separating the Madurese passengers from the non-Madurese by smelling. The Dayak killings often took place in accordance with an ancient Dayak ritual in which the victim was beheaded, part of his blood was drunk and his heart and liver were eaten. Later the heads of the victims were given to the Dayak community to be displayed as a warning and as a sign of the courage of the young combatants (Bernardinus 2006, NY 2001).

The killing of the Madurese took place until the spell caused by the mystical red bowl lost its hold. Some say the magical trance continued until they drank blood, but obviously some of the interviewed young men did not stop after their first kill. On the contrary, they describe the festivity of violence as an addiction to blood. However, after the spell had worn off, combatants experienced an "unbelievable tiredness," and later they regretted the atrocities they had committed. However, they still tended to feel that violent operations against the Madurese were needed for the sake of the common good of the Dayak community, and that they were proud of their overall participation in the Dayak force.

The Dayak rituals solve many of the crucial problems met in mobilizing violent action. Media reports often describe the disorganized style of Dayak fighting (Lloyd Parry 1998), but in fact this does not seem to be the case in most places. The rituals performed before the fighting did indeed solidify the role of customary community leaders and highlight the role of the traditional (*adat*) hierarchy, thus making the killings more systematic (Bernardinus 2006). Furthermore, the magical elements of the trance and the loss of consciousness after the ritual provided ways around the everyday norms against violence. Actions committed in an unconscious trance were beyond moral consideration; they took place without conscious decision, just like the beating of the heart or the growing of nails. Furthermore, the Madurese were often described as black dogs by the Dayak combatants interviewed for this research. This perception of the enemy as sub-human also eased the problems of morality: it is easier to kill an enemy that is seen as a dog rather than a human being.[28]

The idea of Dayak fighting taking place in a context outside ordinary morality was often demonstrated by exaggerating those actions that broke everyday norms against violence. A reporter on *The Independent* (March 22, 1999: 1, 12; see also Horowitz 2003) described the festive atmosphere surrounding the extreme

---

28   The logic of circumventing morality by dehumanizing the enemy is theorized in Kelman (1973: 25–61).

violence of a cannibalistic Dayak mob: the message conveyed by the combatants was that normal notions of morality were irrelevant here. The fact that combatants punctually follow a collective community ritual also emphasizes collective rationales and obscures the fact that violence was sometimes clearly motivated by sick, sadistic lust. One of the interviewed Dayak combatants (YMT 2001) said that some of his friends participated in the mob killings "just for fun."

The magical invulnerability and the fearlessness it induced address the problem of fear—the strongest hindrance and emotion in all conflicts. According to beliefs in the sub-district of Sanggau Ledo, it is the *matek* prayer and the spells of the bird commander (*ketua burung*) that make the Dayak combatants invulnerable to the bullets and knives of their Madurese opponents (Andoth 2006, Bernardinus 2006). Some believe it is the trance or the magical water (*air teriu*) that perform this task (YMT 2001). The invulnerability and the magical nature of the Dayak rituals are believed in by most people in West Kalimantan, regardless of ethnic background, religion or even level of education.[29] Finally, the extreme brutality of the Dayak warfare serves the purpose of scaring the Madurese away, which, according to many Dayak combatants interviewed, was the main aim of the operation.

In the case of Malay revenge, the conflict process was slightly different. Since the Malay participation in the Sambas conflict (1999) was a continuation of the Inner Valley conflict of 1996–97, and since after the murder of a Dayak man outside of Pemangkat on March 16, 1999 many Dayaks also participated in the fighting in an alliance with the Malays, many of the traditional Malay and Dayak practices were mixed. In a surprisingly high number of cases, Malays participated in the Dayak rituals, and, according to one informant interviewed for this study, the Dayaks' role was the most important as they lent their traditional doctors (*Dukun*) and magical powers to the protection of their Malay brothers against the Madurese.[30] The Malays, who normally defined conflict avoidance as one of their ethnic characteristics and who took pride in being the ones who run from conflicts, were often found in Sambas parading around and carrying the heads and skulls of the Madurese they had killed. In some cases, Malay combatants carried the skulls of their own victims together with skulls they had found (YD 2001).

In a different ritual, Malays also participated in drinking and taking a bath in the charmed protective water (*air tolak*), which tended to have effects similar to those of the red bowl (YD 2001).[31] None of the interviewed non-Malays used the protective water, but according to Professor Syarif Ibrahim Alqadrie, who has observed and analyzed violence in West Kalimantan since the early 1970s, Dayaks, Bugis and Madurese sometimes do use the protective water (Alqadrie

---

29 Some critical observers do notice, however, that "sometimes the spell does not work, because occasionally Dayak combatants do die" (interview material).

30 There is a good study on the Dayak involvement in the Sambas conflict in Hermanto Juleng (2003).

31 This practice seemed local as some others claimed it never happened (Abdurrahman 2006).

2010). While the magical spell for the Dayaks, Malays and Bugis originates from a non-religious tradition, in the case of the Madurese the magical power comes from Islam. Malays did not, however, fall into a trance, but fought consciously, and according to one informant this is why Malays tried to avoid killing Madurese women and children (unlike Dayaks, according to an anonymous Malay non-combatant informant in the Telok Ramai sub-district of Sambas, interview March 2003). Yet, according to all the Malay combatant-interviewees who were aware of the use of the protective water, it was precisely the protective water (*air tolak*) that made them bloodthirsty. After the effect of the charmed water wore off, they also began regretting the atrocities they had committed (MT 2001, YD 2001).

Furthermore, Malays were able to get around the norms against violence by using the myth of "amok." According to traditional "wisdom," Malays can yield to a point, but if pushed further, they run amok, get irrational and wild and are no longer in control of their actions (Horowitz 2003: 102–109). The explanation of some Malay community leaders (Darwis 2009c) that Malays are like a spring which can be pushed to a degree, but which then eventually has to bounce back, also externalizes the moral responsibility. The bouncing back is a natural response, not a decision by the spring (=the Malay individual). Thus, if there are no conscious decisions, but simply a "natural response," moral judgments do not apply. In addition, the idea repeated by many Malay combatants that the conflict was "an accident" seems to serve the purpose of making the events morally less controversial: one cannot be morally condemned for accidents. Furthermore, the problem of morality was often tackled by discursive strategies to construct offence as defense: "Madurese houses were burned in order to stop the killings by the Madurese" (TK 2003).

Protective water (*air tolak*) tackled the question of fear by making Malay combatants invulnerable. At least one Malay fighter blamed it for his neglect of his family during the conflict (YD 2001). In some cases magical science (*ilmu ghaib*) made the Malay combatants interviewed immune to some threats: one of the combatants lost his fear because of the immunity to sharp objects that he gained through magical science (TB 2001).

Violence as an Argument for a Particular Construction of Order

In addition to normative constructs not preventing violence, social constructs can also actively facilitate violence and offer opportunities for it. Horowitz (2003), in his chapter "Say it with a murder," develops the idea of communicative violence, in which conflict behavior is interpreted as communication.

In West Kalimantan the language of political argumentation involved violence, and only violence could communicate some of the grievances and claims for terms of interaction. Davidson (2008) sees this as a function of the routinization of violence. However, there are factors that made violence more than a routine; they made it a way to communicate and to create social realities that affect all inter-community relations.

Violence in business negotiation, in political bargaining, in fundraising for traditional institutions, in the settlement of disputes, always creates new rules whereby stronger people have more space to maneuver. If the traditional institutions could not give space to newcomers, violence could always find this space. Many of my informants among both the Sambas Malays and the Bengkayang and Landak Dayaks emphasized the fact that with violence by Madurese individuals the rules of the transportation business, land ownership and politics gradually changed, and this gave the "newcomers" more space (Abdurrahman 2006, Luna 2006). Many Malays and Dayaks felt that the success of the Madurese in some business sectors was largely due to this change of rules, induced by violent practices. According to an MA student from Sambas, "Madurese were often regarded as an exclusive ethnic group ... they also had a bad habit of breaking the *adat* by occupying land belonging to a local. Malays could not accept this sort of attitude" (student assignment in June 2010).

However, the fact that norms against blood-letting were at the core of Dayak tradition (Acap 2006, Luna 2006)[32] and local order made violence a perfect way of arguing against the meaningfulness of the local customary norms in Bengkayang and Landak. By creating a practice in which the norms against blood-letting did not exist was thus an effective means to demonstrate the non-existence of the customary rules of the Dayaks in Bengkayang and Landak.

In some cases it seems that humiliation of the Dayak custom was indeed the intention of some of the criminal individuals from the Madurese ethnicity, while in other cases it is clear that crimes were committed merely for private gain. In any case, violence was seen as a demonstrative argument against the Dayak norms against blood-letting, and regardless of what the motive of the Madurese individual was, his action was treated as a collective Madurese challenge against the local order; a challenge that needed to be met: "The Madurese were no better than us in terms of education, and yet they behaved arrogantly, disrespected our ways, and stole our chicken ... our people simply had to do something to all of this" (TK 2003).

The Dayak and the Malay violence was always related to either defending the locals against Madurese arrogance or to asking the "visitors" leave Sambas. This reveals the demonstrative argument behind indigenous violence. Violence was saying to the Madurese:

---

32   This was explained to me also in one of the sessions of the Bengkayang Ethnic Communication Forum (a branch of the West Kalimantan Ethnic Communication Forum). Whether this norm matches the reality of Dayak behavior is another matter. According to Choy (1999), a Singaporean diplomat who has studied Indonesian ethnic stereotypes as objective primordial realities, anyone going against the Dayak *adat* will be subjected to bloody violence. However, the existence of the norm as a declaratory reality is sufficient to trigger bloody resistance to it.

1. that the Madurese are not superior (as their arrogant behavior framed it), and
2. that they were "visitors" with no ownership in the local social realm unless they assimilated into the local culture.

In the absence of assimilation they are "visitors" who can be asked to return "home." While the first of the arguments was often explicated to me by some of the fighters and observers, the latter has not been confirmed to me by any of the Dayak or Malay fighters. Every time I have asked about it, the response has been an effort to convince that Dayaks and Malays are the locals and that there is no need to argue for that with actions. However, the receivers of this demonstrative argument, the Madurese, have helped me with the interpretation of this demonstrative action. The first thing most Madurese informants said in describing their expulsion from Bengkayang and Sambas was that the Dayaks and the Malays had no right to do this, as the Madurese were Indonesians with equal rights in Indonesia as the Malays and the Dayaks. For the Madurese informants the expulsion was an enactment of an incorrect interpretation of "local" rights (Sedau 1, 2, 3, 2006).

The problem for peace was that these arguments could be demonstrated with violent action rather conveniently. Meeting the challenge of the violence from Madurese individuals was almost needed to avoid a situation where local norms were not valid. Without a reaction, fear of Madurese violence would have downplayed local customs. According to Davidson's (2008: 130–31) interpretation, which seems to correspond to my experiences too, the Malay message in violence was also that the Malays were not weak. Malays were not "krupuk"—as easy to break as prawn crackers.

When violence and terror were used to expel newcomers, this was clearly demonstrating the interpretation that the Madurese people were, indeed, visitors rather than landowners or citizens with rights equal to the local population. Thus, violence fitted perfectly into the local vocabulary of argumentation on the rules of inter-ethnicity.

In addition to knowing why violence could be used as an argument in inter-community communication, it is important, from the pragmatic point of view of diverting paths to conflict, to ask why violence was the most credible and useful way of arguing a point concerning inter-ethnic rules. Why, for instance, was non-violent, verbal argumentation not available?

The lack of channels for inter-ethnic communication made it difficult for frustrated young men to negotiate their grievances with those people who had caused these grievances. According to members of the West Kalimantan Ethnic Communication Forum, there have been efforts at the promotion of inter-ethnic communication, but the lack of any resources from outside has made it inconvenient for any of the ethnic groups to take the initiative and fund such communication. As a result, even peace rituals have not involved genuine dialogue across ethnic boundaries. While inter-ethnic (or perhaps de-ethnicized) communication takes place in cities, in rural areas, ethnic divisions effectively molded structures of communication.[33]

Even religious communities were ethnically divided. Madurese people were not welcome in Malay mosques, and the other way around. The idea of brotherhood among Muslims could not have been further from reality. In an interview with a youth leader in Tanjung Keracut, Sambas (TKK 2003), it was demonstrated that Malays did not really consider a Madurese mosque a holy place or the Madurese as Muslims. As evidence of this, the informant claimed that their youth had found indecent, pornographic pictures in a Madurese mosque. This is the same logic of argument presented against the Muslim identity of the Madurese after the Parit Setia raid: real Muslims would not conduct a violent raid on Idul Fitri. I have seen Madurese mosques that have been burned and destroyed by fellow Muslims of Sambas Malay ethnicity. Religion, therefore, did not offer a channel of communication or reflection about what was right and wrong in the relations between the two communities.

Verbal dispute was also shied away from because of the culture of prudence and harmony in West Kalimantan (and in fact most of East Asia: see Kivimäki 2011, Svensson 2011). This harmony is often not seen to be threatened by corruption or power abuse or exploitation, but instead by open discussion of such issues. This attitude does not encourage verbal dispute and the airing of grievances. Yet debate, even an angry one, is often needed to offer demonstrative, violent argumentation a non-violent alternative to physical violence.

In tandem with the culture of harmony is the Indonesian myth of conflict provocateurs. Conflicts are often suspected to have been provoked by malign behind-the-scene movers. Many informants who contributed their knowledge to this study, even some who had themselves been party to very violent behavior, felt that the conflict was triggered by provocateurs, while ordinary people just acted in response to the provocation. This kind of thinking, while taking the blame from the actual violent actors, also discourages open debate. Statements by General Wiranto saying that West Kalimantan has experienced cannibalism have also seriously been proposed as mechanistic causes of the deadly violence. When a group of intellectuals (Harsono et al. 2009) suggested that the people actually involved in the killings in Sambas in 1999, and Bengkayang in 1996–97 should be convicted, leaders of several Sambas Malay and Dayak communities suggested that the authors should be put in jail for inciting violence (Darwis 2009a, Harsono et al. 2009).

The idea that actual violence could be caused by an opinion that the agents of violence violently resisted is not a useful one if demonstrative violence needs non-violent, verbal alternatives. Yet, the position of many West Kalimantan intellectuals is that the media has to be "responsible" and thus it has to avoid

---

33   This observation is based on the discussion among ethnic leaders during the first, joint preparatory meeting of the inter-ethnic class of ethnic leaders in Pasir Panjang Beach on October 15–16, 2007.

divisive issues. For example, the dean of the Faculty of Social and Political Sciences at Universitas Tanjungpura suggested in a public seminar on the media and conflict that the media should be silent about issues that anger people, and that the media would be well advised sometimes to sit on issues where revealing the truth could cause a popular outcry (Tangdililing 2003).

Violence is in part triggered by the lack of alternatives to violent demonstrative action and the lack of channels of explicit negotiation on the terms of inter-community interaction. Under these circumstances West Kalimantan has developed a tradition of demonstrative argumentation, which reduces the need for explicit conflict resolution. Demonstrative behavior is often appreciated and it offers a way to demonstrate not only the community's arguments but also one's own commitment to the community.

Furthermore, the Bengkayang rioting, which was triggered by the protection of the honor of a local girl, clearly exemplifies the tradition of a violent assertion of one's masculinity. An incident that became to be portrayed as a case of protecting a female icon of a village gave ample opportunities for young men to demonstrate their heroism and brutal masculinity. The tradition in general supported violent solutions. My visit to several Madurese IDP camps indirectly testified to the use of violence as a means to demonstrate masculine potency.[34] It seemed that many of the men who had escaped from the atrocities were more traumatized and emasculated by their decision not to fight than men who in fact did. Discussing with wives of the men revealed the other side of the trauma. Some of the wives had great difficulties talking about the family's escape from Bengkayang or Sambas. In some cases women, clearly full of shame for their husbands, presented several reasons why their husbands were unable to defend the Madurese community, but instead had to escape from the scene (Bhakti Suci and Satuan Pemukiman 2003). As suggested by Henri Myrttinen (2003: 44) in the work for reducing options offered by violence, "One needs to work with the alternative unarmed, non-violent concepts of masculinity and femininity already existing in the society in question, further developing and opening possibilities for these and empowering them, thus laying the groundwork for a sustainable peace."

Many people both in Bengkayang and in Sambas feel that the demonstrative action against the Madurese in 1996–97 and in 1999 worked much better than conflict resolution: it led to a more comprehensive solution, as the entire community of the Madurese was expelled from the two districts. Yet, since no explicit rules were negotiated for the interaction between "locals" and "visitors," the situation continued to be unsettled between the Madurese and the Sambas Malays, and caused fear among Sambas Malays whenever they were visiting Pontianak, where they were in the minority. Furthermore, the same principles of local rights applied also within ethnicities, and thus negotiated rules could have

---

34 My observations resonated very much with the observations of some other scholars on the baggage of masculinity. See, for example, Jacobs, Jacobson, and Marchbank 2000 and Myrttinen 2003.

helped inter-community relations amongst Sambas Malays. According to the deputy head of the district (discussions on November 12, 2008 in Sambas city with the author), there have been conflicts between villages that closely resemble the logic of the conflict between the Sambas Malays and Sambas Madurese in 1999. In August–September 2008, for example, at a wedding party somebody from village B hit somebody from the local village A. In a very similar manner as between the Madurese and Sambas Malays this incident quickly escalated into a sub-community, inter-village feud. There was group revenge by 300 young men from village A against village B. As a response 600 villagers from village B took revenge against village A, and many houses were burned. Due to rapid police action and help from community leaders casualties were avoided. This incident shows that the problems between "locals" and "guests" could not be ended by my means of the demonstrative action of expelling the Madurese from Sambas.

Failure of Law Enforcement

One of the peculiarities of the conflict was the passivity of law enforcement in the face of blatant violent criminality before and during the episodes of mass violence. It has been established elsewhere (Herriman 2006, Welsh 2008) in a study of Indonesian mob violence and lynching that the fact that law enforcement is not seen as legitimate and efficient is crucial in the decision of mobs to enforce their own justice. This was clear also in West Kalimantan. The first two recommendations of Human Rights Watch (1997: 5) for an investigation into the conflict in Bengkayang were:

1. Why was there so little effort on the part of the security forces to stop the attacks?
2. Why were no arrests made for organizing attacks, even when the names of alleged perpetrators were known?[35]

One of the answers to these questions was simply the lack of resources. After the transition to democracy, reform and decentralization of 1995 and the economic crisis of 1997–98, turbulence, confusion and the lack of resources created a situation that hampered the ability of modern norms and law enforcement to block the path to conflict.

The ratio of police and military personnel per inhabitant or per square kilometer in West Kalimantan was one of the lowest in the world (Haseman 1999). According to John Haseman only six infantry battalions were regularly assigned to the expanse of Kalimantan. The military forces in West Kalimantan totaled fewer than 1,200

---

35   The Human Rights Watch observation might have been entirely correct at the time of the writing of the report (1997). Yet, in the conflict of 1999, in Sambas, one of the interviewees, YD, a 35-year-old Malay fighter, was condemned to jail for a year for killing two people and for not surrendering the skulls of his kills to the police.

troops, while the police force numbered less than 800. Furthermore, according to a report by Syarif Ibrahim Alqadrie to the National Police Headquarters in 2000, the inadequate number of policemen in West Kalimantan was exacerbated by the inadequacy of funds for police operations and the low salaries of the policemen (classified report referred to by its author in discussions with the current author in October 2002). The last factor contributed to the low morale and the need for the policemen to engage in extra occupations which often took a considerable amount of time away from police duties.

The fact that law enforcement was suffering could be witnessed in the entire country, not only in its periphery. Street justice gained prominence both in peripheral areas such as West Kalimantan and in the center of the nation, Jakarta. According to the central hospital statistics in Jakarta, during a mere six months in 1999 hospitals in the city treated 73 suspected victims of lynching (*Jakarta Post*, June 25, 1999). At times, even the work of the police in the capital city reminded one of street justice: in 1998 the police shot 191 suspected criminals, and 90 of these died (*Jakarta Post*, January 4, 1999). On the nation's highways, the police shot and killed another 41 "road bandits" (*AFP*, March 16, 1999). During the same time period, the police arrested only 326 people on the same highways, which meant that they shot every eighth suspected criminal. Street justice was an even more serious problem if one looks at all cases, not just those where the police were involved. Lynchings became very common during the transition from a centralist autocracy to democratic decentralism. "Newspaper accounts ... record 4,037 incidents involving 5,506 victims, from 1995 through 2004. Nearly a quarter of the incidents (23.7 percent) involved more than one victim" (Welsh 2008: 475).

The relative lawlessness itself contributed to conflict, even if its main impact was its weakening of the obstacles to community violence. With the decline of law enforcement, the coercive apparatus itself felt no hesitation in engaging in opportunistic violence. Some of the bureaucracy played the part of "peace spoilers"[36] who aimed at reducing chances for peace, as they had personal reasons to be opposed to peace. People who feared losing their unfair, corrupt privileges if the democratization of Indonesia proceeded saw lawlessness as a golden opportunity. In Aceh, East Timor, West Java and the Moluccan Islands some rogue elements of the army were suspected of provoking, supporting and committing violence.[37] Furthermore, in addition to maintaining disorder, the failure of legal obstacles to violence gave some provincial police officers and military officials opportunities for personal enrichment. Whenever the police or the military could use their coercive power with impunity, outside the reach of political surveillance, coercive means were used to guarantee illegal businesses (Crouch 1978, Robison 1986).

---

36 On the general problem of "spoilers" of peace processes, see Stedman 1997.

37 On army confessions to this in Aceh, see the *Jakarta Post*, June 30, 1999. In the Moluccan Islands, see *Time* 2, 2000, and in East Timor, see the *South China Morning Post*, January 5, 2000.

Conflict statistics show that the poorly supervised coercive apparatus was the biggest national contributor to violence in Indonesia. For example, in Aceh in 1999, out of the 325 casualties, 243 (about 75%) were killed by soldiers or the police. In West Papua, the ratio of killings by soldiers to that by rebels tilts even more to the side of the soldiers.[38] Naturally, many killings by the military and the police were within the context of government-authorized "control" against the independence movements, but there is plenty of evidence that a lot of them are not. The police and the military had deliberately killed children (*AFP*, June 3, 1999, *AFP*, May 5, 1999), stole livestock and cut off water to a refugee camp (*Waspada* May 30, 1999). They shot and killed a large number of escaping demonstrators (*AFP*, May 5, 1999), and, instead of making arrests, shot down fleeing people/ suspected rebels (Reuters June 28, 1999, *AFP*, June 13, 1999, *AFP*, June 5, 1999). In East Timor, the Indonesian law-enforcement forces attacked the UN office (UN mission head in ABC News bulletin, June 30, 1999) and apparently participated in the ousting of the UN mission from the territory in the fall of 1999, after the referendum on independence and before the arrival of international troops. Also, police corruption was often referred to, especially by Malay informants in Sambas, and the police suffered the same structural problems even though the morale of the police and the military in West Kalimantan never got as low as it did elsewhere in Indonesia.

Political parties were also able to exploit the decline of order in a violent way. Political campaigns involved a lot of intimidation, threats and open violence—in many cases, party supporters were armed when attending party rallies (Porter, *South China Morning Post*, May 29, 1999).

However, the failure of law enforcement as an obstacle to conflict and criminal violence was most harmful for the relations between communities in West Kalimantan. As the chances of getting caught for crimes were reduced due to the lack of police resources, heavier penalties were used as disincentives against violence and crime. Ordinary people were mobilized rather than discouraged from taking the law into their own hands. All this was related to the economy of law enforcement. Those looting food stores were threatened with the death penalty (*AFP*, September 8, 1998), while in some parts of Indonesia the police instructed students to kill provocateurs of violence (*Waspada* May 12, 1999). This situation brutalized society, and ethnic communities were encouraged to deal with their problems with crime using their own means. Instead of the police being an obstacle to community violence—as an impartial, monopoly source of coercive law enforcement and arbitration between local ethnic groups—the conflicting parties in Kalimantan were empowered to enforce their own orders. Since different communities had different perceptions of what kind of order was to be enforced, they ended up fighting with each other over their interpretations. The example of

---

38   In East Timor and the Moluccas, the role of soldiers is as yet impossible to estimate, but more of the violence there is expected to have been exercised directly by civilians and unofficial military forces.

the Dayak enforcement of their customary law against the Madurese is a good example of this. As a result, the structure of a classical security dilemma among the community self-defense neighborhood watches/militias emerged: one militia's strength was perceived as a security threat by another militia, which was thus motivated to strengthen itself (Fearon 1995).

The police also failed as an obstacle to conflict behavior because of the perception in the communities of partiality among the law enforcers. The military was accused of siding with the Madurese,[39] while the police were often seen to favor the Dayaks (Human Rights Watch 1997). Davidson even claims that *most* of the Dayak victims of the Bengkayang riots were victims of open battles between Dayaks and security forces (Davidson 2008: 102), but while such clashes clearly did happen, especially with military units that protected the Madurese temporary displacement centers, my interviews have not found evidence to support such an extreme statement. However, the roles of these organizations and the patterns of Dayak and Madurese violence explain these accusations, at least partly. It is natural that the police were more involved in containing the criminal patterns of Madurese violence, while the military were more concerned about the mass rioting and warlike type of violence of the Dayak mobs. Thus, it was the military's duty to protect the Madurese from the Dayak mobs and it was the duty of the police to take the side of Malays and Dayaks (and other communities) against Madurese criminal violence.

The Madurese suspicion of police bias against their community was especially clear in Pontianak, where the local Madurese community have a history of hostility to the police. In 1993 the police allegedly tortured a Madurese to death, triggering a riot in which Madurese mobs systematically targeted all the local police stations (Human Rights Watch 1997). However, many of the Madurese from the coastal Sambas who were interviewed for this study at a refugee camp in Pontianak in 2000 mentioned that they had sought protection for themselves and their families from their local police stations. If the Madurese suspicion of the police had also been prevalent in those areas, it would have been unlikely that Madurese families would have sought protection from the police.

The Dayak suspicion of the army favoring the Madurese is naturally based on several incidents in which Madurese people were protected against Dayak mobs. In many cases, such as in the case of Bengkayang, where an army unit fired on a large crowd of Dayaks (December 30, 1996), and in the case of Singkawang (April 7, 1999), where the troops shot and killed three Malays and a Dayak (*Pontianak Pos* December 31, 1996, April 8, 1999). Dayak fighting against the military took place in a context where the military was defending fleeing Madurese from lynching by an angry mob. The fact that the army represents the nation, while Sanggau Ledo is used to local rule based on Dayak customs, does make the perception of the military as a partial institution more understandable. According to a prominent

---

39   Human Rights Watch 1997, YMD 2001, several other interviews with the Maduese informants 2000–06.

Dayak peace-maker, Suherman Acap, many years after the massive riots there have still been many incidents in which the Indonesian military has been in direct confrontation with the structures of traditional Dayak leadership in the district of Bengkayang. There have, for example, been traffic accidents with military involvement, and they have occasionally given rise to tension between the military and the Dayak community (Acap 2006).

The perception of their lack of impartiality hampered the legitimacy of the police and further contributed to their failure to prevent crime and conflict. The lack of legitimate law enforcement especially affected the initial stages of war. If individual crimes had been dealt with early on and individual perpetrators captured, the need for ethnic community action could have been avoided. The riots in Sanggau Ledo are a case in point. According to an eye-witness (Dede 2006), the activities of the two Madurese men who first harassed (or kidnapped, as the local Dayak witness puts it) a Sanggau Ledo Dayak woman in Ledo were known to "everybody" (but apparently not to the police). After being chased away from Ledo by the uncles of the abused girl, they returned with a number of Madurese friends several times, looking for the uncles. Yet, the police failed to do anything about this. The violent incident of the stabbing of the girl's two uncles in Ledo on December 27, 1996 took place within the context of a music festival with a large crowd of young people. Even there, the presence of the police was missing (Dede 2006).

The lack of police presence was amplified by the fact that the frustrated Dayaks did not always learn about what the police had done to preserve order. The arrest of the Madurese perpetrators went unnoticed by the Dayak mob and the assumption that the police had not done anything was further provoking the Dayak community (DF 2006). It seems that the triggering incidents as well as the emergence of a perception among the Dayaks of Bengkayang and the Malays of Sambas of the Madurese as a criminal race can largely be explained by the lack of police resources for tackling violent crime. This, of course, is partially due to the notoriously low levels of police resources in general in West Kalimantan (Haseman 1999) during the time of the conflicts.

The lack of response by the police to the triggering incidents stemmed partly from insufficient cooperation between the police and the strong civil society of West Kalimantan. Since the police were unaware of the growing ethnic tension and the harassment of criminal individuals, something most of the people already knew about, greater resources could not be assigned to areas where they were needed at the time. This lack of collaboration could have been partly due to the remaining uneasiness between the modern administration and the traditional leadership.

The issue of law enforcement does not only affect the initial provocations, but also the mass actions. It became clear to me that the Malay officials in Sambas and the Dayak officials in Sanggau Ledo and elsewhere in Bengkayang recognized the importance of law enforcement in the prevention of the initial provocations by the Madurese, but not in the prevention of the mass action (Andoth 2006,

Yon Gedean 2006). When talking about the lack of police protection, most of the other communities automatically focused on the lack of punishment for crimes committed by the Madurese people. However, once their massive riots started, opportunities were lacking for the protection of the Madurese community.

Furthermore, the conflict was constructed in a way that made the circumstances so special that the normal deterrent provided by law enforcement did not apply. If I asked whether it was possible to investigate the motives of the violent Malay or Dayak combatants by interviewing Malay or Dayak perpetrators in the jails of West Kalimantan, I often got the surprised response: "But surely we no longer have anybody in jail for the Sambas riots. That was many years ago" (Pandjiwinata 2003). Interviews with the head of the provincial police, the district head of Sambas and the village head in Tanjung Keracut showed that all these people felt it natural that only 2–3 years after the mass killings in Sambas and 4–5 years after the killings in Bengkayang there were no perpetrators left in jail. A Malay mob member interviewed for this study was carrying three skulls in his belt, one his own victim, when captured by the police, and yet he only received a one year sentence (YD 2001). It became clear in many of the interviews with officials in Sambas and Bengkayang that many known participants in the feast of violence were not convicted at all. In a lecture at Sambas (March 2003), the district head (H. Burhanuddin S. Rasyid) introduced the audience of community leaders to me, laughingly saying that he knew that many of the individuals there were involved in the Sambas violence.

An important explanation for the riots (and not only the pre-conflict violence) in Sambas and in the Inner Valley (Sanggau Ledo area) was the culture of impunity in relation to violent reactions by the Dayak and Malay mobs. Looking at the cases of lynching and mobbing more broadly in Indonesia, this seems not just specific to West Kalimantan. There do not seem to be strong norms against taking the law into one's own hands (Welsh 2008). This is clear also in police reactions in cases where targets of public outcry and mob violence are taken to the police after they have been beaten. In many cases only the beaten target of mob violence is investigated for his violations that "caused" the violent "reaction," while the violent mobs are not tried (Welsh 2008). In West Kalimantan, running amok was perceived as the effect of an objective cause, and as such it was not something intentional that could be sanctioned by law or by morality (Burhanuddin 2008, Muksin 2006). When sanction for violent rioting is non-existent, weak motivations are sufficient to mobilize large crowds of violent young men. To some extent, this impunity was caused by the prominence of local custom in the conflict areas. Customary law and institutions on each side of the conflict were blind towards offences committed by the community in which these laws and institutions were based.

Furthermore, the modern sentiments of the West Kalimantan people failed to prevent traditionalist reactions among the perpetrators of violence. It seems clear, though, that a majority of Sambas and Bengkayang people feel awkward—perhaps collectively ashamed—about their sudden belief in very traditional myths that are not easily reconciled with their current modern lives.[40] Some informants even felt that a statement labeling West Kalimantan indigenous people as cannibals was the trigger for much of the violence (Abdurrahman 2006). However, this violence strengthened the credibility of the statement, as traditional man-eating rituals were mobilized.

Instead of explicitly talking about this shame or explicitly distancing themselves from the violent aspects of the invented tradition, West Kalimantan is silent about the traditions of which people are ashamed. For example, it is a taboo to call the Sambas or Sanggau Ledo riots "cannibalistic," despite the fact that nobody denies the eating of body parts by some Dayak and Malay combatants in the conflict (Davidson 2007: 231). This is because cannibalism is naturally regarded as something shameful and primitive. Still, people do not denounce it or decide that it will not belong to the future of modern Dayak communities.

It is also inappropriate, in the local thinking, to consider the offences committed in this conflict by the indigenous people as morally wrong or criminal. The local communities, and especially the modern people of Sambas and Bengkayang, stay silent about this moral issue, rather than defend it publicly. This silence and the moral justification of the local atrocities are part of a process of contextualizing the atrocities in a unique, special context in which modern norms against violence do not apply. In a way, the conflict acts are taken out of a normal framework and put into a security or conflict framework (this framing was very clear in the discussion with the police chief, Pandjiwinata 2003). This throws the power and the deterrence of law enforcement out of the window and makes it possible to imagine special conditions under which normal ethics do not apply.[41]

The failure to treat the Malay/Dayak violent rioting as criminal behavior is a very dysfunctional feature of West Kalimantan conflict dynamics. The taboo regarding the traditional injustices and the sense of exceptionalism (or securitization) of inter-ethnic violence prevents West Kalimantan from learning from its past mistakes. Yet, it is one that many local power-holders want to defend. Instead of discussing the morality of violent mass action, many leaders in the province discuss the morality of reporting it, as if it was the reporting that created the horror, not the actions themselves (Darwis 2009a, Statement by the Dayak Community 2009). A paper presented by the head of the district of Sambas in a conference on conflict prevention in Sambas expressed regret at the behavior of sensationalist media in exposing the violence against the Madurese; an irresponsible behavior that fueled conflict (Darwis 2009b). Most of the conference participants shared his view. While the discussion of awkward topics might be difficult due to the traumas of war, it

---

40   This sentiment is occasionally very clear among the students of my lectures in West Kalimantan, especially in Pontianak and Singkawang.

41   The creation by interpretation of special conditions, security, which apply to an issue area such as ethnic violence, has been theorized and studied by the so-called Copenhagen School of Security Studies, see Wæver 1995.

seems that the prevention of an open discussion on the violence also prevents West Kalimantan from changing the myths that make violence possible in the province.

Diagnosis

As the analysis of the three main theoretical junctures on the path to conflict has revealed, the real path to conflict bounces between changes in identities and agency, and motives of and opportunities for violence. Developments on the opportunity-side give rise to new identities, which again affect motives, then again identities, and these identitive changes might again create new opportunities, and so on. This means that in order to summarize the entire path to conflict we need to move from the examination of the three theoretical junctures (agency, motives and opportunities) in the path to conflict separately, into more detailed chronological presentation of junctures on the path to conflicts in West Kalimantan. In order to build the presentation into an illustration of the path to conflict, I will give iconic terms in italic letters when describing a specific juncture in this path.

The starting point for the path to conflict could be as far away in the past as one wants to, but most of the antagonism, motives and opportunities for violence can be traced back to the early 1970s. The military-backed authoritarian central state of President Suharto (1966–98) was strong, and this strength was reflected in the relationship between the political elite and its opposition as well as between the center and the peripheries. The difficult relationship between the Indonesian center and its peripheries for decades had been expressed by the suppression by the central government of its peripheries and by an assimilating nation-building linked with efforts to modernize the country on the terms of the center. A less explicit manifestation of this modernization was the dominance of the Javanese people over the non-Javanese local populations in the peripheries (*non-responsive, modernizing, centralist, discriminatory, Javanese state*).

As a result of both discrimination and insensitivity to needs, all communities, not just the indigenous communities, were frustrated (frustration to central administration). Due to an illegitimate formal political system people were tempted to seek public goods, even security, from their ethnic communities rather than from the state (*communalization of politics, economics and security*). This tendency was strengthened by the gradually increasing democratic and decentralist opportunities and the anticipated power transition from Suharto to his successor, in the 1990s. Competition for democratic and decentralist opportunities created a need to mobilize local forces, and due to the communalization of politics these forces were ethnic: new opportunities in both business and politics were sought by mobilizing ethnic civil society and bureaucracy. This happened first among Dayaks, and the success among Dayaks encouraged and forced the mobilization of both the Malays and the Madurese. Even though mobilization of ethnicity did not express itself as separatism, it linked ethnicity to the control over a defined territory to ethnicity. This involved competition mainly between Malays and

Dayaks: it was a reaction to Javanese discrimination, yet it found a way to express its frustrations against the Madurese.

It seems that during the years of Malay-Dayak competition a consensus emerged whereby the majority indigenous ethnicity was to have a dominating role in each area. In the current Bengkayang district this meant that Malays did indeed submit to the local rules and Dayak norms, while in Sambas Dayaks had to accept a Malay dominance (*emergence of the demand for a "local rule"*). This dominance was made possible by the poorly defined and enforced rules regulating the relationship between the center and peripheries and between communities. Rules of indigenous dominance and agency were born: the indigenous local majority ruled, while others could achieve equality only through assimilation to the local customs.

Since these rules were only shared between the Dayaks and the Malays, and not the Madurese, who were in most conflict areas the third biggest ethnic group, a Madurese frustration of the local dominant rules followed and this led to the criminal mobilization of the Madurese underground. Local interpretations could have been negotiated in an explicit process of dialogue between ethnic communities. However, explicit confrontation between competing interpretations is not encouraged in West Kalimantan. Verbal dispute is often seen as a prerequisite for violence and the breakdown of harmony. Due to this Indonesian tradition of not confronting problems head-on (*culture of demonstrative communication*), crime also became a strategy to articulate and construct an order free of hierarchy between locals and non-local ethnicities (*emergence of violent crime as a way to demonstrate irrelevance of the local rule*). This mobilization was possible especially due to the insufficient resources and legitimacy of the police. Even though it is debated if and how much the Madurese presence actually increased criminal violence, it did create an impression of an arrogant and criminal Madurese, which on the one hand served the Madurese interests in inter-community bargaining (*people were afraid of even perfectly peaceful Madurese*). On the other hand the stereotype of the criminal Madurese also legitimized indiscriminate violence against every member of the community, once the local aggression had started.

While the Madurese underground sought ways to consolidate their power and do away the discriminating local dominance (*emergence of violent crime as a way to demonstrate irrelevance of the local rule*), it was natural that the local groups felt frustrated by the Madurese crime (*Dayak/Malay frustration of Madurese crime*). Crime and especially arrogance towards local norms by some Madurese youngsters created a situation where either the local communities had to yield to the irrelevance of local norms, or they needed to argue for the reinstatement of the local normative code. Again in the culture of demonstrative communication, action to ask the Madurese either to assimilate or to leave articulated a framing where the Madurese were seen as visitors, who could be asked to leave by the hosts (*Dayak/Malay demand for the Madurese to leave, as a way of constructing "hosts" and "visitors"*). Since this did not bear fruit, the Dayaks and the Malays had to mobilize for an offensive (*mobilization of violent communal offensive by the Malay and Dayak communities*).

Violent demonstrative argument on both sides was not limited to disagreement about the terms of inter-ethnic relations. Violence was also used in the demonstration of belongingness to ethnic and religious communities, and of masculinity (*violence as a way to enact masculinity*). Why young men could demonstrate their masculinity, Christianity or commitment to Islam by killing other people was related to the language of conflict and in the definition of loyalty and masculinity in West Kalimantan.

In a precarious situation like this, the ignition of communal violence was in many conflict episodes an incident of inter-community crime. Violence was made easier through the mobilization of ethnic mythology for the purposes of circumventing fear and peaceful norms. The material reality of weak police resources was translated into a securitized conception of ethnicity and into the mobilization of traditions for war. This was the first phase in the collapse of resistance to the temptation of violence.

Once the community tradition was mobilized for defense and war the outnumbered police were no longer able to react to the communal disturbances. This created a special context of communal tension where the usual legal norms did not apply (*conflict as a norm-free zone*). The memory of the sanctioned ethnic cleansing of rural areas of the Chinese in Sambas further strengthened the de facto impunity with which the conflict actors committed their murders without fear of legal retribution. This further contributed to the collapse of resistance to the temptation of violence.

Finally, after the events, strategic elements of the conflict were interpreted as primordial qualities of ethnic cultures. While for some Madurese youth crime had been means of resisting the stranglehold of local norms, criminality was seen as a quality of all Madurese individuals (*stereotype of the Madurese as criminals*). Similarly, after the violent reaction to the crime by the indigenous groups, cannibalism and brutality became seen as qualities of the two indigenous communities of West Kalimantan (*stereotype of cannibals*). As a result, in addition to the collapse of resilience the societal capacity to resolve conflicts collapsed. If the conflict problem could be reduced to the qualities of opposing ethnic groups, conflict could only be ended by defeating (or expelling) the enemy.

The diagnosis specific to West Kalimantan can be summarized the path shown in Figure 3.1. In this illustration the main junctures, the birth of agency (first column), the development of the motive to violence (second column) and the emergence of the opportunities (third column), are still clearly visible. For these junctures I will now try to identify remedies so that the path to conflict can be blocked or redirected.

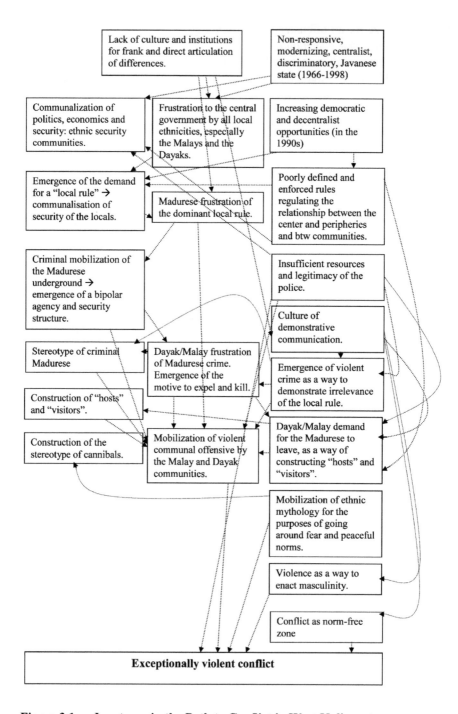

Figure 3.1   Junctures in the Path to Conflict in West Kalimantan

Chapter 4
Can the Path to Conflict be Blocked or Redirected?

Introduction

In this chapter, I will, firstly, look at the opportunities for the prevention of antagonistic agency, the resolution of conflicting interests and the strengthening of obstacles to war, one by one. In my identification of opportunities I will focus on 21 junctures on the path to conflict as identified in the diagnosis in the previous chapter and aim at designing interventions that could block or redirect these junctures. Secondly, the aim is to generalize the recipes for West Kalimantan into something that could be seen as a lesson for other cases of conflict that show structural similarities. But instead of aiming at one parsimonious prescription on how to remove "the root cause of all conflict," the attempt here is to identify many ways of reducing the risk of violence. In order to facilitate the integration of my findings into existing peace research, I will return the junctures into the three main clusters of agency, motives and opportunities.

Particular attention will be paid to the ways in which scholars could play a positive role in conflict prevention. The main focus will be in the opportunities that can be identified in West Kalimantan, but since some of the work I have been doing and observing in converting a university class of ethnic leaders into an ethnic communication forum under the vice president of Indonesia has exemplified the ways in which scholars can be useful for peace, I will also analyze the scholarly action that has in fact been taken to transform the agency structure, resolve the disputes and block opportunities for violence.

Can Antagonism be Reconciled?

In a democratic society it is not possible to fight antagonistic agency by means of state propaganda or enforced harmonization. Thus designing strategies based on strong state influence in debate would be futile: while diverting paths of conflict, we do not want to build paths to authoritarianism. Instead, as was concluded in the diagnosis and the analysis of antagonism, what is needed is dialogue across the ethnic lines. Only cooperation that fights with words rather than with demonstrative arguments, dialogue that explicates the obligations and rights of communities, can reconcile the relations of the "migrants" and "locals." Such activity belongs to a strategic cluster that could be named Strategy of Democratic Dialogue, echoing the strategies prescribed by several theorists of intra-state democratic peace (Davenport 2007, Gurr 2000, Pruitt, Bettye and Thomas 2007). It is a democratic peace strategy as it is based on dialogue, and free communication and negotiation. In addition to examining here the use of the strategy in preventing antagonism, I will reveal later more elements of this strategy in my examination of ways to remove motives and opportunities for violence.

The first step in the strategy of democratic intra-state peace is an increase in inter-community and inter-religious communication. Interventions to enable this are useful also to democracy, but they are also feasible and relatively costless. In West Kalimantan this has been attempted by means of two forums, the West Kalimantan Ethnic Communication Forum (ECF) and the West Kalimantan Inter-Religious Communication Forum. These forums are the main instruments in the transformation of conflict agency in West Kalimantan. I will explain these two instruments by starting with the more important: the West Kalimantan Ethnic Communication Forum.

The Transformation of Conflict Agency and the Emergence of the West Kalimantan Ethnic Communication Forum

In antagonistic agent structure, it is not easy to build bridges between the conflicting parties. Bridges are needed for communication and if there is hostility between communities, there is little interest in communicating anything but threats and insults. Furthermore, when there is coercive bargaining between alternative interpretations of the inter-community relationships (framing of equality versus framing of locals and visitors) eagerness on one side to improve relationships would easily be treated as a sign of weakness. This is why the linking of ethnic communities often needs external help and indirect strategies. In West Kalimantan the original objective of ethnic leaders for becoming engaged in conflict prevention was prestige. Ethnic leaders represent traditional culture and they cling into old, traditional sources of power and prestige. Conflicts in West Kalimantan offered tradition-based prestige and thus power.

However, studies in conflict prevention also put them into the center of activities. Since West Kalimantan conflicts were perceived as communal, it was natural that community leaders were also central in the prevention of such conflicts. This is why I decided in the year 2000 to link up with a local university, Universitas Tanjungpura, and offer my own experience in peace research and some European resources for the training of these ethnic leaders in conflict resolution. Offering university-based training on conflict resolution and conflict prevention for ethnic leaders underlined the centrality of ethnic leaders in a new function, peace building. University studies were also a way for the ethnic leaders to broaden the foundation of their authority beyond the tradition, into more modern platforms of authority and respect. It was a way to offer them a new identity that served the same interests they had had in their conflict involvement.

University courses for ethnic leaders were not possible with local efforts only. On the one hand, local universities lacked resources for teaching extra classes. On the other hand, the province did not have a university with peace research or conflict studies in their curriculum, or scholars with competence in these topics. Furthermore, and here I would need a third hand, most local actors were considered partisan. Giving any credit for moves to peace for local actors was not easy for leaders of those ethnic groups who had an antagonistic attitude towards the ethnic group that the local facilitator might have represented. This is where the international research network, the Indonesian Conflict Studies Network, became handy.

The Indonesian Conflict Studies Network (ICSN) was an initiative I had launched during the Finnish EU presidency in 1999 for the buildup of scholarly contacts that could help Finland in its new role keep in touch with different conflict realities that the EU could be interested in. The network had activities and coordinators in each of the Indonesian conflict areas and it gave university teaching on conflict prevention, dispute resolution, conflict transformation and peace-building to various stakeholder groups in these troubled regions. Activities in West Kalimantan started in spring 2000 as cooperation between the institute I worked for at the time, the Nordic Institute of Asian Studies (NIAS), and the Universitas Tangungpura. Teaching capacity was largely imported from Europe and adjusted to local conditions by the local professor, who had experience of conflict in West Kalimantan, even if not of education in comparative conflict studies. The local contact, Professor Alqadrie, is an anthropologist with a specialization in forestry management and cultural studies. Teaching worked originally without funding, occupying a large share of my free time as well as my research time. However, in 2003 teaching activity in Indonesia as a whole managed to secure funding from the EU's Asia Link program. The Asia Link project was, again, all-Indonesian in focus, but West Kalimantan was one of the areas where it was most successful. Teaching in this category of funding has only educational, and no conflict prevention, objectives. In the absence of a mandate for anything political, this limited the scope of activities. Yet, university teaching can be capacity-building that empowers local peace actors for conflict prevention. The agenda of conflict prevention was kept hidden from the sponsors until the project had clearly proved its usefulness in the buildup of a local network of peace actors that helped the pre-negotiation efforts in the Aceh peace process. Success in Aceh brought some new leverage in West Kalimantan too. After this, the European Commission obviously made several declarations implying that conflict prevention was among the original intentions of this particular Asia Link project.

Later in 2006, after Finland had received some positive publicity from the mediation by President Martti Ahtisaari of the Helsinki Talks on Aceh peace, and after Indonesian Conflict Studies Network had received a small part of the credit for the European help for Indonesian success in Aceh, the Finnish Foreign Ministry had become more active in Indonesia and the teaching project in West Kalimantan started receiving funding from the Finnish Embassy's Regional Cooperation

Funds. Yet, the contract for the activity emphasized that the mandate of the project remained purely educational and academic, and that the project did not aim at political or conflict prevention objectives. This was a bureaucratic necessity as the embassy wanted to avoid diplomatic problems if Indonesian officials began to perceive the teaching as controversial. To negotiate arrangements that insulated the embassy from all political criticism but allowed it to take political credit from potential successes was difficult, but in the end it was possible for the project to be open about its full set of objectives. After the successful handing over of the project to the vice president of Indonesia, the embassy, for the first time, publicized the project and the objective of the embassy to support peace in Kalimantan (Vuokko 2010). Good cooperation with the Kalimantan police and military intelligence ensured that none of the wishes the teaching operation had regarding being able to contribute academic concepts and pragmatic knowledge for Indonesian peace actors in West Kalimantan had to be kept secret.

Academic peace diplomacy is often made impossible by the lack of funding. Decisions on funding fall between the academic and development cooperation categories, and since preparation for funding decisions on such small projects, especially in the latter category, are taken care of by rather junior officials, they often lack perspective and are intended as "safe decisions." A decision not to fund can always be based on the fact that there are other good projects and an insufficient amount of funds to sponsor all of them, or that innovative projects do not fall into the categories that are the foundation of the funding instruments. Thus a decision not to fund is always a safe one, while funding a project that can cause political problems could be disastrous for a diplomat who has sided with the funding. Funding a project that does not really fit into the definitions of the funding instrument is always a risky decision, and thus difficult for junior officials. The funding of the Helsinki talks (on Aceh) from the EU Jakarta delegation's counter-terrorism funds (rapid reaction mechanism) is a fantastic exception to the rule of safe decisions in funding bureaucracies. It was only possible to make because the decision was made at a very high level of seniority. The decisions by the EC and the Finnish Embassy to fund the West Kalimantan capacity building in conflict prevention were also exceptions.

International facilitation of peace work in West Kalimantan was met with a lot of suspicion. It seems that some of the international media people were seen as Madura-sympathizers, while especially in Muslim communities, Westerners were often seen as anti-Islamic. In Sambas, the Indonesian Conflict Studies Network was met with suspicion on the part of some religious leaders and teachers, as the initiative was seen as one with the hidden agenda of bringing the Madurese community back to the province. Only with very stern support from the head of the district, Ir. H. Burhanuddin A. Rasyid, could activities continue through the years until it became clear for all communities that the teaching program did not intend to impose any specific terms of peace on the district.

In several classes in Sambas, I was accused of being a CIA operative, and at times local officials demanded to see my notes from the seminars I gave in the district. My notes, written in Finnish, did not help a lot to alleviate these suspicions. Only time, and close cooperation with trusted locals and the Malay co-facilitator, Professor Syarif I. Alqadrie, made it possible to develop more trusting relations with the local conflict stakeholders. Appearing as the guests of the district head, Mr. H. Burhanuddin A. Rashyid, also helped in building trust and confidence.

International cooperation, while suspicious, was also prestigious, and thus local politicians were eager to host events in a way that showed the subordination of the international component of the project to the local administration. As a result, the project got authoritative local support, while at the same time subordination to local bureaucracy alleviated suspicions. Later as the Indonesian Conflict Studies Network program became part of the activities of the ASEM Education Hub for Peace and Conflict Studies, the existence of a trusted international platform of our activities helped to alleviate the suspicion that I was a CIA agent. This international platform was, after all, created by European and Asian leaders (in the London ASEM Summit in 1998), with Indonesia's president included. Local bureaucrats were generally eager to participate on platforms that sounded like they were high-profile and international, yet politically safe.

Another way around the local suspicion regarding international collaboration in conflict-management capacity-building was the strong leadership in local operations by the local university's then director of the MA program in social sciences. Professor Syarif I. Alqadrie is also a mentor and former teacher of most of the leading media personalities, the governor of the province and the heads of the main conflict districts.

Furthermore, the entire teaching program was designed in a way that aimed at dispersing the suspicions surrounding international cooperation on such a controversial topic as conflict resolution. Teaching in West Kalimantan was based on the assumption that, while recognizing the expertise of local intellectuals in understanding the local conflict conditions, comparative research can still offer something to deepen this understanding. Every lecture started with a general introduction I (or in some cases some other European professors) gave on the basis of comparative conflict studies.[1] This introduction was focused on a theme that was crucial for the understanding of the conflict in West Kalimantan and attempted to carry lessons from conflicts all over the world for scrutiny in West Kalimantan. Next the local teacher briefly applied the global lessons to the West Kalimantan context. In the third phase, the "students"—the stakeholders in the

---

1 In addition to the author, who led the training project together with Tanjungpura's Prof. Syarif I. Alqadrie, some other European and Asian scholars from the Muhammadiyah University (Pontianak), STAIN (Tinggi Agama Islam Negeri, National College for Islamic Studies, Pontianak), the University of Helsinki (Katri Kyllönen), The Peace Research Institute, Oslo (Stein Tønnesson), the International Crisis Group (Henri Myrttinen), the Finnish Embassy, KITLV (Gerry van Klinken), the Universitas Syah Kuala (Aceh, Delsy Ronnie) and members of the Finnish media participated in the program over the years.

West Kalimantan conflict, for example elected leaders of ethnic associations of each major ethnic group from the five conflict-affected districts—discussed the Kalimantan experience, trying to think what went wrong in the run-up to the conflict, and what should be done to prevent the conflict from beginning again.

Even though education could be perceived as neutral and non-intrusive, the teaching of conflict studies was still somewhat suspicious. Security considerations and a security mentality became a problem for these international peace efforts. In many Indonesian provinces, universities act as mobilization centers rather than forces for conflict prevention. In Central Kalimantan, a university professor took a leading role in the violence against the Madurese, while in Riau a separatist uprising in the 1990s was led by a university professor. Dissidence against President Suharto's authoritarian rule was led by students of Universitas Triksati in Jakarta, while the separatist movement in Papua has a stronghold in the universities of Abepura. As a result, conflict studies were viewed with suspicion even if they were merely framed as educational activities. This is why our activities were open about the pragmatic purposes of conflict prevention attached to the teaching.

However, we were also very open about the ways in which peace was being promoted. The intention was to offer lessons from other conflicts that local experts could then utilize for their efforts at conflict prevention. The stakeholder classes were always considered as the main experts, while the international teacher (99% of time, this was me) only offered international experiences and the local teacher (almost always Prof. Alqadrie) tried to apply these lessons to the context of West Kalimantan. Thus instead of facilitators aiming at taking control of peace promotion, the experts and legitimate actors, such as the ethnic leaders, were the ones in charge.

Given that knowledge is power and the framings presented in the class did affect the realities on the ground, this total local ownership was naturally a bit of a myth and a dream. Yet, the effort to give the ownership and control to the ethnic leaders together with the strict publicity policy (the operations of the class were followed from the beginning by the local media) emphasizing the role of the ethnic leaders as the main decision-makers, helped, after years of cooperation. The feeling among ethnic leaders was that this was not a foreign conspiracy, but a genuine effort to empower local conflict stakeholders. The idea of empowering ethnic leaders, again, boosted their motives to participate. If leaders had not been able to claim credit for progress for peace, they would have had one motive fewer to make any compromises.

In addition to the suspicion of the training participants, the authorities' suspicion had to be tackled. Domestic conflicts are a problem for the image of a province and thus most areas would not like an international focus on their violent episodes. Furthermore, foreign interference in sensitive issues is dangerous as foreign operatives could act as provocateurs, or they might simply act in an insensitive manner that could unintentionally stir conflict.

The provincial military intelligence followed our program closely and the police occasionally summoned some of the program's key local actors.

Furthermore, occasionally as the international project leader I was "made aware" of the fact that my moves were being followed. Sometimes "a student" raised questions in the class revealing that he knew exactly which villages I had visited in my preparation of the lectures. This way, and in many other comparable ways, I think I might have been kept in check, sometime a bit harassed, in order to remind me that my role was educational, and not "subversive" in any way.[2] However, the program was never disturbed by this surveillance. On the contrary, Indonesian officials had a legitimate right to be informed about what I was doing in sensitive areas. The project's links to the Indonesian military intelligence proved useful in the organization of military classes in conflict resolution. In the end, the head of the provincial military intelligence participated in the inauguration of the West Kalimantan ECF and the transition of the MA class into a peace process.

By adhering closely to various legal norms such as visa regulation and by having a strong backing from the Indonesian central administration, suspicion was overcome. Furthermore, funding from respected international partners such as the European Commission and the Finnish Embassy, and the platform of the ASEM (Asia Europe Meeting) Education Hub for Peace and Conflict Studies helped the official acceptance of the program. In the end, the transition from an educational program into a peace process was led by the office of Indonesia's vice president, Jusuf Kalla. This put the proper authorities in the driver's seat, instead of trying to keep control in foreign hands.

The suspicion and security mentality of the international securocracy can also be a great problem for border-crossing peace activities. It is often assumed that democratic Western countries have democratic securocracies simply because of the existence of democratic practices and general norms. This impression is surprisingly persistent despite the evidence of the atrocities and secretive behavior of Western intelligence apparatuses, especially in Muslim countries. However, since secret organizations are insulated by secrecy and since their exceptional methods are justified by security-exceptionalism (security is so important that those who enforce it cannot respect all the norms of democracy and human rights), it is my observation that the intelligence apparatuses of Western democracies behave in very similar manner as their sibling organizations in totalitarian countries.

Even within the legally regulated spheres of their operations, there are limitations that are relevant for international conflict prevention, and for my work in West Kalimantan. If the conflict involves parties that are listed as terrorist organizations, or if peace work involves cooperation with foreign intelligence operatives, the intelligence officials of the foreigners' own country can also become a problem. In some cases, especially when dealing with Islamic conflicting parties, as was the case with the Madurese and Malay militias, the Western securocracy tends to

---

2   Elsewhere in Indonesia, noticeably in Papua and Aceh, I was occasionally assisted by airport officials who knew my name, where I came from and where in Indonesia I was heading to. I think these officials were instructed to let me know that I was safe and being checked on.

make its own definitions of who is and who is not a terrorist, and this affects even conflict prevention activities that do not involve anybody who has been formally listed as a terrorist. It is not uncommon, even if it is something scholars tend to be silent about, that their intelligence communities make contact with scholars to warn against (and forbid) cooperation with certain groups. Sometimes they interrogate the scholars about the programs with conflict stakeholders whom the intelligence officials consider terrorists or spies. I was interviewed for the first time by the Swedish secret police (Säpo) after preparatory meetings for the Aceh Helsinki talks with the leadership of the Gerakan Aceh Merdeka in June 2004, and in this context I was informed very bluntly of the preference the Danish secret police had against my meeting with "suspicious people."

Later, when I was investigating the mindset of radical Islamists for the Danish Foreign Ministry's work for the development of cooperation that could address the root causes of terrorism, the Danish secret police insisted on getting briefings on the people I had interviewed confidentially for the project. I could not do this, and soon I found a "bug" (a secret listening device) under my office table (this during the Helsinki talks).

Later I was informed officially that the Danish secret police had for a long time listened to my telephone conversations and had read my emails including those on my West Kalimantan activities. The legal ground for this was a suspicion related to my advocacy work for another peace process for diplomats whom the Danish Security and Intelligence Service suspected of being foreign spies (activity that I conducted without ever using either my email or my phone). Part of an earlier version of this book had been recorded as "evidence material B-9" in a criminal investigation by the Danish Security and Intelligence Service against me. This activity on behalf of the Danish secret police was framed as security-enhancing activity and as law enforcement. Even if contacts and confidential communications were needed for the promotion of peace, partisan security interests overrode the interests of peace.[3] Confidentiality needed for peace work was overridden by the partisan confidentiality norms of the Danish securocracy. A very good example of this was an incident where a member of the Danish secret police insisted that I had to explain my notes of a confidential discussion with President Ahtisaari related to the Aceh peace process. As I declined, he insisted that he had a top-secret classification that meant that I had to tell him everything.

In a peace mentality one country cannot insist even in its own territory that they can unilaterally dictate the norms of information sharing, and, of course, demanding that a scholar reveal his confidential discussions was also not legal in the Danish democracy. But since the context of this demand was secrecy, the demand could be made, and it could be denied later that this demand was made.

---

3   This activity by the Danish secret police took place after the Danish right-wing government had closed down the Copenhagen Peace Research Institute and denied any public funding to peace research in the entire country. At that time Denmark was, according to its own soldiers' publications, participating in the CIA's secret interrogation programs.

This intrusion for the sake of Danish "security" into the facilitation of West Kalimantan peace process eventually ended my activities there, but fortunately only after the conflict-resolution capacity-building had been taken over by the office of Indonesia's vice president, and transformed into a peace process in the framework of the West Kalimantan ECF.

Teaching among ethnic groups was first conducted in two streams. On the one hand, there were classes of intellectuals from different ethnic groups in bigger cities, first in Pontianak and Singkawang and later also in Ngabang (Landak). Some of the ethnic leaders that later became the core of the negotiation between ethnic groups participated in these meetings of the pre-influentials (Kelman 1997). On the other hand, lectures were given to local ethnic leaders. Identifying ethnic leaders in West Kalimantan was easy due to the semi-official status of most of the ethnic organizations. With only a few exceptions, there was no real competition or alternative interpretations regarding who represented which ethnic leadership. The tremendous prestige in the province of my local collaborator, Prof. Alqadrie, together with the genuine interest in conflict prevention of many of the ethnic leaders made it easy for our project to attract the main ethnic leaders from each of the main conflicting ethnic communities to the classes. The setting offered prestige, and eventually national and even international attention, to the ethnic leaders for their peace work, which helped to prevent the diversion of some of the paths to conflict. Thus, as discussed in Chapter 3, this managed to reconstruct the path to peace by articulating meanings for non-violent strategies that have the same value as some violent strategies, attracting the conflict actors to choose the former rather than the latter. To some extent this was one the main strategies that was repeated in several stages during the process of establishing the West Kalimantan ECF.

After several years of lectures that involved ethnic leaders, there was a sufficient foundation and consensus to the organization of joint classes to the very same ethnic leaders that had mobilized their ethnic militias against each other in the conflicts of Bengkayang and Sambas. The organization of the first meeting was well coordinated with the provincial police to safeguard each of the participants of the first lecture. To emphasize the importance of this event in the development of West Kalimantan, I accepted the request of a Finnish documentarist, Janne Savin from CajaVision (who took the cover picture for this book), to let him come to follow my work in Aceh and West Kalimantan. He was making a documentary for Finnish television on my efforts to contribute to conflict prevention in Indonesia. We agreed that he would come to West Kalimantan to take footage of the historic first meeting of all of the leaders of the communities that had waged war in 1996–97 and 1999. This way the second day of this meeting of ethnic leaders dressed in their best customary clothing was covered by a small "European TV crew." Also, this move was planned to create a setting where, instead of waging war, making peace was what raised the status and prestige of the ethnic leaders. While used to attention from their own community, attention from the provincial media, let alone the national or international media, was rare for them. The venue for the first meeting in Pasir Panjang Beach on October 15–16, 2007 was carefully planned, and some of the ideas of the first joint declaration by all relevant ethnic groups were pre-negotiated among the ethnic leaders.

The original idea was to invite ethnic leaders to the beautiful beach resort with their families for a few days. This would have served the idea of transforming demonized perceptions ethnic leaders had of each other, which is often prescribed in textbooks on pre-negotiation (Kelman 1973, Stein 1989, Zartman 1989). There is nothing as "re-humanizing" for feared, dehumanized leaders of conflicting parties than seeing each other being given the run-around by children or grandchildren. At the same time, the discourses that ethnic leaders have to mobilize in interactions with their families rather than with their military institutions are useful also for peace-making. Family discourses are not obsessed with abstract notions of security of collectivities like ethnic groups, but instead they are more focused on everyday survival and pragmatic problem-solving, not to mention love and compassion (Turshen and Twagiramariya 1998). Being there with their families have the potential to reframe their perceived images in a way that could have emphasized the common basic issues shared and valued by all the ethnic leaders. After all, ethnic leaders were mostly people with large families whom they valued. This could have been the start for these leaders of seeing each other as fundamentally similar, and as people who have similar basic interests.

However, despite this good plan, it seems that the leaders had decided among themselves that this kind of a meeting was not dignified or appropriate given their high positions. It seemed also that the local facilitator from Universitas Tangungpura had decided that he could cut costs by not pushing the ethnic leaders into bringing their children. In the end, I was the only person who turned up with my family. Yet, the atmosphere in this beach resort was relaxed, and in addition to the first day of lectures a lot of careful socialization took place. Some of it, not much though, took place between ethnic groups.

The second day was spent discussing how to develop the inter-ethnic class. I suggested that the local classes would start developing ideas for a declaration of an inter-ethnic code of conduct that would then be submitted to each of the local classes for discussion and further development (in Sambas, Bengkayang, Singkawang and Pontianak). Finally, these ideas related to the code of conduct would be discussed in a similar meeting to the one in Pasir Panjang in October 2007. The code of conduct would set the ground rules regarding the rights and responsibilities of ethnic groups towards each other.

However, soon enough it became clear that the ethnic leaders wanted to develop more frequent dialogue and an institution of permanent dialogue between ethnic leaders to discuss problems of inter-ethnic interaction. While the ethnic leaders were always keen on emphasizing the role of the traditional institutions, they were also perfectly realistic about the tendencies towards more formal democratic, modern representation, and thus it was decided that the role of the emerging dialogue forum was mainly to define what ethnicity and community loyalty should not be used for, rather than trying to extend ethnic power towards areas where it would be resisted by forces of modern administration. It was important to ensure that the emerging elements of consensus on the terms of inter-ethnic interaction were given a formal status. In order to ensure that inter-ethnic peace efforts were not hijacked by any ethnic group or political party inside West Kalimantan, the Pasir Panjang group (or the Pasir Panjang Group for Ethnic Harmony, as the group named itself before the eventual establishment of the West Kalimantan ECF a year later) asked me to seek protection for the group from the vice president's office. Despite the fact that the vice president was also the leader of the Golkar party, the vice president's office was seen as sufficiently outside the party politics of West Kalimantan, which was important for the ethnic leaders. Similarly, attention from the central government boosted the prestige of both the province and the ethnic leaders themselves.

Thus the process that followed was, on the one hand, based on the efforts of local classes in Pontianak, Singkawang, Sambas and Bengkayang (and later, in 2008, also Landak), to prepare ideas for another round of discussions on the inter-ethnic code of conduct. It is natural that in such a setting, as is often the case with stakeholder training and stakeholder seminars (Kelman 1997), a lot of practical negotiation takes place between the main conflicting community leaders. However, a university class cannot pretend to be a negotiation venue. It would have been a great waste to keep the cooperation purely academic, and not to utilize the confidence built in the class to get a "pre-negotiated" consensus around such crucial issues as how to prevent violent inter-ethnic crime from turning into communal conflict, how to help the police react quickly in the case of conflict-triggering events by offering them community-based early warning, and how to foster communication and confidence-building between communities.

Thus to create a setting where partisan actors would not take credit for the achievements of West Kalimantan's ethnic leaders, I contacted people I knew from the Aceh peace process in the Indonesian vice president's office in spring 2008. At the time, I had been contracted by the Danish Foreign Ministry to establish a PhD class at the University of Helsinki for students from Southeast Asia, who were directly involved in practical conflict-resolution processes. One of the students was Mr. Santos Winarso from Vice President Jusuf Kalla's office. This way communication and arrangements for meetings with the leadership of the office were easy to organize. The vice president's deputy for political affairs, Prof. Djohermansyah Djohan, quickly became the hub of the action. The vice president accepted the idea of taking over the inter-ethnic class and participating in the inaugural meeting of the West Kalimantan ECF, and to chair the first meeting. The vice president's office, however, sent Kalla's political deputy, Prof. Djohermansyah, to chair the first four meetings of the West Kalimantan ECF, and nominated an official to liaise with the facilitators of the forum. In 2010 the forum selected a secretary with whom the vice president's office would liaise. The fact that the vice president's office held the records of the meetings meant that ethnic leaders would feel much more committed to the decisions they made in the forum than if the forum had remained just a dialogue forum on an educational platform. The forum being sponsored by the vice president clearly constructed a situation where the prestige received from the vice president's office's frequent visits to the forum in the province was translated into greater commitment from the ethnic leaders to keeping their promises and doing their best to persuade politicians, businessmen and other members of their communities to keep to the jointly agreed code of conduct for peaceful inter-ethnic relations.

The work of the forum was from the very beginning very public, as the local media followed its work closely. Media releases were given collectively, this way avoiding the use of the media to push for partisan interests inside the forum. The inauguration ceremony was attended by public officials of the province on all levels of regional administration, as well as by the provincial police chief, chiefs of all the police districts as well as the province's chief of military intelligence.

Originally the West Kalimantan ECF consisted of leaders of Madurese community organizations from Singkawang, Pontianak district and Pontianak City. Later in 2009 Madurese from Bengkayang and Landak were also represented. Dayaks and Malays were represented by their community leaders from Bengkayang, Sambas, Singkawang and Pontianak. Smaller ethnic groups, such as the Chinese, Javanese and Bataks, were represented from the districts where they had a substantial presence. In 2008 ethnic organizations from Landak district joined the forum, and in December 2010 the forum expanded to include each of the communities from each of the districts of West Kalimantan. With enlargement communication covered more communities, and lessons could be drawn more broadly. However, at the same time expansion has created practical problems as the costs of dialogue grow. The province has taken co-responsibility for the financing of activities, and this has made continuing biannual meetings possible. But there is a risk that the forum will become more entangled in politics and will lose its broad-based political support as a non-political initiative. The initial idea of the vice president's sole coordination was to avoid provincial political competition: if the forum was facilitated by outsiders, the credit for its initiatives could not be claimed by one of the province's partisan groups. Yet, for practical reasons the province's co-facilitation after the inauguration of the forum has been welcomed.

In addition to the province-wide communication forum, similar forums have been initiated in the main conflict areas by districts (Sambas, Bengkayang, Singkawang and Pontianak City). The forums in Sambas and Bengkayang at the initiative of the districts have mixed religious and ethnic members. Official and traditional leaders participate in these forums together, and they actively discuss the place of various communities in the district. Furthermore, the forum in Bengkayang has already become involved in preventing the transformation of individual incidents of violent crime into communal riots. In Bengkayang, a Javanese individual had killed a Dayak individual. Instead of a communalization of this crime, the Bengkayang ethnic communication forum managed, with the ethnic leaders' authority, to persuade the Dayak youngsters that this incident was not a communal one. The cooperation between the Dayak and the Javanese leaders in doing this was crucial: joint public appearances by the two made it difficult for the younger generation of Dayaks to legitimize any action against the Javanese population in general.

The establishment of the district-level communication forums will not mean the sudden transformation of the province's antagonism. Even though I will be able to show the linkage between what the ECF did on the one hand, and pragmatic theory-based and comparative lesson-based prescriptions on the other, it is difficult to prove the causal relationship between the forum and the decline in violence in West Kalimantan.

There are still problems with the project of reducing inter-community antagonism in West Kalimantan. Firstly, communication between ethnic groups on the grass-roots levels is still insufficient to show to ordinary people the humanity of people of all ethnic groups. Broadening of the province-wide cooperation to the districts addresses this problem. Also, the attention the ECF gets from the media is important for the re-humanization of people from other ethnicities.

Secondly, another crucial question-mark is the indigenous commitment to and guidance of inter-ethnic dialogue. International and national attention has been rewarding cooperation (and made it financially feasible), and there has been a strong trend of the province and the districts showing a greater commitment and ownership in the process. However, the crucial test of commitment will be whether this survives and whether there will be resources that sustain this cooperation on the long run. There have been many comparable good initiatives that have, however, died down after the initial interest as resources and the political capital that only new initiatives (but not continuing programs) offer to politicians have waned. Whether the ECF continues to be a competitive platform for ethnic leaders that keeps them interested and focused, or whether there are more tempting partisan community platforms that attract ethnic leaders to activities that are incompatible with the peaceful constitution of the ECF remains to be seen.

Thirdly, even though ethnic leaders used to mobilize forces to conflict, their role was often less central than is visible. Ethnic leaders tend to go with the flow in order to create an illusion of their leadership. When tension is high and conflict is about to emerge, it is often a good power strategy for an ethnic leader to switch from a peaceful mode into a belligerent one, in order to stay in touch with their constituencies. There is nothing that would prevent this from happening in the future. The rioting in 2010 in Singkawang against Chinese cultural expressions is a good example of this. Despite the fact that collectively the ECF emphasized that criminal vandalism should be treated as individual criminality, rather than considering it as an effect of inter-ethnic provocations, Singkawan's ethnic leaders were unable and unwilling to go against the flow by explicitly taking stands against violence and destruction.

Furthermore, while ethnic leaders could mobilize many people for war, mobilization for peace would mean authority over everybody. Since only a small percentage of the members of each community are needed for extensive destruction, the prevention of this small percentage would require the widespread authority of leaders in peace. Thus it is clear that permanent communication for the removal of antagonism between communities is just "fair-weather cooperation" that could not survive a storm (as Rüland 2000 says about all ASEAN security cooperation). Yet, in the long term, inter-ethnic communication, especially if it spreads from the top to the grassroots, could be effective at "changing the weather," and safeguarding that "storm cooperation" is not needed.

Finally, while the ECF was initially mobilized as a modern peaceful platform for traditional leaders, it did offer greater prestige to *adat* and its representatives. But the original intention was not to boost the power of traditional leaders at the expense of modern democratic leadership. So far there has not been much competition between the ECF and modern, formal leaders, and the cooperation has been mutually helpful. However, if the ECF becomes another platform for the expansion of the power of traditional leaders, it can become a vehicle for the development of a new antagonistic communication structure. Since the focus of the forum has been on ethnic and community relations, it was not designed as a forum that strengthens the power of ethnic leaders politically or economically. Ethnic leaders can gain prestige from this forum, but this does not necessarily mean that they would derive power from modern democratic administration. On the contrary, the original idea was to discuss how to avoid the abuse of communalism for violent purposes. Yet, creating expectations of expanding power is one of the risks in this development. The creation of an agent structure where the modern and traditional leadership view each other as competitors, perhaps antagonistic ones, would be a disservice for conflict transformation in West Kalimantan.

Inter-Religious Communication and Conflict Agency

The prevention of antagonism between religious groups is not so much to reconcile existing conflict (as the existing conflict has not been primarily religious) as it is to prevent the rise of a new type of conflict in the future. There have been a few conflict episodes between Dayak and Malay communities, the most well known of them in Kuala Mempawah just before the expansion of the Sambas riots in February 1999. However, this conflict was not directly religious even though it involved a power battle between a Dayak community leader (Cornelius Kimha) and the Malay candidate (Agus Salim). The rioting of the Dayak youth eventually led to the burning of the parliament[4] and to the Home Ministry imposing a Dayak candidate rather than his standing for election (Alqadrie 2004). Religious harmony will be crucial especially for the prevention of tension between the two biggest ethnic groups, the Muslim Malays and the Christian Dayaks. Due to the fact that these groups are relatively large and, if antagonized, threatening to each other in all districts, the potential magnitude of conflict between these communities could be much greater than in previous conflicts. This is why preventing religious antagonism will have a high priority despite the fact that relations between Dayaks and Malays have largely been harmonious up until now.

---

4   Alqadrie 2004. According to Davidson (2008: 125), just cars and property around it.

Measures have already been taken, at both a national and provincial level, for the purpose of religious communication. The Inter-Religious Communication Forum, Forum Komunikasi Umat Agama, is a national creation for each province, inaugurated by a presidential decree (Djohermansyah 2009). However, its inauguration and activities are dependent on the activities in each province. While in many Indonesian provinces ethnic communication forums have been inactive (Djohermansyah 2009), in West Kalimantan activities have had good leadership. The ASEM Education Hub for Peace and Conflict Studies and the Indonesian Conflict Studies Network have participated in the training of the core team of the forum, and they have contributed some ideas for activities. Administratively the forum is under the direction of the rector of the Pontianak branch of the National College for Islamic Studies, STAIN (Sekolah Tinggi Agama Islam Negeri), and Prof. Haitami Salim, who was nominated as the chairman of the Inter-Religious Communication Forum. His university dedicated one of their centers, CAEIRU (Center for the Deepening of Religious Harmony), as an intellectual secretariat for the forum. This secretariat helped in the development of the program of the forum, and under the rector its director, Mr. Eka Hendry, devised ways of invigorating inter-religious communication. With help from the Dutch government and a Dutch consultancy company, the drivers of the religious forum received some mediation training. To create an impact on the grass root levels this education has been passed on to Sambas and Bengkayang, where this forum (and its core staff from CAEIRU) has conducted some tens of hours of mediation training (Eka 2009, Haitami 2008).

However, limited resources have made the active promotion of inter-religious communication difficult. The religious forum as a fully local initiative is also very dependent on contributions by local politicians, and this puts its local neutrality at risk. The lack of national and international attention might have given religious communication a head-start as this forum has not had to prove itself against suspicions like external actors have. Yet, this has also meant that the activity has not had the resources inter-ethnic communication has had. In the absence of broader attention, inter-religious dialogue has not managed to offer politicians the political capital they have been able to extract from cooperation with the ECF, and thus the local funding of inter-religious funding has also suffered. At the same time, STAIN has managed to integrate the forum's activities in national scholarly networks to get resources to training and intellectual activities (Atio 2009, Eka 2009).

The link between activities—religious mediation and facilitation of dialogue between religious leaders—and theoretical prescriptions of pragmatic peace research are naturally quite clear. How the inter-religious forum reacts to concrete issues of tension will be an interesting test for the activity. The strong leadership of Islamic scholars in activities, the local approach, and the political ambitions of the rector of STAIN, Professor Haitami,[5] could be the weak links of this effort to transform religious agent structures of conflict in West Kalimantan.

The Deconstruction of Community Stereotypes and the Socialization
of a More Positive Picture of Communities

When following the processes of conflict episodes, it is easy to trace the contribution of negative ethnic stereotypes to the agency structure in West Kalimantan. The assumption that there are collective characteristics of the Madurese or the Malays or the Dayaks that somehow are shared by all or most members of the ethnic group makes it easier for violence to move from one member of an ethnic group to another. If it is the collective characteristics of ethnicity that determine the actions of one member of a group, it is also logical to hate all members of the group for deeds done by only one of the members. This makes collective punishment possible and helps the transition of conflicts from individual to communal.

Stereotypical views of members of community or ethnic groups reduce the activity of people to their characteristics, not their interests or desires. This makes it impossible for conflicting parties to try to reconcile their interests. If Madurese violence were seen as caused by a conflict of interests, the solution could have been one of dispute resolution. But since violence was seen as the character of the Madurese people, it was something objective, and therefore irreconcilable. The solution had to be to remove the people with that violent character. This clearly shows the centrality of negative stereotypes in the path to conflict, and thus is an issue that peace strategies should address. Since getting rid of derogatory stereotypes will mean work for inter-community prudence, this could be part of the Strategy for Peace by Prudence. Such a strategy has been outlined in some of the classical work on peace dialogue and work on activity to re-humanize conflicting parties in the eyes of each other (Kelman 1973). In addition to analysis of the elements related to getting rid of antagonism, an analysis of world efforts against opportunities for violence will reveal more elements to this peace strategy.

Academic capacity-building among local civil-society actors aimed at revealing the conflict consequences of racist/communalist stereotypes could bring about more success than the government's efforts to change people's approach to communities. This is the case in societies where politics is viewed with suspicion (as in West Kalimantan), and where intellectuals are therefore more trusted as opinion-leaders. In such environments academic interventions to stereotypical constructions of communal agency are often likely to be more cost effective. If West Kalimantan is such an environment we should seek strategies to deconstruct stereotypical agency by means of critical scholarship and academic socialization.

_____

5   Professor Haitami ran for the mayorship of Pontianak in 2010. Discussions with him have at times suggested that his willingness to keep partisan interests apart from the interests of peace are a source of worry. He has asked if my program or the Finnish embassy could support his candidacy, since he is a candidate that supports peace.

If it were possible for the enlightened segments of the communities in cooperation with some media people to make an inter-community alliance against racism, it would be possible to create more progressive approaches to community relations. In a place like West Kalimantan, the educational elite is very narrow and the main newspaper journalists and main local administrators are almost all former students of a handful of social science professors; for example, the main university offering MA-level education in the area, Universitas Tanjungpura, has only one graduate school for all the social sciences, so just one professor has been responsible for all its students. Thus the dominant interpretations of ethnicity and communities are dependent on only a few people. It is easy to imagine a coalition of civil society actors that could fundamentally change the general attitude between communities. Defeating the most harmful stereotypes should therefore not be impossible if the local opinion-elite could agree on some ground rules for the usage of community identities and for views of ethnicity. At the same time Universitas Tanjungpura has been a bastion of partisan Malay interests. The former leader of the MA school, Prof. Alqadrie, is a relative of the Malay sultan of Pontianak, while the current leader of the MA school, Mr. Gusti Suriansyah, is a Malay customary leader in Landak. This could limit the role the university is able and willing to play in the playing-down of pejorative community stereotypes. Furthermore, until recently the West Kalimantan media has been dominated by the Jawa Pos group with its own partisan interests. This, too, could have complicated the non-partisan efforts to get rid of ethnic stereotypes (Widjaja 2003). A more independent Indonesian Conflict Studies Network has tried to help in this project, and the community leaders have taken a strong role in the activity. Community leaders have discussed the problem in two of their communication forums and they are in agreement on the need to tackle the problem of stereotypes.

Also the media has had meetings with scholarly opinion-leaders on the issue in classes organized by the Indonesian Conflict Studies Network/ASEM Education Hub. However, the focus of discussion on conflict-sensitive media is mostly on how to limit conflict-insensitive media exposure. The problem with this discussion is that when conflict-insensitive reporting is limited, the ones with power to do this tend to insert their own interests in limiting media also about issues that are sensitive to their groups. In many of the discussions of Universitas Tanjungpura some interests regarding to forestry management and logging have been associated with conflict insensitivity, and in fact censored (by conference chairmen) even in conferences about conflict-sensitive reporting.[6]

This practice is problematic as revelations about corruption in forestry business or in politics are necessary to curtail such abuse of power. After all, corruption and

---

6   This observation is based on experiences of one of the media-related conferences of the Indonesian Conflict Studies Network in March 2003. In this conference conflict sensitivity was explicitly associated with silence about the abuse of power and corruption in the forestry business, and this association was strongly resisted by some Dayak organizations.

abuse of power are often associated with the emergence of motives for violence. The fact that criminal logging arrangements have such a clear linkage to conflict in West Kalimantan, as has been revealed in Chapter 3 of this book, underlines this conclusion. Furthermore, hesitance to report on issues that give rise to anger discourages verbal disputes and explicit debates on the terms of peaceful interaction, and encourages the demonstration of one's arguments by means of violent action. This obviously is counter-productive. Prudent crime reporting should not deviate from truth or avoid controversial topics.

Yet, there is a need for prudence, too, in conflict-sensitive reporting. Framing individual criminality as communal or presenting a picture of crime being associated with one ethnic group only (by reporting the ethnic origin of criminals only when they are Madurese, for instance) are related to these deceptive reporting practices. On this issue there is already an agreement (this time not affirmed by any authority, just an agreement reached in university classes) about a practice of avoiding reporting the ethnic origin of criminal perpetrators, unless the incident really was such in which individuals stole or killed for their communities and not for themselves.

However, when communal tension rises, the media tends to reveal circumstances that make it easy for the reader to guess the ethnic origin of the perpetrator. Instead of reporting on a stabbing, newspapers or the local radio sometimes report a stabbing with a sickle-shaped knife (implicating the Madurese community) (Syukur 2003). Thus, more explicit agreements are needed. So far dialogue has been conducted among journalists, but these discussions should be extended to the editors of the province's main newspapers in order to enforce a policy of conflict-sensitive reporting. If the rules for the public reporting on crimes, for example, were explicitly agreed upon between the main newspapers, radio stations and ethnic leaders, it would be difficult for a reporter, even during times of tension, to feel it was a communal responsibility to reveal the community identity of a perpetrator. Furthermore, if newspapers were part of an explicit agreement, community leaders whose community had been implicated in a crime could refer to an agreement in their complaint against the radio station or newspaper, creating a motive for a stronger media policy within media outlets.

In addition to the limitations of unfair ethnic labeling, the fight against stereotypes in the media should involve re-humanization of the individuals behind ethnic labels. Re-humanizing human-interest stories about the lives of the law-abiding Madurese majority (Gubara and Kivimäki 2005, Kelman 1973) and stories that reveal greedy interests in the ethnic policy of divide and rule (Kivimäki 2005) are both generally associated with the reduction of ethnic stereotyping.

Sometimes the commitment of intellectuals to avoiding ethnic stereotypes is limited. For example, some intellectuals and politicians (Burhanuddin 2003) avoid blaming the characteristics of ethnic communities, but instead, for example, claim that the characteristics of their culture make the Madurese violent. Thus ethnic stereotypes are replaced by cultural stereotypes and not much has been achieved by the abandoning of ethnic stereotypes.

One way to deconstruct ethnic stereotypes is to try to emphasize the human agency of all individuals regardless of ethnicity. Ethnic communication forums, and especially the (failed) efforts to promote interaction in humane roles (for example, as the parent or grandparent of small children) could have emphasized the humanity of the opponents.

Another scientifically theorized and empirically tested way to do this is to try to create inter-ethnic cooperation by utilizing cross-cutting cleavages (Simonsen 2006). Cases of post-conflict peace-building have shown that the utilization of the common interest of, say, Malay and Madurese women in questions of gender equality could build a gendered bridge between the two antagonistic communities. Thus supporting gender advocacy could, as a side product, help alleviate problems of inter-ethnic conflict transformation (Kivimäki and Pasch 2009). The use of cross-cutting cleavages is based on the idea of re-articulating meanings relevant to conflict agency. If interaction can be facilitated within groups that consist of people from "enemy ethnicities," but which clearly have common interests against some of the people of their own ethnic groups, this experience helps re-articulate the conception of group identities. The realization that this interaction forces on its participants is that there are cross-cutting identities that can all be useful for the mobilization of cooperation for one's own interests. This conception is in contradiction to the framing where the antagonistic division is fundamental and all-encompassing.

Using cross-cutting cleavages as a bridge between antagonistic actors, Universitas Tangungpura could, for example, establish a research program for its Malay students who live in Bengkayang and Dayak students who live in Sambas, on problems of the protection of minority rights. Here Sambas Dayaks and Bengkayang Malays, who are both minority groups, would have a common interest and channels of communication to their communities for the collection of information on the perceived problems in minority status in the two districts. Advocacy for minority rights would then be easy for both groups as they could simply utilize their common Malay or Dayak identity in the districts where their own groups are in the majority.

This Sambas/Bengkayang project could then be expanded to the two main cities of the province and broadened to cover other minorities, too, including the Madurese. Principled academic debate and analysis using the method of "bridging by cross-cutting cleavages" on minority rights could help transform the potential antagonistic divide between Malays and Dayaks, while in the expanded version of the program it could also directly address the existing antagonism between Dayaks and Madurese, and Malays and Madurese.

The Malay sultan of Landak (Suriansyah 2004) has suggested a similar cross-cutting arrangement on a national level. With national representation of and communication between different ethnic groups, it would be possible for members of the same ethnic group in different positions (as minorities/majorities; as "local"/"migrants") to discuss the rules of localities, and the rights of minorities. This communication could make it easier for members of ethnicities to sympathize with the rights of other communities in their own areas, since people of their own communities are in similar positions elsewhere in Indonesia.

Efforts to create commonness between the Malays and the Madurese by using their religious commonness and difference from others have not been very successful yet, but there are also efforts that have been fruitful. Muhammad Saad Munawar (2003) has mentioned as an example of this the work of the inter-ethnic boarding school Pesantren Hizbullah in Singkawang. It seems clear that prospects of building a religious bridge across the most antagonized identities of the Malay and the Madura should be fully explored, to dispel the stereotypical images many members of these communities have carried in their minds since the conflict in 1999.

Deconstructing Communal Security Agency

In the analysis and in the diagnosis I have shown how the assessment of people of the inability of the police to guarantee their security pushes people to seek protection from their communities. Kalimantan's conflicts reveal that this contributes to the province's vulnerability to sudden escalations in tension in communal relations. The situation can change quickly from bad to worse if there is a violent individual criminal incident involving two antagonistic communities. The link between individual criminal incidents and communal reactions is one of the main things that the communalization of security causes. There is a need to break this central linkage in order to reduce conflict potential in West Kalimantan. While the starting point in breaking this linkage is in the increasing of police capacity and the legitimacy of the police, this part of breaking the linkage is mostly related to the obstacles to violence. The opportunities that limitations in police performance offer for violent actors is naturally related to the opportunities for and obstacles to conflict and will be dealt with later in the chapter on the building-up of obstacles to violence. However, communities can themselves do many things to avoid the communalization of security and the communalization of crimes.

In West Kalimantan communal leaders learned lessons from comparative conflict studies about the rationalist explanations of conflict and about the domestic security dilemma that arises from a situation where each of the communities organizes its own defense. As their conclusion they decided in their class that three steps were needed for the containment of developments from crime to communal reaction.

The steps are the following:

1. The leader of the perpetrator's community together with the leader of the victim's community makes a public appeal (in the local media) to their communities to help the police to settle the criminal case.
2. The leader of the perpetrator's community bans any hiding of the perpetrator, and declares that the crime was not justified in the name of the interests of the community.

3. The leader of the victim's community urges members of his community not to take the law into their own hands and punish the perpetrator or his community, and declares that the incident was private and has no implications for relations between those members of the two communities who were not responsible for the crime.

These steps were accepted unofficially by all the main ethnic groups in the first meeting of the leaders that later formed the ECF in October 2007, but at the inaugural conference that established the ECF in December 2008 it became clear that communal leaders of Landak could not accept the promise not to organize the community's own self-defense in case the police failed to act in a criminal case. In a longer discussion on this principle in a district-level ECF in Landak in October 2009 it became clear that in Landak the distrust of the police was more fundamental than elsewhere, and therefore it was not possible for the Landak ethnic groups to accept the idea of ruling out communal mobilization for revenge in the event of the police and the system of positive law failing to do its best to capture and punish the perpetrators. If this ability was ruled out, a window would be opened for the kind of Madurese terror that Landak Dayak representatives in the district-level ECF explained that they experienced before in 1996 and in 1999. It is also possible that this issue was difficult for the Landak groups as they did not participate in the meetings of ethnic leaders in 2007 that prepared for the first common meeting, where these steps were endorsed. This way, because of a psychological mistake on my part, for them this suggestion of the steps was "imposed" on them and thus they did not feel they had ownership of it. Thus the last of the three steps has not yet been accepted by the collective meetings of the community leaders. Leaving out the third step was the "fingerprint" of the Landak Dayaks that ensured the ownership of the remaining steps to the Landak community leaders.

While ethnic community leaders wield some power in their communities, it is not likely that they can "command" their communities effectively. There has been previous agreements trying to tackle the communalization of inter-ethnic crime, including the Malino 1 and 2 Accords that both emphasized the cooperation, in Ambon and in Poso, between the police and the religious groups. In both agreements community leaders advocated cooperation with the police instead of encouraging a community response to crime. Yet, there have been cases in both places, and undoubtedly also in West Kalimantan, where, for example, perpetrators of inter-ethnic crimes are being hidden by relatives and members of the perpetrators' communities. Yet, even in Poso and in Ambon, this has no longer led to massive violence comparable to the conflicts at the turn of the millennium. Communalization of crime has no longer been as complete as it was then.

However, in West Kalimantan the steps of what to do have been defined in much greater detail than in the Malino Accords, which only define the principle of cooperating with the police. In West Kalimantan the provincial police have nominated an official whose task is to liaise with the relevant members of the ECF in the case of inter-ethnic crime. Furthermore, links have been created to like-minded (peace-minded) journalists who have shown interest in publishing the declarations of ethnic leaders of the perpetrator's and victim's communities. This way, when the agreed behavior has been better operationalized, the ECF group can be more efficient in demanding its members to comply with these agreements. Yet the impact on the ground needs a more careful analysis, to identify the mechanism of how these steps could divert or block a path to conflict.

The intention behind the three steps is to demonstrate the opinions of the leaders of the ethnic communities in order to make it difficult for other members of the community to interpret the community interests in a hostile manner. Even if community leaders cannot prevent violence, they can affect the way in which the violence is framed and prevent it from being framed as communal. Also, even if the perpetrator is still hidden by his relatives, this does still not constitute a community action, especially if the victim's community hears on the radio news that the perpetrator's community leader condemns the crime and forbids his community members to hide the perpetrator. This in itself makes it more difficult for the violence to grow along community lines.

Yet, to be realistic, when there are pressures from the communities for a communal revenge and for the framing of an ethnic crime as a communal event, it is probably likely that community leaders do not in every circumstance feel committed to the steps, despite the fact that they have promised to uphold them in a meeting with the deputy of Indonesia's vice president. Furthermore, it is not guaranteed in cases where the ethnic leaders are willing to comply with their commitment to the steps that they will be heard. It is possible that the media will fail to give voice to the ethnic leaders in time to prevent community violence. And even if the community leaders are given the floor, it might be that enraged people do not hear. Yet, there are already cases where the steps of de-escalation have actually been followed and in these cases the result has been peaceful. But this does not necessarily prove that this will always be the case nor that the ethnic leaders' publicity was crucial in the prevention of community violence. To be realistic, therefore, one should see these steps as useful and meaningful, but in no means a guarantee against community antagonization in the event of a visible inter-community violent crime.

Can Disputes be Resolved and Conflict Motives be Tackled?

The macro-context of removing motives for conflict depends on the responsiveness of the political system. The long-term economic and cultural grievances of the traditional Dayak communities, for example, and the political grievances of all local groups except the ruling Javanese were at the core of early motives of conflict during the Suharto period. If non-violent democratic channels for change are missing, grievances and the need for change become motives for violence (Gurr and Duvall 1973). Authoritarian modernization lay at the root of cultural grievances, while ethnic discrimination to the advantage of the ethnicities of the center, especially the Javanese, was the macro-context for political frustration in West Kalimantan. The corrupt authoritarian system caused both economic and political grievances by sending corrupt and incompetent rulers from the center to West Kalimantan. This created the motive and urgency for the Malay and Dayak races to compete for local power as soon as this was possible in the 1990s. Clearly, the general Strategy of Democratic Dialogue seems then relevant for the tackling of these grievances on the national level.

However, while grievances on the national level were real, the poorly regulated decentralization and democratization processes that followed non-responsive centralist authoritarian rule tended to be marred by greater violence than authoritarianism (Barron and Madden 2003). The political system that served local West Kalimantan people badly could have been part of the explanation for the urgency of local rule, and thus feverish communal political and economic competition. However, it was the lack of rules and law enforcement that mainly created the context for violence, not the preceding authoritarian conditions. Thus, it is likely that the maturing and institutionalizing of democracy in the Indonesian political system will contribute to the reduction of violence in West Kalimantan. Once the rules of decentralization are clearer violence will not be as tempting an option for power-greedy political leaders. In general, democracy should reduce long-term grievances as the political system is more responsive (Gurr 1993), and it can offer ways to change policies that cause frustration, by means of democratic non-violent action (Gurr and Duvall 1973).

Undoubtedly, with globalization some economic grievances cannot have a reaction at the level of national politics. Nations often have their hands tied because of the realities of a global economy, and then tackling grievances could require a more inclusive and responsive international system of governance (Rodan and Hewison 2004). Even though this level of political governance will have to be kept in mind for the future transformation of conflict, capitalism and peace seem to be closely tied in East Asia, and so the main challenge related to responsiveness is still the national political system. Thus, in the future, it is possible that the advantages in tackling conflict motives that are caused by democratization could be outweighed by the fact that an increasing share of economic grievances will be related to global and regional rather than national political governance.

Perhaps more important for the removal of conflict motives and for the resolution of conflicts is open, honest and frank communication between communities. The capacity for conflict resolution must be built among a core of people in the communal, political and administrative elite, including the police. There have been local, national and international efforts towards such a buildup, and recently an academic institute (CAEIRU) has been established at the local religious college (STAIN) under the Inter-Religious Communication Forum, to act specifically as the mediator and the trainer of mediators in local conflicts. Furthermore (until my exit from the province in 2010), the Universitas Tangungpura, and the Indonesian Conflict Studies Network that is based at the university, gave 60 hours of annual training in conflict resolution to conflict stakeholders, such as community leaders.

All this could contribute to the structural strength for peaceful dispute resolution at various levels. However, in addition to general conflict-resolution capacity, peace-research education in West Kalimantan can potentially remove a number of epistemic orientations that have hindered conflict resolution. Perhaps the most urgent of them is the general negative attitude of West Kalimantan people towards conflict resolution. Focusing on divisive issues such as disputes is often seen as provocation.

The Deconstruction of the Myth of Provocateurs and Harmony

One of the main obstacles to conflict resolution in West Kalimantan that needs to be overcome is the local interpretation of the principles and requirements of harmony, which prevents people from debating openly. Yet conflict resolution requires debate on disputes. It seems that the typical way in which conflicts terminate in East Asia as a whole is through inaction. Explicit peace negotiation has become very rare in all areas of East Asia since the end of the 1970s (Kivimäki 2011, Svensson 2011).

Verbal dispute is often equated with violent conflict and thus angry debate is avoided, as it is associated with brutality and violence. This is the more widespread type of negative epistemic orientation that Herbert Kelman attacked by shocking his audiences, saying that conflict is good and necessary; only violence and destruction is bad (Kelman 1997). The avoidance of boisterousness associated with democratic practices prevents the democratic culture of debate from entering West Kalimantan. Yet, peace research and Kelman's prescriptions suggest that the borderline between the strategy of prudence and that of democratic dialogue in West Kalimantan should be moved closer to the ideals of democracy, even at the expense of prudence.

The negative impact of the exaggerated prudence of West Kalimantan political debate was clearly demonstrated in the communal reactions towards the Pontianak Appeal, which suggested that the perpetrators of violence and human rights violations in the conflict in Sambas and in Bengkayang should be tried. Bengkayang Dayak community organizations reacted to the suggestion by saying, "We appeal to all parties not to make provocative statements which may cause anxiety among the people of WK as the people in this province now enjoy harmony and peace" (*Pontianak Pos*, September 30, 2009).

The idea of provocation being at the root of conflict makes it difficult to present controversial viewpoints that could be seen as provocations to riots and violence. If the perpetrator of violence is not himself responsible for his actions, but if instead political violence is modeled as puppet theatre where the puppets have no will of their own, while the puppeteers hold the strings, any verbal provocation can be seen as a violent act of the puppeteer and a contribution to violence rather than peace. The Dayak reaction to the Pontianak Appeal illustrates this, as they considered the initiators of the appeal responsible for whatever angry and violent reaction followed from this "provocation." As the leader of the Sambas Malay community, Mr. H. Darwis, pointed out: "We call on the West Kalimantan police to summon the initiators of the appeal to ask for their intention regarding the appeal." Mr. Darwis went on to be even more explicit on this. He asked, "If something happens, will they [the signatories of the Pontianak Appeal] be responsible for their actions?"

The exaggerated harmony thinking can be deconstructed and socialized away by means of critical social science practice. In this activity peace and conflict research scholars could do a lot, and the work of some inter-ethnic human rights organizations shows the direction in which this activity could go. The group of 77 intellectuals from all West Kalimantan ethnic groups that signed the Pontianak Appeal deserves examination concerning their action in this area.

This group of relatively young intellectuals—mainly scholars, teachers, journalists and activists—has been busy focusing popular attention on human rights issues and conflict violence. They represent Dayak, Malay, Chinese Indonesians, Bugis, Javanese, Madurese, Banjar, Indonesians of Arab descent (Alawiyyin), Sunda, Batak, Minang, Dutch, Manado, Aceh, Nusa Tenggara, Balinese, Ambon and Gorontalo ethnicities, and they are thought of as young opinion leaders. The Pontianak Appeal was published in major West Kalimantan newspapers on Monday, September 28, 2009. In this appeal the 77 drew attention to the pattern of resolving even the smallest disputes by means of massive demonstrations of violence, and to the pattern of expelling whole communities from areas where some of their members have been suspected of being responsible for crime and violence. The Appeal suggested that the first of these large-scale incidents, which led to the expelling and killing of the Chinese population from the rural areas of Sambas, was the example that created the precedent that now haunts the entire province (the Davidson thesis). Then by taking the problem to the level of individual perpetrators of violence and human rights violations the Appeal attempts to deconstruct the reality that the causes of anger are responsible for individual actions of violence. Instead, the Appeal emphasizes the rule of law, which focuses on the act of violence rather than exceptionalizing the context of such activity and giving the responsibility for these actions to some provocateurs. The Appeal demands a retroactive punishment for those that were responsible for atrocities and human-rights violations during the Bengkayang and Sambas violence in the 1990s as well as in the 1960s. While fundamentally challenging old ideas about the responsibility of provocateurs and the conflict's context, and while placing responsibility directly on the final actors of the violence, the Appeal also demonstrates a new culture of frank and open, even confrontational, articulation of opinions and concerns.

The Pontianak Appeal is a good example of the deconstruction of the old dysfunctional harmony thinking, but it is not the only one. For a few years now, several human rights organizations, most prominently the West Kalimantan office of the Indonesian Human Rights Council, have promoted a more frank exchange of views on issues of rights and conflicts of interests. Starting with less controversial issues—such as women's rights, or rights to unpolluted air, water and soil—these institutions have been an important part of the creation of a culture that is more open to explicit conflict resolution. Also, ethnic organizations in their activities of advocating ethnic rights have given space to a younger generation who have been much more open to a frank exchange of views. Even the Institute of Dayakology (and, to a lesser degree, Betang Raya Dayak Youth, the Dayak Students' Forum, the Youth Communication Forum, the People's Solidarity Forum for Justice and Peace, and the Dayak People's Solidarity Forum), though accused of creating legitimacy for Dayak violence, supports free and frank discussion (Bamba 2003). Madurese organizations, such as the student organization HIMMA, and the religious organization Gamisma, have been more modest and careful, but they have nevertheless tried to create openness to a polite and discreet but explicit conflict-resolution culture (Ali 2005, Rupaat 2007). Madurese influence through human rights organizations has been more direct in its construction of the culture of a frank exchange of positions.

It is easy to see how this Appeal, let alone the similar activities of several human rights intellectuals and activists, goes a long way towards creating a social reality alternative to the traditional focus on harmony and on the responsibility of conflict contexts and intellectual provocations. Despite the fact that both the Sambas and Bengkayang local communities reacted strongly against the Appeal, one thing testified that a new social reality was emerging. Both Sambas Malay and provincial Dayak organizations shared the worry of the 77 intellectuals about the enforcement of law. In doing so, they also accepted the responsibility of individuals for their violent acts, since law enforcement is clearly focused on direct action rather than on some exceptional climate that provokes violence.

Professor Alqadrie explained in his powerful media articles (see, for example, Alqadrie 2009) and in his university teaching, after the strong reaction to the Pontianak Appeal, that conflict violence should be conceptually separated from explicit articulations of conflicts of interests. Building on the classical ideas of Louis Kriesberg (1998)[7] of the difference between constructive conflict (of interests) and violence, he tried to explicitly challenge the mainstream notion that any expression of conflict is shied away from as something that automatically induces violence.

In Maluku, the belief in provocateurs exhibited, for example, by the closure of many social media sites by the police, has been countered by means of an interesting intellectual exercise in the rearticulation of conflict concepts. There, some NGO and religious blogs started to redefine provocations as sources of inciting false information, instead of seeing all inciting information as provocation. This way it was possible to introduce a new concept, "peace provocateurs," with reference to journalists who correct false information and tell the truth even when this means communicating about wrongdoings and things that give rise to anger.[8] By this

---

7   In his article Alqadrie referred to the book by Simon Fisher (2000) which repeats Kriesberg's idea.

8   See for example Rijoly-Matakupan 2011, Agenzia Fides 2011.

conceptual exercise these intellectuals have managed to uncouple false agitation from truthful reporting about wrongdoings that give rise to anger. By doing this they manage to make open dialogue and democratic peace more feasible, and to prevent untruthful hate-reporting from tarnishing the image of a responsible but open spread of information.

While the idea of provocateurs as the "root agents" of violence and the idea of silent harmony are still very much alive, it seems that the thinking in West Kalimantan, especially among younger generations, is changing, and this change has started to create the cultural foundations for the direct addressing of conflict grievances and motives of violence. The increased focus on law enforcement is a good example of thinking where the final responsibility is not with puppeteers but with the puppets—the violent actors themselves. When explicit articulation of positions has more space, conditions for open conflict resolution improve.

Grievances that Need to be Tackled

The creation of communication forums and the tackling of the main issues related to the antagonistic communal groups are steps that facilitate the serious resolution of disputes. Yet, confidence building and the tackling of antagonistic communal relations are not enough. It will be necessary to tackle, head-on, some of the interest and value incompatibilities that lead to conflicts. This is at the core of what I call the Strategy of Democratic Dialogue in West Kalimantan.

So far, West Kalimantan conflict resolution has achieved some immediate successes in Bengkayang, while no conflict resolution has even been attempted in Sambas. Even in Bengkayang, conflict resolution has not dug to the depths of the main grievances of the conflicting parties, nor has it resolved the main disputes of the previous conflicting parties or set rules for peaceful coexistence in the future. Davidson undermines the value of these efforts as efforts of the authorities to deploy "'cultural' tactics such as holding 'traditional' peace ceremonies" (Davidson 2008: 102). The status of these peace rituals is not simply a question of empirical truth in the traditional sense of the word. The interpretation of these rituals as insignificant or "election rallies of Golkar" (Human Rights Watch 1997: 32) constitutes their insignificance, while an effort to try to see the peaceful seeds in such processes could be more constructive for the future of peace. Davidson (2008: 103) in his analysis seems to recognize this and according to him ceremonies have kept minor clashes minor by offering a closure to the conflicts they have "ended."

According to Suherman Acap (2006, 2009) who, according to my sources, was (instead of the "authorities") the main architect of Bengkayang peace process, negotiation was not really focused on the disputes that had given rise to the conflict. Instead, the focus was on the future friendship between ethnicities, and on the rituals to foster this friendship. "These disputes were part of the history of Bengkayang while the peace process wanted to end the conflict and look forward" (Acap 2006). However, in order to look forward, it would be necessary to learn from the conflict and try to find the terms for future cooperation (Zartman and

Kremenyuk 2005). Furthermore, as the losing party, the Madurese were not really allowed to participate in the ritualistic peace negotiation process. However, their leader was later consulted and he accepted the "negotiated" future friendship and that it was up to the Dayak community to decide when or whether Madurese individuals were to be allowed to return (Acap 2006, Andoth 2006). However, since this was the first process in conflict resolution it is useful to look into it in some detail.

The first steps towards conflict resolution after the mass riots of the 1990s were taken early on, right after the first episodes of the Bengkayang riots. Then, the courageous activity of some leading Dayak individuals, especially a Christian priest, Suherman Acap, the Dayak customary leader (*ketua adat*) at the time, made it possible to have a peace process focused on the immediate conflict issues. This process was led by the Dayak customary (*adat*) leadership, and in cooperation with the Indonesian Army, the police and some Madurese (Muslim) religious leaders. Cooperation between these actors managed to bring to the safety of the Air Force Base thousands of Madurese people, and probably rescued the lives of several hundreds of them. Instead of becoming marginalized as a traitor, Acap managed to maintain his leadership within the Dayak community, while at the same time communicating with Madurese religious leaders and the national forces—the TNI and the police.

Activities initiated by Mr. Acap's customary village area early in January 1997 persuaded customary leaders against taking large-scale action against the Madurese. The decision of the Dewan Adat Dayak (an organization consisting of the leaders of customary villages) on January 3, 1997, broadened the process to include the officials in a body that coordinated cooperation between the official governing bodies and the traditional customary authorities (Muspida on the level of sub-districts and Mustika on the level of the district) (Acap 2006, Andoth 2006). The expanded meetings on the following day and the day after reached a consensus on ending the hostilities and the safe transportation of the remaining Madurese from the local air force base, but failed to involve the customary leaders of the Madurese. Thus, the peace process managed to tackle the immediate issues, but failed to involve the Madurese customary leaders in a direct dialogue. The frightened Madurese were, however, in touch with the initiator of the process, Suherman Acap, and agreed to the main principles of the consensus of the Mustika/ Muspida meetings of January 4 and 5 (Gedean 2006).

Madurese refugees also tended to have a very positive attitude towards the peace process and its initiators (Ali 2003). While the peace agreement declared that there would be good relations between those Madurese who subjected themselves to the local Dayak customary norms and the Dayaks themselves, it did not specify in detail the terms of Dayak-Madurese coexistence. When asked, it seems that no officials or any of the customary authorities even remembered what the peace treaty of Bengkayang said about the terms of peace (discussions with the sub-district administration of Sanggau Ledo, February 2006).

The memorial statue of the peace treaty in Sanggau Ledo is not a monumental creation, and, judged by the long grass surrounding it and the poor shape it is in, it would be safe to say that this symbol of a peace deal is not much valued in the sub-district of Sanggau Ledo. The function of the peace process was, however, important as a confidence-building measure rather than as a conflict-resolution measure. The peace agreement broke down in just weeks and the rest of the Madurese had to flee from the province (Prasojo 2009). Still, this effort to build trust could help in future negotiations on more substantial issues. In fact, Mr. Acap is one of the founding members of the ECF, and the fact that this forum has been established is in part due to the confidence built during the first peace process.

Many Madurese families have during the past few years been allowed to return to Bengkayang (Acap 2010), and the Bengkayang Madurese people are already represented in the provincial and district-level communication forums.[9] Yet, the rules of coexistence are not clear yet. The inter-communal interaction has not yet resolved the fundamental issues related to the rights of people and communities.

On the Madurese side, the core grievances that would need to be settled are related to the safety of their members when visiting Bengkayang or Sambas (Sedau 2, 3, 2006). The issue of opportunities for the Madurese to return to Bengkayang or Sambas has been less pertinent, since not many have been interested in returning. However, as a matter of principle, this issue should also be settled and it seems that there is some progress. Some Madurese families have already returned to Bengkayang, while the Malay organizations of Sambas are currently discussing the possibility of allowing those Madurese families to return whose members were not involved in crime (discussion in the inaugural meeting of the Sambas district communication forum, November 12, 2008). The two organizations involved in this discussion are the main cultural organization Dewan Adat Malayu Sambas, which is more positive about the return of the Madurese, and the Sambas Malay Youth organization, Forum Kommunikasi Pemuda Malay, which was more involved in conflict mobilization and which is still very much reserved about the possibility of Madurese return.

Also, the question of the Madurese's lands has become a pressing issue. After the Madurese were expelled these lands were largely taken over by local inhabitants or outsiders of Malay or Dayak ethnic origin. No rental agreements were made, and according to local officials, this would not be tolerated. Madurese are allowed to sell their lands in some areas, but they are not allowed to lease them. If they are allowed to sell, the Madurese must first pay an "incentive payment" to the people who have used their lands for free, just to create an incentive for the occupiers to vacate the lands. According to the head of the Sanggau Ledo sub-district, this payment is also compensation to the Dayaks for the "maintenance of the lands" (Andoth 2006, Gedean 2006)! However, according to the organization

---

9 I was first introduced to the Madurese participant of the Bengkayang ECF in Bengkayang in November 2009. The Madurese representative participated in the third and the fourth province-level ethnic communication forum meeting.

for the preservation of the Dayak culture, Dewan Adat Dayak, in Bengkayang (which is now headed by Mr. Suherman Acap), the practice of the unpaid leasing of the Madurese lands is unfair. Some officials (Muksin 2006) also see the current situation as unsatisfactory and try to change it, but many others do not. The issue of their lands is the key local issue for the Madurese, and it will not go away unless solved to the satisfaction of all sides of the conflict. The illegality of Sambas land practices should be considered a problem for Indonesia.

The issue of permanent settlement has not yet been resolved, either, and this issue has at times had implications for the voting rights of the Madurese IDPs (internally displaced people), as voters are registered locally in the place of permanent residence. Camps for IDPs have often been bases for the mobilization of criminal and communal violence by the Madurese, at least as long as there has been no prospect of them voicing their discontent in non-criminal, non-violent ways. Camps have also occasionally been attacked by Dayak and Malay mobs.

On the part of the "local" communities, the issue of efficient crime prevention will need to be resolved before a durable solution to conflict can be found. Furthermore, the transition to a modern way of life has to be cushioned, especially for the traditional Dayak population, in a way that does not threaten the collective cultural existence of the Dayaks. Part of this is the question of traditional and religious norms and their role vis-à-vis state law in modernized Indonesia. Without clarity on the rules, mini-conflicts cannot be avoided as communities try to enforce their own interpretation of rules by means of violence (Barron and Madden 2003). These smaller events can escalate into larger-scale violence.

With an inter-ethnic communications forum established under the auspices of the vice president's office, it is important that dialogue does not stay at the level of confidence-building, but that the confidence and contact that are built are swiftly used to form agreements on a code of conduct for inter-communal co-existence and, especially, rules for how ethnicity can and cannot be used in economic and political life. Ethnic leaders cannot control the abuse of ethnicity, but explicit norms could still help to make the selfish use of ethnicity in business or political competition illegitimate, especially when this usage goes against the norms decided upon by one's own ethnic leader. This code of conduct would also need to outline basic principles and definitions related to indigenousness, religious tolerance, and the rights and duties of "visiting communities."

So far the ECF, with its permanent dialogue between ethnic leaders, local administration and the office of the vice president, has been disappointing on these crucial issues of dispute. It might be that part of the problem has been in the sensitivity that this forum with foreign facilitation and initiation. This is related to the fact that from the beginning the Sambas Malay community leaders have been suspecting that the foreign push in West Kalimantan is to push the Madurese community back to Sambas against the will of the Sambas Malay community. In order to respect this sensitivity it has been difficult for me to maneuver the agenda of the forum towards discussions on these sensitive issues. The lectures have been the foundation of the forum's effort to tackle many of the other conflict issues.

The ECF's decisions to appeal against the mobilization of ethnicity for elections (see the section on gainful motives of conflict and political election campaigns on pages 134–6), the decisions of ECF's reaction (the three steps, see the section on communal security agency on pages 122–4) against the communalization of inter-ethnic crimes and the ECF's decision to declare that ethnic loyalty does not justify violence even in the context of ethnic tension and conflict (see the section on ethnic/traditional norms on page 144–6) have all been decisions that have been reached after a long academic discussion on similar general problems in conflicts overseas. However, it has not been possible for me to push the ECF to serious dialogue, let alone decisions, on the crucial issues of the rights of the Madurese without my neutrality being suspected.

Measures to protect Madurese individuals visiting Sambas, measures to protect the selling or renting of Madurese lands, and measures to ensure that modern advances do not threaten Dayak cultural existence need the attention of the ECF. They will also need to be negotiated within a broader forum, under the leadership of the public authorities. Conducting a hearing of the ethnic representation in this process would be necessary, but constructing a reality that would exaggerate the role of ethnic leaders in issues that legally belong to the realm of modern public administration would not benefit the preparation of West Kalimantan for its inevitable modernization. Collaboration between ethnic leaders and the modern public sector would be needed in order to socialize a constitutional order on the roles of *adat*, religious law and state law, and on which rules which issue areas. Collaboration between the central administration, the ECF, the Inter-Religious Communication Forum and the local administration would be necessary. While democratic dialogue and negotiation are one side of this strategy, clarity and enforcement of the rules of decentralization are the other side. Thus, negotiating for clear terms of inter-ethnic cooperation in the context of decentralization belongs both the general Strategy of Democratic Dialogue, and the strategy of Peace by Strong State.

The main actor on the central administration's part in the establishment of the West Kalimantan ECF, Professor Djohermansyah Djohan, has recently been moved to the Home Ministry with a portfolio of director general in charge of decentralization issues. In this task he will be the main facilitator for agreements between regions and the central administration about the practical rules of decentralization. For West Kalimantan it could be extremely positive that now the center's action in the clarification and negotiation of the meaning of decentralization in West Kalimantan is handled by an official who has intimate understanding of the conflict context of West Kalimantan, and who is well advised by the lessons of peace research from other conflicts involving incompatibilities of interests regarding to the terms of decentralization.

Gainful Motives of Conflict that Need to be Tackled

Many of West Kalimantan's conflict motives are gainful, mainly related to economic and political competition. While the issue of law enforcement will be dealt in the next chapter on obstacles to violence, the buildup of consensus between communities about the rules of political competition is an issue where negotiation on the rules of the game is genuinely and primarily focused on gainful motives. It is instructive to look at what peace research education and its spin-off, the West Kalimantan ECF, have managed to achieve in terms of negotiating rules of ethnic mobilization in elections. This is especially pertinent if one looks at the centrality of election motivation in sparking gainful violence in West Kalimantan.

Gainful Motives of Conflict and Political Election Campaigns

Just a bit more than a week before the general elections in spring 2009, on Saturday, March 28, the leaders of the Malay, Dayak, Madurese and Chinese communities in the main previous conflict areas of West Kalimantan gathered in Pontianak and made the important decision to disallow politicians from their own ethnic communities to utilize their ethnicity as a platform for political campaigning.[10] This, I think was an important measure in the Strategy of Peace by Strong State.

Cynics would say that Indonesia is a modern democracy with little space for decisions by ethnic leaders, and thus this unanimous decision by the West Kalimantan ECF had little or no value. There have been many agreements on not mobilizing ethnicity for election campaigns by many district-level election supervisory boards in some other conflict areas such as North Maluku, Maluku and parts of Java, and their impact has been negligible.

However, the fact that the declaration in West Kalimantan was made and initiated by ethnic leaders themselves, instead of government officials pushing such agreements on paper, could have been the reason why in West Kalimantan ECF declaration was associated with successful, non-violent elections. Since the ban on ethnic mobilization is part of the strengthening of the state and part of the pushing of ethnicity and locality out of politics, it is natural that such a ban would be more efficient if the genuine ownership and initiative for it came from the ethnic groups, not from the state. If communal power and traditional leaders are seen as an alternative to national domination, it is likely that local decisions on ruling out ethnicity from election campaigns could be better locally owned than decisions arbitrated by bodies instituted by the central government. An analysis of the meanings and roles of ethnicity in elections could illuminate the possibilities of the usefulness of the kind of declarations that the ECF made in March 2009.

If one looks at Indonesian political debate, the issue of ethnic representation still rules political campaigning in many parts of the country. Ethnic campaigning is a

---

10   Second meeting of the West Kalimantan Ethnic Communication Forum, Pontianak, March 27, 2009, art. 6.

problem in Indonesia for two main reasons. Firstly, democracy will not be successful if elections do not produce a test for the existing rulers. When politics becomes a matter of ethnicity elections fail to force popular accountability on the political elite. If people can be mobilized to vote only for candidates from their own ethnicity they will not vote for the candidates whose programs reflect their wishes best. This means that political leaders do not need to deliver in order to be re-elected. An American political scientist, Professor I. William Zartman (1995), says that this is what transforms an election into an ethnic census. If elections are no more than ethnic censuses they will not offer the needed responsiveness that helps prevent conflict grievances from emerging and which offers non-violent channels for change.

Secondly, political disputes can easily spill over into tension in ethnic relationships if politics takes place in an ethnic framing (Brown, Coté, Lynn-Jones and Miller 1997). This could be dangerous for ethnic harmony and peace in Indonesia. Thus there is a need for activity that counters ethnic mobilization in politics. Again we can match the objectives of the ECF with theoretical prescriptions of peace research. However, the question is whether the ECF declaration can be matched with the fact that the following elections were indeed the first non-violent elections in the democratic history of West Kalimantan.

The ECF's decision to ban ethnic mobilization for elections was made at the third meeting of the forum under the facilitation of the office of the vice president. Thus the format was serious and the decision was made officially, while the record of the decision is kept both at the secretariat of the forum, and at the office of the vice president. Wriggling out of these commitments would not be possible for ethnic leaders, even if they wanted to. However, the decision was made unanimously, and despite the fact that some of the ethic leaders themselves were running for office, everyone in the forum was committed to the ideal of promoting democracy and peace through disallowing ethnic election strategies.

The reason why it is likely that the decision by the forum is meaningful is not because ethnic leaders would have a lot of power as such. It is because of the fact that they have authority over the interpretations of communal tradition and ethnic norms. They have been selected and elected as traditional community leaders, and thus they define what can and what cannot be done in the name of ethnic solidarity. This means two things. Firstly, a politician who has intended to run mainly as a Malay, Madurese, Dayak or Chinese candidate will hesitate. He no longer has the right to claim that it is the obligation of his fellow Malays/Madurese/Dayaks or Chinese to show ethnic solidarity and vote for him. The fact that ethnic mobilization is not legal, and that there is a formal partnership between the ECF and the police of West Kalimantan, could mean that ethnic mobilization could also have negative legal consequences. Secondly, and more importantly, a person who has to make a choice—is this candidate the best choice simply because he is from one's own community?—will think twice. If the leader of his community himself does not recognize the obligation he has towards his community by listening to the advice of his ethnic leader, then why should an ordinary member of an ethnic community feel obliged by his ethnic loyalty to vote for this candidate? This is why it is possible that the decision reached on Saturday, March 28, 2009 by the ECF was a meaningful one.

Yet, it is clear that it did not prevent the fact that voters still calculated for the benefit of their ethnic groups rather than for the benefit of the entire province, district or city. To change this ethnic dialogue will have to reach entirely different depths. Grassroots levels will have to be involved to make ethnicity less relevant in politics. Furthermore, the public sector will have to show that it can offer the services that are expected, so that people will not need to resort to their ethnic communities to provide them. Thus, if people still vote "ethnically," ethnicity will still be relevant for the candidates even if they do not explicitly mobilize it. Thus ethnicity remains a problem of democracy, and ethnicity might still give rise to conflicts if supporters of candidates still consider members of other ethnicities as threats to their candidates. Thus, despite declarations from their ethnic leaders, popular mobilization against specific candidates during election campaigns or after the result is publicized is still possible. However, if candidates are more hesitant about openly mobilizing ethnicity, campaign violence could be substantially less probable. Thus it would be important that ethnic leaders will continue to declare and publicize their "ban" on ethnic campaigning in the future elections, too.

Can Obstacles to Conflict be Strengthened?

Strengthening Law Enforcement

In the realm of security the clearly perceived monopoly of the strong state for violence is essential for the ruling out of the fragmentation of the security structure, elimination of a security dilemma among ethnic groups, and for the prevention of a situation where potential belligerents can feel that they can benefit by using force. The strategy of enforcing law and the monopoly of the state in law enforcement is at the core of the Strategy of Peace by Strong State.

The assessment of the opportunities for benefit from using violence is always subjective. Gochman (1990) noted that in most conflicts all sides are overconfident of their own position and assume that they have more benefit-opportunities than they actually do. In the case of West Kalimantan, this mutual overconfidence was based on the different framings of the conflict. Madurese individuals that were the main perpetrators in the first phase of the conflict trusted the local capacity of their gang, despite the fact that as a community they were regionally a small and weak minority. The reality that the violent individuals of the Malay and Dayak communities perceived was exactly this regional rather than local reality, and in that reality they were stronger. The way in which scholarly activity relates to these subjective assessments and overconfident approaches can be harmful. There is a temptation for researchers to try to sympathize with both parties when interviewing them, simply in order to gain confidence and to get more information. However, by being overly sympathetic, for example of the justifiability of the "defense of the rights of the locals," researchers inadvertently feed the overconfidence of the conflicting parties, and encourage subjective assessments that suggest that the party a scholar is interviewing will be stronger than its adversaries if there was violence. This is a disservice we scholars should try to avoid providing to conflict situations.[11]

In the realm of material realities it seems clear that law enforcement would require substantially more resources than were available for West Kalimantan during the time of the main conflict incidents. One of the clearest strategy-elements of peace in West Kalimantan is related to the strengthening of the state and its law enforcement, the Strategy of Peace by Strong State. This strategy has been theorized in the literature of rational intra-state conflict (Fearon 1995, Kaufmann 1997, Lake and Rothchild 1997). Communalization of defenses happens because of the lack of credibility of the state in securing its people. Furthermore, crime can terrorize people and create motives for larger-scale responses only when the police are unable to tackle crime. Mass reaction against the whole community whose individuals have committed crimes is considered attractive only if there is no significant risk of a strong reaction from the state (police or army). Finally, a culture of violent demonstrative communication and articulating loyalty and arguments by means of violence all become possible only if the police does not work properly.

What peace and conflict research has been able to do in relation to the insufficient material resources of the police in West Kalimantan has been relatively significant. At the request of the national police, Prof. Alqadrie drafted a policy paper suggesting prescriptions for the purpose of preventing massive riots after the 1999 Sambas riot. In his report, Alqadrie not only suggested an increase in the number of police officers in the province, but he also suggested the doubling of their salaries. Alqadrie based this suggestion on the fact that police officers in West Kalimantan had traditionally supplemented their salaries with external income which sometimes caused a conflict of interest that compromised their roles as police officers. The harmfulness of police side-funding in Indonesia has been revealed by several critical studies of the political economy of the security in the country (Aditjondro 2001, Kingsbury and McCulloch 2006). If the level of salary does makes such side-income necessary, salaries have to go up. The wisdom of Sir James Goldsmith, the European industrialist who said, "If you pay peanuts, you get monkeys," seems to be relevant to West Kalimantan. Yet, while salary raises might be a necessary condition for improved security, they are not enough on their own. The main monkeys in the security business—such as Presidents Ferdinand Marcos, Suharto or François Duvalier (Papa Doc)—never stopped running after extra income despite their massive wealth. Needless to say, the rich monkeys cause a lot of insecurity with their shady security businesses. This is why I think peace research should advise that extra income for the police of West Kalimantan should

---

11   This accusation is made against the scholars of the Dayakology Institute by many scholars of the West Kalimantan conflict; see for example Davidson (2007).

come with strings attached. Police officers who get salary increases should be subjected to more stringent surveillance of their incomes so that increased salaries would not be supplemented with protection deals with the private sector.

This type of conditional thinking seems to guide President Susilo Bambang Yudhoyono's policies of security-sector reform. The substantial increases in the prestige and pay of security personnel have come with strict legal restrictions prohibiting security personnel from many of the extra-income-generating deals they were used to during the time of President Suharto.[12] The crucial issue determining how much this positive development will affect security in West Kalimantan depends on how the surveillance of the security personnel can be instituted in practice. Good laws will not have much influence if they are not well implemented and enforced. The practice in West Kalimantan seems to vary from area to area. In general, it seems that the level of professionalism in the police has drastically improved since the early 2000s.[13] This could be one of the reasons why the security situation seems better now than it did in the 1990s.

All in all, the material setting for physical obstacles to conflict has improved since the massive conflicts in Kalimantan. With the modernization of the province, the police have gained new resources and new access to areas that previously were difficult to administer. Furthermore, the overall quality of police staffing is higher now in the main conflict areas. The West Kalimantan police participate in the conflict resolution and conflict transformation training of the Indonesian Conflict Studies Network, and show progress in their capacity to understand methods of conflict prevention. With the establishment of the communications forum between civil society and the police there is an institutional capacity for creating cooperation that potentially can multiply police resources: if the police can tap into the expertise of local populations on communal or religious tensions, they will be able to be in the right place at the right time, and to concentrate power geographically in a way that optimizes conflict-prevention efficiency. Collaboration with civil society will require financial resources, though, and these resources are still not easy to acquire. Despite the small size of the police force and the relatively small size of the population in West Kalimantan, it is not easy to finance the modest efforts the provincial police make to keep contact with community leaders and the people. Yet, efficient law enforcement requires just that. The role of the police is crucial in blocking the path to conflict, and it is the first step in the strategy to prevent criminal incidents from becoming communal riots.

Scholars can also do something concrete to create obstacles to criminal violence. Those individuals whose acts require political legitimacy are often inhibited in their violence by transparency. Thus the mere existence of scholars (who could

---

12   The most explicit expression of this conditionality is the Law on TNI No. 34/2004 article 39 paragraphs 1 and 2, which prohibits TNI members from involvement in politics and business.

13   This observation is based on my experience in training the West Kalimantan police in conflict prevention for ten years.

report and publicize political violence) could be useful for the strengthening of law enforcement. Development workers and the transparency they brought with their presence had a very strong role in post-tsunami Aceh. In some conflict areas (at least in Southern Thailand) development cooperation has facilitated, at the initiative of scholarly intervention, some specific measures for the increasing of transparency as a structure that helps law enforcement and also the control of the police. The idea has been to give four things to selected villagers in an area that has suffered from violence, especially human rights violations. These four things are cheap cameras, training for use of the cameras, non-traceable email addresses and access to email; this way they would be able to send stories about human-rights violations with verifying digital pictures to third parties with a minimal risk of being punished for their revelation.

All sides of the conflict are likely to accept this kind of project in general, as not accepting such transparency would clearly indicate that this side of the conflict is taking advantage of the secrecy for the illegitimate use of violence. The idea is that this way villagers can document human-rights violations by writing a short story about the event, and by attaching pictures that aim to verify the events. This all should take place in areas that otherwise remain outside media attention.

In addition to human-rights violations people would also be able to send pictures and stories about everyday life as it is affected by tension and conflict. Adding an element of publicity that helps publicize also a more harmonious picture of areas in West Kalimantan makes the project more appealing, as it then does not only give bad publicity to the province, but also positive publicity. Many book publishers would be interested in publishing positive life histories "behind front lines," and this by-product of transparency-based obstacles of illegitimate violence can also serve the "rehumanization" of conflicting sides.[14]

Part of the law-enforcement problem was pinpointed as being the lack of cooperation between civil-society organizations and the police in the diagnosis of conflict. There were individual actions attempting to bridge the gap between Dayak customary organizations and the police. The Sanggau Ledo peace process initiated by Suherman Acap was a good example of this kind of activity. As part of this process, the local police and the traditional authorities worked in collaboration to transport the Madurese to safety and to create lines of communication between the conflicting parties towards a peace agreement (Acap 2006, interview with an anonymous Ledo police official, March 22, 2006).

The West Kalimantan police also made many efforts to build a community-based conflict early-warning structure in order to allow a more effective use of police resources before major conflicts arose. For example, in 2004 the West Kalimantan

---

14 This type of camera project has been implemented in Southern Thailand by the organization Friedrich Ebert Stiftung with some success, and similar projects have been accepted for implementation by the rebel leader of the Moro National Liberation Front, MNLF (Prof. Nur Misuari) and they are being initiated for the main conflict areas of Mindanao.

police district eagerly participated in and supported a conference organized by the West Kalimantan branch of the Indonesian Conflict Studies Network together with UNESCO and International Media Support (IMS). This workshop aimed at creating an NGO and media-based cooperation structure which could be used as an early-warning system in the case of conflicts in West Kalimantan. This clearly constitutes one of the ways in which academic diplomacy can help conflict prevention. Later, in 2007, the police established a communication forum, Forum Komunikasi (antara) Polisi dan Masyarakat (FKPM) for the purpose of enhancing communication with civil society.

Finally, for them to be able to contain conflicts by means of law enforcement, the law enforcers will have to change their mentality. West Kalimantan will have to accept the idea that murderers can be prosecuted, even if they have committed their atrocities within the context of a riot or communal conflict. Without that, the deterrence of law enforcement cannot reduce conflict potential. Here, the communal mindset has to change, and there is already some proof that this is happening. This change will be discussed further in the section on the mobilization of communal/traditional norms for peace (see page 144–6).

Deconstructing the Language of Violence

In addition to a realistic subjective assessment of opportunities for violence, and sufficient material capacity for the prevention of criminal and conflict violence, rules and laws that the police will have to enforce have to be clear. This has not been the case, and part of the demonstrative violence by communities against other has been caused by the lack of clarity on how decentralization should be interpreted. If legal norms are unclear, the practice of decentralization will be constructed in the interaction between communities. If even a relatively small number of Madurese youngsters manage to ignore the reality of local norms, and if they get away with it, the practice of decentralization will not have much space for local rules. At the same time, if local mobs and militias get away with murdering and expelling communities (including their totally innocent members), the practice of decentralization becomes one where ethnicities that are, in the local practice, viewed as indigenous will have a disproportionate say in local matters.

In order to be on top of the "language of violence" the people of West Kalimantan should be conscious of the ways in which their action speaks. If people realized when there was a perception of growing crime committed by people of a non-indigenous community, and when there were voices in favor of terrorizing the entire community out of the district, that these actions were articulating arguments, it would be possible for community leaders, the police, or the district government to invite some representatives of these communities for discussions on the arguments that would otherwise be argued by means of violent action. Here the method of articulating alternative, non-violent strategies with the same symbolic meanings as violence could be mobilized. Consciousness of the demonstrative argumentation and the ability to understand what these demonstrative actions "mean" could make it possible to replace violence with debate and thus transform conflict into a verbal dispute. In this task the role of intellectuals who can see the meanings of action has to be central in revealing the meanings of demonstrative behavior in public debates. The transformation of conflict and violent demonstrative action into debate and verbal dispute has to be initiated by those well conscious of the meanings of demonstrative action, and it will have to be done by means of public debate, newspaper articles, radio interviews and so forth. People have to be provoked into explicit debate on issues about which they have previously been violently demonstrating.

This way of rerouting the path to conflict leads to verbal dispute and non-violent debate. As it is based on direct argumentation, free media and popular participation in debates it clearly belongs to the general Strategy of Democratic Dialogue in West Kalimantan. While it will not offer harmony, and the peace it offers is at best a noisy peace, it is clear that its socialization could take time. Yet, democratic peace in West Kalimantan would be able to offer more than just absence of violence; it could also offer wider opportunities for people to participate in agenda building and the expression of grievances.

Instead of the conscious transformation of violent demonstrative action into debate, the systematic study of conflict elsewhere in Indonesia, Southeast Asia and East Asia reveals another way for the transformation of conflict. Violent demonstrative action can be replaced by non-violent demonstrative action. If one looks at more modern areas of Indonesia (and the rest of East Asia), one realizes that the culture of violent demonstrative action has not been replaced by explicit verbal debate, and yet most areas have avoided conflict. This is due to the fact that while in West Kalimantan masculinity and group identity may be articulated in violent action, development and capitalist competition have replaced violence as a means of masculine self-articulation in the more modern areas of Indonesia. Due to the developmentalist tradition in modern Indonesian centers, the way of showing one's power and masculinity is by means of economic success. Instead of manipulating traditional community norms the Indonesians in modern centers articulate their belongingness to modern society by demonstrating their loyalty to the norms of capitalism. A demonstration of a commitment to modernity and to capitalist norms does not require violence, as do some of the manipulated norms of community loyalty.

While in West Kalimantan economic competition tends to be violent at times, this competition is often not consistent with modern capitalist norms. Rather than being based on free competition, it is based on licenses and public subsidies, and the competition is not about producing products and services of superior quality or price, but about monopolizing the incentives and privileges issued by the corrupt public sector. Priorities of liberal and fair economic competition, on the other hand, have led conflict areas of Indonesia and East Asia into decisions that are helpful for conflict prevention. Conflict is not good for Indonesia's competitiveness, and it hinders economic input, most particularly investments from outside. Furthermore, partial treatment, and communal privileges instead of the rule of law, make economic activities difficult for the province.

Commitment to development seems to be related to the drastic decline of conflicts and battle-related deaths within ASEAN since the establishment of the organization. Two-thirds of conflicts and 93% of battle-related deaths disappeared from ASEAN after the transition from the turbulent revolutionary 1960s into the development-oriented ASEAN regime (Kivimäki 2001, 2008). The same development took place in East Asia after China abandoned the Cultural Revolution and started promoting economic development under the leadership of Deng Xiaoping. In East Asia, the number of conflicts was reduced by one-third while the number of battle deaths was down by 95% (Kivimäki 2010a, 2011). While commitment to development has been only part of the explanation of Southeast and East Asia's stability, it is an important and necessary part of it.

This kind of developmentalist thinking is emerging also in West Kalimantan and one can already see how it can contribute to peace in the province. A very clear example of these pressures is the need for Sambas, for example, to show that Madurese lands have not been confiscated, but that instead the rule of law applies to land ownership titles despite communal affiliations (Burhanuddin 2008). This is helping the conflict settlement, while its main purpose obviously is to show to potential investors that Sambas protects their investments, regardless of the investors' race, religion or ethnic origin. Developmentalist norms are thus coming to West Kalimantan, and this is likely to be a positive factor for the province's peace potential.

The path to peace focused on transforming violent demonstrative behavior into developmentalist demonstrative behavior could be called a developmentalist peace strategy, to highlight how development is at the core of it. The success of the strategy elsewhere in Indonesia and in East Asia speaks in its favor. Yet, developmentalist peace is not in contradiction with democratic peace. There is no reason for seeing the revelation of the meanings of violent demonstrative behavior, and the vigorous direct debate on the terms of communities' co-existence, as an alternative for non-violent, developmentalist, demonstrative behavior. Competition by means of economic success within commonly accepted norms can be a complement to vigorous debate.

As mentioned in the analysis and in the diagnosis, conflict has also been an opportunity to enact masculinity. Violence in Sanggau Ledo was sparked by a representative case of Madurese violence against a Ledo woman, and the communal reactions to this violence offered young men in Bengkayang a concrete opportunity to enact their masculinity in a symbolic defense of an iconic female of their community. This opportunity exists as an attractive option only due to the language of masculinity that associates weapons and violence with masculinity and does not offer sufficient alternative symbolic ways for young men to demonstrate their resolve and capacity to defend and project power. This resolve and capacity is connected to the primal roles of men as protectors of their families.

The strategy of changing the language of masculinity could be developed from the starting point of the realization that some of the features of what some gender specialists call hypermasculine identity (Nilan 2009, Nilan, Broom, Demartoto, Doron, Nayar, and Germov 2008)—heroism, power and a tendency for violence—are not very useful in conflict situations. Whenever these features are hegemonic in the culture of masculinity, whenever they represent a normative or 'ideal' type of masculinity occurring in specific times and places (Connell 2002), masculinity becomes a source of conflict. Yet, hegemonic masculinity is not an ideal that would be detached from social rationalities. Masculine identity naturally, as does any identity, interacts with other identities, with other social constructs and with material realities. If peace research can reveal realities that make alternative, less destructive identities seem more attractive, the meaning of masculinity can be changed.

The strategy of removing the negative impact of the language of masculinity on peace, the transformation of masculinity, has been theorized by Myrttinen (2003), and Jacobs, Jacobson and Marchbank (2000). This transformation could theoretically take place by derailing the impact of traditional primal masculinity, hypermasculinity, to less destructive expressions, and by changing the definition of aggressive hypermasculinity altogether. I will shortly look at these two options with two examples that seem relevant for West Kalimantan.

In modern society there are many non-violent types of alternative symbolic opportunities to the violent ones for the enactment of primal masculine roles. In general, these alternative opportunities can be encouraged and made more attractive in West Kalimantan. The close association between defeating an enemy in sports and defeating him in a fight has been extensively studied, especially in critical feminist literature (see for example Messner 1990, Messner and Sabo 1994). While most of the literature focuses on the symbolism of masculine violence in sports and on the primal stereotypes of men in the language of sports, my interest in this literature is related to the pragmatic possibilities of seeing sports as a substitute for violence for men that feel the need to enact their masculinity.

My un-systematic observation, when driving through villages in West Kalimantan, some of which have been theatres of violent episodes and some that have not, is that in disproportionally few of the violent villages there is a volleyball field in a central place of the village, while in disproportionally many of the peaceful villages such a place can be found. Sports achievements can be a symbolic opportunity for young men to demonstrate their primal capacities. In societies where such symbolism develops, deadly demonstrations of the same capacities could become less attractive. Thus, encouragement of participation in sports (rather than offering just spectator roles for sports events) could be a way to derail some of the opportunities that are crucial for the path to conflict. A volleyball field as such does not naturally create the meanings that make sports achievements an alternative for violent enactment of masculinity. Yet it is the necessary material infrastructure for the development of such a language of masculinity, and thus offering sports opportunities at the village level could be a way to redirect the path from conflict to peace.

While offering non-violent ways of demonstrating primal capacities could be a way to crowd out violent ways, it is also possible to try to support more sophisticated, artistically expressed ways of articulating and enacting masculinity. Pop culture, for instance, offers violent and non-violent role models for young men and boys, but the very potential popular art offers in the articulation of more sophisticated and less violent masculinities should be explored. While pop culture in Indonesia has so far been associated with violent Western decadence, indigenous pop culture is developing, with opportunities for the articulation of alternative masculinities. In this development local and national Indonesian pop stars can have an opportunity to help the West Kalimantan culture of masculinity to develop from its primal expressions towards a more modern and sophisticated direction.

Finally, research on the enactment of masculinities and the language of violence will also be necessary for any conscious social engineering and emancipation of conceptions of masculinity away from the current, dysfunctional, violent modes. Redirecting options to enact masculinity in non-violent ways constitute another cluster of opportunities for intellectual conflict transformation: Peace by the Transformation of the Language of Masculinity.

Mobilizing Ethnic/Traditional Norms for Peace

In addition to law enforcement and deconstruction of the demonstrative security practice, traditional norms against violence have to be strengthened in order to build up obstacles to violence. In transition areas where modern norms and law enforcement are not yet strong enough, but where the tradition is no longer very strong either, a manipulation of the tradition becomes a problem when there is tension between communities. The fact that different villages used different so-called Dayak traditions or Malay traditions to get around fear and moral inhibitors suggests that tradition is being abused for violent purposes.

The traditional leader of the main Dayak conflict zone in Bengkayang, Mr. Suherman Acap, has suggested that the traditional norms related to warfare should be put in writing, so that there is something to refer to when warmongers turn to tradition for their own defense. Research and dissemination of the real norms, especially the ones regarding conflict resolution, of different communities could, thus be a contribution peace research could make in West Kalimantan, to mobilize tradition for peace rather than war. This activity is at the core of the general Strategy of Peace by Prudence.

Furthermore, modernization and modern norms could be called upon for help against violent traditions. The people of West Kalimantan will have to be responsible for exposing traditions that are used to remove norms from the conflict situation and to create an illusion of moral and physical immunity. Communities will have to accept the fact that some of the old Dayak/Malay/Madurese wisdom has served the interests of power and war rather than the interests of the community. There seems to be a consensus among most communal leaders on this, and the emergence of a modern normative code and lifestyle could help make some of the violent traditional ideas look primitive and embarrassing. Furthermore, religion and religious leaders could be useful in transforming the violent aspects of tradition, as many of the beliefs and magical rituals are naturally against the teachings of religion. In order to avoid further violence, people in Kalimantan will have to tolerate the obvious:

- that people will get killed despite the spells and amulets,
- that people will be held responsible for their deeds despite the trance, and
- that violence harms the communities of West Kalimantan, regardless of the context.

Ethnic tradition also has to tolerate the idea that even in times of ethnic tension modern criminal law has to take precedence over ethnic tradition: murder should always be a murder so that the deterrent of legal punishment would not be lost even at the time of conflict. The way in which the Pontianak Appeal addresses this problem is by appealing for a tribunal that studies cases of violent action all the way back to 1967. If the province were to follow this advice, the tribunal would make it plainly clear that criminal law rules in conflict situations.

However, this part of the Appeal has raised a lot of anger, certainly among the people that would be likely to be tried for their deeds but among others as well. Anger can be good and it is important that this provocative suggestion could provoke discussion in addition to anger. However, the Appeal is demonstrative in nature. Instead of negotiating and agreeing that the conflicts are not accidents and that they are not outside the normal moral context, it is suggested that all this could be demonstrated by tribunals. These tribunals would then articulate the position of individual responsibility before the criminal law by punishing those who did not take this responsibility seriously. Obviously, the tradition of demonstrative argumentation has affected the Appeal, and despite the fact that accepting the idea of individual responsibility could be good, the way in which it is being argued by means of punishing someone is problematic.

Instead of focusing on the past, and instead of demonstrating one's arguments, it should be possible to explicitly agree that legal order cannot be sidelined by "specific conditions." This was the path of the ethnic leaders in the West Kalimantan ECF. The issue was discussed explicitly in June 2010 by the leaders of Sambas, Landak, Bengkayang, Singkawang and the Pontianak Malay, Dayak, Madurese, Bugis, Javanese and Chinese, and as a result a unanimous decision, the Pontianak Declaration of the West Kalimantan ECF, was issued. According to the declaration, "ethnic tension will no longer be considered as a special condition that would exempt people from the legal consequences of their actions." Ethnic leaders will no longer offer individuals of their communities ethnically based impunity, regardless of how the rationale of their actions might have been based on the defense of the community. Since ethnic leaders, authorities on ethnic tradition, have agreed on this, people will now know in advance that a murder is a murder and results in the legal punishment reserved for a murder according to Indonesian law. This will hopefully deter them from using violence.

It would again be useful for the ethnic peace process in West Kalimantan to take a leap of trust and believe in the effect of this declaration. The Pontianak Declaration can be meaningful only if people believe in it. However, for the sake of scholarly analysis, I will have to be realistic about the impact of this declaration. The principle of not allowing ethnic tension to justify violence in impunity (which was the case before) is great, but when there is a case of ethnic tension, the operationalization of this abstract principle will be tested. Unfortunately, the riots in Singkawang soon after the Pontianak Declaration proved that the operationalization of the Pontianak Declaration is difficult. Some ethnic leaders[15] issued public statements that clearly implicated the Chinese community as a collective for the provocative statements of the Chinese Mayor of Singkawang, and treated the Malay rage as an automatic reaction to these provocations. Despite the declaration stating that criminal reactions to ethnic provocations should be treated as individual, some of the very same people behind this declaration were instantly ready to negate this principle.

It seems clear that the future process of the ECF should aim at operationalizing the Pontianak Declaration further. Only after more concrete operationalizations of what the declaration requires from ethnic leaders in the event of ethnic tension will this declaration meet its full potential.

However, there is another way in which the Pontianak Declaration could be useful. The police have endorsed this statement, adding that the police as an institution will make sure that people know that the social context of a conflict does not matter, but instead that murderers will be tried regardless of the context. While in the past the police had to yield to the interpretation that conflict creates a context of exception to criminal law, this time they have something to refer to if someone tries to prevent normal legal procedures for offences committed in the context of conflict. Collaboration between the police and ethnic leaders on this will also possibly help the communal leaders to remember their duties in the creation of legal deterrence on conflict violence.

---

15   Good academic practice would be to specify the statements referred to here in this note. However, this would mean that I would have to directly point the finger at some ethnic leaders. Due to the close linkages between knowledge and social reality, I, as an actor in the West Kalimantan peace processes, cannot do this.

Conclusions: Strategies of Peace for West Kalimantan

The main objective of this book has been to identify individual acts that different types of peace actors could make to help end violence in West Kalimantan and conflict areas like it. Yet, while it is important to identify all the elements and individual acts that could divert the path to conflict, in this conclusion it makes sense to sum up some strategy clusters in order to reveal the big picture of peace-making. This is the reason why I have been grouping individual peace opportunities in four strategic clusters.

While the conflict problems in West Kalimantan can be grouped in simplified clusters—those related to antagonization, those related to motives and those related to conflict opportunities—interventions to prevent conflict and limit violence can also be gathered into simplifying strategy clusters. These clusters obviously closely relate to the clusters of conflict problems, but they do not each address only one of the problem clusters. Instead, there are peace strategies that each address various elements of all of the conflict clusters.

It seems that four main strategies applicable in West Kalimantan can be identified. I call these strategies:

1. Peace by Democratic Dialogue;
2. Peace by Prudence;
3. Peace by the Transformation of Masculinity, and;
4. Peace by Strong State.

True to the idea of eclectic pragmatism, each of these strategies addresses some problems, while an optimal super-strategy would require a combination of all of them. I will shortly describe each of the strategies and their relation to the conflict problem in West Kalimantan, and emphasize the elements in these strategies that academic diplomacy can address.

Democratic dialogue on various levels is needed to offer:

1. non-violent channels of change (on the level of the nation as well as the village);
2. opportunities for verbal dispute instead of violent demonstrative conflict, and;
3. a deconstruction of the culture of forced harmony that has prevented explicit tackling of grievances and enabled the culture of demonstrative argumentation.

While academic advice based on peace research on democracy can contribute to the democratic transition, academic peace diplomacy can also directly contribute to the creation of non-violent channels of change. Critical approaches to central concepts with which politics is conducted, such as "provocateurs," "harmony," "(positive and negative) conflict" and "democracy," can directly change the social constructions that structure our social reality of conflict. We have seen in detail in this book how these realities change the probability of people being killed by conflicts.

Furthermore, academic diplomacy can transform violent demonstrative action and a shooting war into a verbal battle, for example, by offering academic dialogue and educational platforms as forums for the explication of arguments about the disputed issues. The example of the transformation of the ethnic class into the Pasir Panjang Group of Ethnic Harmony, and finally into the West Kalimantan ECF is a prime example of transformation of conflict behavior into a verbal dispute. Lessons that academic diplomacy can carry from one conflict to another can advise communal leaders on how to devise mutually beneficial strategies that prevent the communalization of inter-ethnic crimes, the escalation of political campaigns along ethnic lines and the exceptionalization of conflict situations so that violence becomes natural or acceptable.

Finally, by disseminating research-based reflection, it has been possible to provoke discussions that have not been possible before due to the overly prudent culture of harmony, as the Pontianak Appeal showed.

Democratic dialogue will introduce democratic noise and it will wipe away the traditional Indonesian harmony understood as an orientation that attaches responsibility for violence to expressions that could give rise to anger, rather than to the violent acts themselves. At the same time it will introduce democratic, institutionalized conflict resolution mechanisms and open cooperation for the definition, within the limits of national legislation, of the rules of inter-ethnic and inter-religious interaction. Practices of institutionalized communication between ethnic and religious groups, and between communities and the police, are an integral part of the strategy of democratic dialogue against conflict.

Prudence is needed:

1. for the deconstruction of the reality of stereotypical agency;
2. for the creation of the rules of inter-ethnic and inter-religious interaction, and;
3. for the cherishing of pluralism and the peaceful traditions of different communities.

Despite the need for openness and frank dialogue, communities need to see the connection between strategies of conflict and the labeling of the Madurese as thieves, the Dayaks as stupid cannibals and the Malays as a lazy *amok* group. This is why a certain self-restraint and prudence is needed, even as people grow freer at expressing their grievances and complaints. What is most important is not that people stop repeating stereotypical expressions, but that people see behind them and are informed about the fact that most Madurese do not carry knives, that most Dayaks are actually very intelligent, and that most Malays are really quite industrious. Seeing the variety of human beings, the variety of collective identities, and the humanness of all individuals frames stereotypical images and puts them into a larger perspective in which people can no longer see a Madurese/Dayak/ Malay individual simply through a stereotypical characterization.

Academic diplomacy can participate in all of these tasks. Research that is empirically more accurate than rumors and common wisdom can alleviate central stereotypes, while a more critical approach to reified concepts of human agency can attack the very foundation of treating individuals as representatives of a groups with objective characteristics that determine an individual's behavior.

Furthermore, educational events can be systematically used to bridge antagonistic divides, and help people make their own observations of individuals from the "enemy communities."

Academically advised information and understanding on traditions makes it more difficult for politicians to manipulate tradition for their violent purposes, while lessons from comparative conflict studies can advise on normative approaches that could complement traditional approaches to peace and security. Dissemination of research-based information on life across antagonistic community divides furthermore helps communities understand each other. It helps them to tolerate or even cherish difference between them. In West Kalimantan progress towards this type of contribution by academic diplomacy has started from the top of communities. Before tangible results can be expected cultural tolerance will have to spread to the grass root levels so that young men of each of the community have tolerance towards people from other communities.

Finally, a strong state is needed for professional, well-funded and legitimate law enforcement, which knows no exceptions to the rules against violence. A strong state means an ability of the state to define explicit, unambiguous rules for the relationships between the center and the provinces, as well as rules regulating the rights of ethnic and religious groups and individuals. Scientifically collected and analyzed lessons from other conflicts that have their roots in the confusion about the rights and roles of the so-called local communities and the relationship between the center and the regions will be crucial for the planning of the rules to be enforced. Furthermore, the role and resourcing of a professional police force in this process needs lessons from conflict research, while in conflict prevention the training of the individuals responsible for law enforcement is one of the contributions in which academic diplomacy can participate.

Dialogue, prudence, transformation of masculinity and strong enforcement of well-defined rules seem to address in a cost-efficient manner the main problems and the most central junctures in the path to conflict. Yet, one should not lose sight of the multiplicity of opportunities to prevent violence. The fact that a super-strategy can be clustered neatly into these four strategies does not mean that peace efforts should or could be neatly coordinated or bureaucratized: successful peace efforts have almost always been chaotic and uncoordinated efforts that have involved many passionately motivated actors operating on very different levels. Academic diplomacy can offer ideas, concepts, dialogue and advice in the process, while it cannot offer representativeness, it is not mandated for official decisions, and it cannot enforce any decision or norms. The fact that an educational platform can offer help in the pre-negotiation of disputes does not mean that academic forums should be authoritative and committing. For the creation of an authoritative setting, educational dialogue forums have to collaborate with official actors. Without the strong role and mandate that the vice president's office offered to the ethnic leaders' classes, the emergence of the West Kalimantan ECF would not have been possible.

The focal points of different traditions of peace and conflict studies make a lot of sense in the case of West Kalimantan. Since a pragmatic study does not need to select the best of the traditions and prove its superiority, it has been possible for this study to offer some wealth of traditions in its investigation of a variety of means to help prevent conflict in West Kalimantan. Opportunities that have been focused on in traditional security studies, motives that have been focused on in the early peace research and conflict resolution literature, and identities of agents that have been the main topic of post-modern peace research are all areas where opportunities for conflict prevention can be found. However, if one wants to identify strategies for rerouting or blocking the path to conflicts, one does not need to explore the best simplified explanation of the conflict. Instead, one needs to seek opportunities from several approaches. Thus pragmatic investigation requires eclectic orientations: pragmatic solutions have to be sought by using various lenses that reveal different sides of the truth. At the same time, pragmatic starting points to truth, theory and explanation can offer a coherent meta-theoretical platform for the various methodological tools of investigation.

If truth is a pragmatic epistemic orientation rather than a mirror of reality, traditional security studies approaches as well as post-modern peace research approaches can be used in the same study just as long as they produce epistemic orientations that put us on top of things in our efforts to reduce violence. The fact that this pragmatic eclectic approach managed to give us prescriptions on what to do, and that these prescriptions turn out useful in praxis, proves its value in the research of conflicts.

The strategy of recognizing the meaningfulness of both material and socially constructed realities has clearly proved useful in the process of creating prescriptions for peace-makers in West Kalimantan. Some of the material factors have a logic of their own: a logic that is independent of the meanings we create to it. One can imagine a peaceful society without sufficient resources for law enforcement. The attitudes and constructions of people certainly influence the need for these resources. Yet, if the security of many can be threatened by few due to the lack of the proper police resources, this material fact makes it very unlikely that the society could be peaceful.

At the same time, operating with social constructions has opened up opportunities for conflict prevention. This is simply because of the fact that some "realities" are social. These realities the stakeholders can change simply by thinking differently. Despite the tradition of highly abstract discussion of the construction, deconstruction and reconstruction of social realities, this study has shown how concrete the changing of social realities can be. By inviting people to university classes focused on conflict studies one can deconstruct negative stereotypical agency, and construct the agency of inter-ethnic peace-makers. By establishing a visible forum of authoritative actors of conflict it is possible to change the language of argumentation from violent into verbal. By fearlessly engaging people through the media in an open debate on the terms of inter-ethnic interaction it is possible to deconstruct the culture of demonstrative argumentation and the association between intellectual "provocation" and violent action. All this can be seen in the reality of West Kalimantan, and it is all very concrete, even though one might have reservations about the practicality of constructivist thinking. Thinking can change the probability of people being killed by conflict.

While this study does not intend to go against the mainstream of West Kalimantan literature in its conclusion that opportunities and lack of resilience and law enforcement explain conflict better than motives or some long-term antagonism, this study does complement the existing West Kalimantan scholarship in several ways. The conflict process has been explained more fully in this study by making a serious effort to explain the pre-conflict criminality that so many stakeholders consider as crucial to the conflict dynamics. The practice of demonstrative argumentation and the meanings that can be given to moves in the conflict game can only be put into their context if one understands that individual crime irritated communal sensitivities. This is, especially since it was seen as a demonstrative challenge to local order and indigenous customs. By seeing the constructs of "visitors" and "guests" in the demand to the Madurese to leave the district as a move that followed the rejection of local rules, the dynamics of conflict makes much more sense.

This study has neither tried to go against the mainstream of conflict studies, nor has it tried to go beyond it in some ways. One of the objectives of this book has been to show how peace can be helped by pushing processes of dialogue. Literature on the facilitation of peace processes often assumes that the role of an expert starts when the parties to the conflict ask the expert to enter the scene. This almost never happens. An important element of academic diplomacy is related to the so-called pre-negotiation process that aims at opening channels of dialogue. The establishment of the ECF would not have been possible in 2001. Without confidence-building on a safe platform of education it would not have been possible to initiate the political dialogue in the forum. Thus, academic diplomacy is not limited to mediation or conflict resolution. In fact, its main role could be in the pre-negotiation and in the opening of channels of dialogue between the conflicting parties.

Conflict in West Kalimantan is complex. There does not seem to be one root cause that can explain or one cure that can end it. Yet, by assuming that civil society actors, together with the political and bureaucratic elite, can be actors in conflict prevention, the menu of options for action for peace can be broadened. This is another contribution this study on the experiences of West Kalimantan offers to the study of conflict. It is often the case that conflict research aims either at very elitist social engineering, or at an almost poetic reconstruction and critique of hegemonic discourses. Neither of these approaches is optimal for the practical aim of preventing conflicts. For that, academic investigation needs to aim for a diversity of prescriptions. It needs to focus on opportunities different actors might have for contributing to peace. Furthermore, if one looks not only at material realities that can be changed but also at the realities that people construct in their practices and in their interaction, a wider variety of methods can be identified for the promotion of a more peaceful future for West Kalimantan. Many of the measures are already on their way, while many others should be initiated. The future of Kalimantan cannot be predicted: it has to be made.

Annex 1

Inaugural Meeting of the West Kalimantan Ethnic Communication Forum with the Pasir Panjang Declaration

List of Decisions, 15.12.2008

1. **Establishment of the West Kalimantan Ethnic Communication Forum:** In order to facilitate a permanent inter-ethnic forum and in order to mobilize ethnic leaders for peace, The West Kalimantan Ethnic Communication Forum was established out of the educational Pasir Panjang class of ethnic leaders and the *Pasir Panjang Declaration* (see Figure A.1) was issued and signed for the explanation of the identity of the forum. The original copy of the inaugural declaration will be kept by the office of the vicepresident of Indonesia. Members of the Forum are the leaders of the ethnic associations of the West Kalimantan ethnic groups from the five main conflict-prone districts of the province (see Figure A.1 for the signatures of the inaugural meeting). Community leaders from other districts in West Kalimantan are welcome to the Forum. Initiators and the office of the vice-president will act in a facilitating role in the Forum.
2. **Principles of Operation:** 10 Principles of the Forum were drafted and accepted.
3. **Conflict Early Warning:** Conflict Early Warning was accepted as one of the functions of the Forum. For the exchange of early-warning information, members of the Forum exchanged contact details. In response to the call for the partnership of the Police Chief of West Kalimantan the ethnic leaders decided to share early warning information with the provincial police.
4. **Crisis Management Action:** As the common diagnosis of conflict incidents in West Kalimantan was that individual criminal incidents often escalate into communal rioting, the Forum decided to include Crisis Management Action in its functions. In a situation where there has been a triggering incident of inter-ethnic crime, the community leaders committed themselves to
   a. Report the incident to the police.
   b. Publicly condemn the incident as an individual crime (including condemnation by the leader of the community of the perpetrator) and publicly forbid the hiding of the perpetrator from the police as an act against the interests of the community.

5. **Meeting Frequency and Schedule:** While the members of the Forum will keep contact whenever the situation demands, the entire Forum will aim at meeting every six months, with the first meeting to be planned in about three months. ASEM Education Hub Network on Peace and Conflict Studies (Timo Kivimäki) will call the members of the Forum for educational events twice in 2009, after which the Forum will hold its meetings every six months. The meeting frequency will be discussed later while possibilities of funding for the meetings from the vicepresident's office will be investigated.
6. **Root Causes of Conflict:** In addition to direct conflict prevention, the forum will discuss issues that influence the root causes of conflict, and ways in which community leaders can help the removal of the root causes of conflict.
7. **Structure of the Forum:** While the office of the vice-president will be asked and has promised to act as a facilitator and chair of the Forum meetings, the next meeting will discuss the structure of the forum in more detail.
8. **Procedure for the Development of the Agendas of Meetings:** All members have the right to suggest topics for the Forum meetings, and pass them to the facilitators (Prof. Alqadrie and Dr. Kivimäki), who together with the vice-president's office will arrange the topics into clusters and issues on the agenda in a way that satisfies the Forum members who have suggested the topics.

ATTACHMENTS:

A. Deklarasi Pasir Panjang (Declaration) with Signatures
B. 10 Principles of the Forum

Translation:

PASIR PANJANG DECLARATION

In the pursuit of peace and harmony between communities and to establish social justice in West Kalimantan, we, on December 14–15, 2008, at Palapa Beach Hotel, Pasir Panjang, Singkawang, West Kalimantan, agree to institutionalize the spirit, initiative, strength and togetherness of the diverse groups in the establishing of a new institution, *The West Kalimantan Ethnic Communication Forum.*

The Forum will implement the mission and the effort of conflict transformation and sustainable peace building in West Kalimantan.

In this spirit, this declaration is based on dialogue and consensus without personal or ethnic interest.

COMMUNICATION FORUM INTER-ETHNIC GROUPS IN WEST KALIMANTAN

Attachment B of the inaugural meeting (translation)

Principles of the West Kalimantan Communication Forum:

1. The Forum is established to respond to the roots of violent conflict, which include unjust structures and relationships, and to solve these sources of conflict.
2. The Forum's work is based on long-term commitment.
3. The Forum will apply integrated approaches that involve various levels of traditional administration.
4. The Forum will develop approaches and methodologies that can be integrated into its programs of conflict prevention.
5. The Forum will apply non-violent approaches to peace-building and conflict transformation.
6. The Forum's activity will be based on solid analysis and a participative approach that will involve various groups.
7. The Forum will be attentive to the needs and problems of people in West Kalimantan communities.
8. The Forum's activity represents a partnership of diverse communities that share and work for the universal values of human rights.
9. The Forum advocates a local, national and global transformation towards more just societies.
10. The Forum aims at supporting and empowering civil society in the pursuit of sustainable peace.

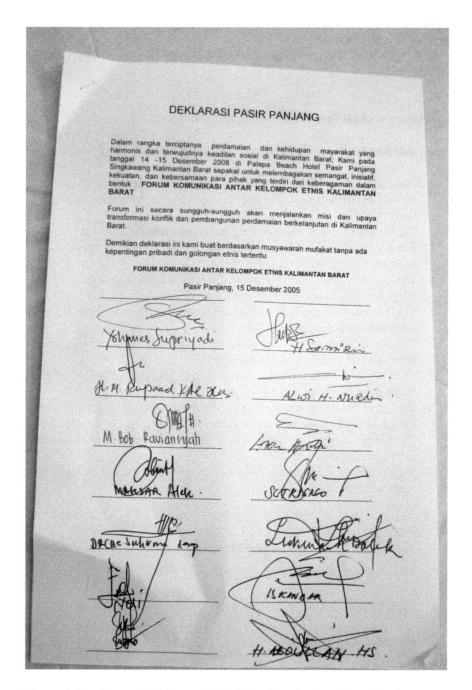

Figure A.1 Annex A (of Annex 1): Pasir Panjang Declaration with signatures

ARIS BAHARIYONO. S.Si.

H. Anwar Mochtar.

ACHMAD RIDWAN.

dr. Don. D. (CoSo SG)

Handra Kurniawan

SIMTITI

Muhammad.

Inisiator dan Fasilitator

Syarif Algadrie
(Syarif. Algadrie)

Timo Kivimäki

Mengetahui:

Prof. Dr. Djohermansyah Djohan, MA

Annex 2
Pontianak Declaration (translation)

Recognizing the fact that, in the previous communal conflicts, conflicting parties have acted with impunity, without the risk of retribution, assuming that the conflict context meant that normal moral and legal norms did not apply, we, the leaders of West Kalimantan's community groups, declare that from now on community tension and ethnic conflict offer no excuse for violent or criminal violence. From now on, a murder will be a murder and a violation of human rights will be a violation of human rights both as regards community custom and as regards the law. The traditions of our communities will no longer be allowed to be used for the legitimation of violence against a member of another ethnic community.

Bibliography

Interviews and Correspondence

Abdul Kadir U. (Haji) 2000. Head, Office of Transmigration and six of his assistants, West Kalimantan. Interview by the author, interpreted by Onga Alqadrie, February 2000.

Abdullah (Haji) 2006. Madurese religious leader in Sungai Pinyu. Interview by Erdi Abidin, in Sungai Pinyu, March 25, 2006.

Abdurrahman 2006. Sambas Malay, Student of UNTAN, Participated in the Sambas riots. Discussions on March 17, 2006 and March 19, 2006.

Acap, S. 2006/2007/2008/2009/2010. Ketua Dewan Adat (Head of the regional cultural organization), leader of Dayaks in Kabupaten Bengkayang, the initiator of the Sanggau Ledo Peace Process. Interview by the author, March 2006, October 2007, November and December 2008, March 2009 and June 2010.

Affendi, M. 2005. Bupati (Regent) of Ketapang. Interview by the author, in Ketapang, January 6, 2005.

AJ 2001. Chinese merchant from Tebas. Interview, based on a questionnaire by the author by S.I. Alqadrie.

Aleksius 2006. Head of the Sub-district of Jagoi Babang. Interview in Jagoi Babang on March 22, 2006.

Ali (Haji) 2005. Then head of Gamisma (a Madurese religious cultural organization in the Singkawang/Sambas area). Interview by the author in Singkawang, January 5, 2005.

Alqadrie, Syarif I. 2000–2010. Interviews and discussion in various parts of WestKalimantan, Indonesia and Europe.

Andoth, F. 2006. Head of Sub-district (Camat), Sanggau Ledo, Interview by the author, Sanggau Ledo, March 22, 2006

Anonymous IDPs 2003. Interviews with one religious leader (PS2), two Madurese wives and one elderly womanin Bhakti Suci and Satuan Pemukiman 2 IDP camps. (Team: author, Delsy Ronnie, Yulia Sugandi, Iqbal Firdiansjah), October 10, 2003.

Anonymous Madurese refugees 2000. Interviews by the author in the City of Pontianak, February 15, 2000.

Asam Djarak 2003. Graduate student and official of the Sanggau district government. Interview in Sanggau, March 31, 2003.

AT 2006. Head of a village in Sanggau Ledo. Interview with the author in Sanggau Ledo on March 22, 2006.

Atio, S. 2004/2005/2006/2007/2008/2009/2010. Indonesian Conflict Studies Network Translator and CAEIRU Researcher. Interviews 2004–2010.

Awang, I. 2003. Mayor of Singkawang. Presentation in an ICSN Conference, March 6–8, 2003, in Pontianak.

Bachtiar, H. 2005. SEKDA (secretary of the regency). Interview by the author in Ketapang, January 6, 2005.

Bamba, J. 2003. Executive Director of the Institute of Dayakology. Interview in Pontianak, November 10, 2003.

Benediktus 2007. Dayak Student of Singkawang in UNTAN officials class, discussion at UNTAN class, October 21, 2007.

Bernardinus, B. 2006. Ketua Benua (Head of the regional cultural order of six villages). Dayak fighter-chief, Sanggau Ledo. Interview by the author, March 22, 2006.

Boni, D. 2009. Head of Dewan Adat Dayak, Sambas. Discussion and speech at UNTAN Conference on Ethnic Communication Forum, March 28, 2009.

Burhanuddin A.R.H. 2003/2007/2008. Head of the Sambas District. Interviews and discussions by the author, 2003, 2007 and 2008.

Cornelis, M.H. 2009. Governor of West Kalimantan. Discussion on November 3, 2009.

Darwis, 2009b. Head of Sambas Malay Organization (Ketua Dewan Adat Malay Sambas). Comment at a meeting of District officials, all Sambas head of sub-districts (Camaats), deputy head of district police (KaPolRes), all secretaries of the district (KaPolSec), leaders of ethnic, religious and youth organizations, October 29, 2009.

Darwis 2009c. Head of Sambas Malay Organization (Ketua Dewan Adat Malay Sambas). Discussion in Sambas, October 29, 2009.

Dede 2006. Eye-witness and friend of the two victims of the Ledo case 1997. Interview by the author, March 23, 2006.

DF 2006. Police official in Ledo. Interview by the author in Ledo on March 22, 2006.

Djohermansyah D.D., 2008–2010. Until 2010 political deputy of the vice-president of Indonesia, after that Director-General for Decentralization, Ministry of Home Affairs. Interviews and discussions with the author.

Eka H. 2007–2010. Director of CAEIRU, Center for the Deepening of Religious Harmony at the STAIN, National Higher Education College for Islamic Studies. Interviews and discussions.

Female student of STAIN, Sambas Malay, Interview in Pontianak on March 24, 2006.

Finnish Forestry consultant in Kalimantan 1999. Interviews by the author in Helsinki, March 15.

Haitami, S. 2008–2010. Rector of STAIN, National Higher Education College for Islamic Studies. Interviews and discussions.

Haryadi, S. 2005. Member of the core group of Gamisma. Interview by the author in Singkawang area, January 5.

Hilarinus 2009. Discussion at UNTAN S2 class. November 2, 2009.

Javanese transmigrant 2003. Graduate student. Discussion in Sanggau, March 29, 2003.

JM1 2001. 47-year-old organizer of Madurese neighborhood watch, a militia in Sari Makmur. Interview by S.I. Alqadrie, based on a questionnaire by the author.

JM2 2001. Madurese fighter. Interview by S.I. Alqadrie, based on a questionnaire by the author.

LBH 2001.A Chinese shopkeeper from Sambas. Interview by S.I. Alqadrie, based on a questionnaire by the author, 2001.

Leo, G. 2007. Head of the district police. Interview in Bengkayang (together with his staff), October 23, 2007.

Liswan, H.S.E. 2005. Member of the Gamisma board. Interview by the author in the Singkawang area, January 5, 2005.

Luna, J. 2006. Head of District (Bupati), Bengkayang. Interview in Bengkayang, March 21, 2006.

Maksal, A. 2007. Leader of the Chinese Traditional Community in Bengkayang District. Discussions in Pasir Panjang, October 2007.

Marsat, S. 2005. Member of the core Gamisma board. Interview by the author in Singkawang area, January 5, 2005.

Mastro, Head of Sub-District (Camat), Singkawang Utara. Interview by the author in Singkawang Utara, March 16, 2006.

MJ 2003. Student activist from Jawaii. Interview by the author with a Malay, March 2003.

MT 2001. Malay teenage fighter from Sambas. Interview by S.I. Alqadrie, based on a questionnaire by the author.

Muhammad R. (Haji Muhammad) 2005. Madurese habib (Islamic teacher), member of Gamisma. Interview by the author in Singkawang area, January 5, 2005.

Muksin, F.A. 2006. Head of Sub-District (Camat) of Samalantan, Sambas. Interview by the author in Selamantan, March 24, 2006.

Munawar, M.S. 2003. Senior Teacher at the IAIN Pontianak. Discussion in Pontianak, March 6–8, 2003.

Nagian 2003. Madurese student activist. Interview in Pontianak, March 6–8,. 2003.

Ngusmanto G.M. 2003. Lecturer at Universitas Tanjungpura Graduate Program (S2). Interview in March 2003.

NY 2001. Ledo Dayak fighter, 25 years old. Interview by S.I. Alqadrie, based on a questionnaire by the author.

Pandjiwinata, I., Brig. Gen. 2003. Police Chief of West Kalimantan. Interview in Pontianak, March 23, 2003.

Razi, F. 2006. Deputy Chief of Academic Affairs, STAIN. Interview by the author in Pontianak, March 20, 2006.

Refiansyah 2007. Member of Gamisma board. Interview by the author in Pasir Panjang, October 15, 2007.

RR 2001. Chinese party to West Kalimantan conflict. Interview by S.I. Alqadrie, based on a questionnaire by the author.

Rudiman 2007. Leader of the Malay Community of Bengkayang District. Interview by the author in Pasir Panjang, October 15, 2007.

Rupaat, H.M. 2005/2007. Member in 2005 and leader in 2007 of the core group of Gamisma. Interview by the author in Singkawang area, January 5, 2005 and October 15–16, 2007.

SA 2001. 32-year-old Dayak fighter from Kecamatan Tebas. Interview, based on a questionnaire by the author, by S.I. Alqadrie.

Sabran, (Haji) 2006. Madurese religious leader in Sungai Pinyu. Interview by Erdi Abidin, in Sungai Pinyu, based on a questionnaire by the author, March 25, 2006.

Sahyudin, H.S. 2004. Former head of the subdistrict of Mandur in Landak. Interview in Mandur, Landak, January 19, 2004.

Sedau 1 2006 Anonymous IDP from Semelautan, Bengkayang, now living in Sedau, South of Singkawang. Interview by the author in Sedau, March 15, 2006.

Sedau 2 2006. Anonymous IDP from Selakau, Sambas, now living in Sedau, South of Singkawang. Interview by the author in Sedau, March 15, 2006.

Sedau 3 2006. Anonymous IDP from Selakau, Sambas, now living in Sedau, South of Singkawang. Interview by the author in Sedau, March 15, 2006.

Sedau 4 2006. Anonymous IDP from Sandayang, Sanggau Ledo, now living in Sedau, South of Singkawang. Interview by the author in Sedau, March 15, 2006.

SN 2001. 52-year-old organizer of Madurese neighborhood watch, a militia in Penjajab. Interview, based on a questionnaire by the author, by S.I. Alqadrie.

Sugandi, Y. 2003. MA student at the University of Jyväskylä. Interview in Copenhagen, October 7–12, 2003.

Suratman 2006. Sambas Malay, Student of UNTAN, participated in the Sambas riots. Discussions on March 17, 2006 and March 19, 2006.

TB 2001. 28-year-old Malay fighter. Interview, based on a questionnaire by the author, by S.I. Alqadrie.

Thoha, A. Md. 2005. 37-year-old Madurese businessman (construction, large-scale), member of FKBM and Gamisma, interviews by the author in Singkawang, January 4–5, 2005.

TK 2003. Anonymous village head. Interview by the author in Tanjung Keracut, Sambas, October 4, 2003.

TKK 2003. Anonymous youth leader in Tanjung Keracut, Sambas. Interview by the author in Tanjung Keracut, October 4, 2003.

Tobing, E.T. 2010. Head of police in West Kalimantan (KAPOLDA KalBar). Discussion in conjunction with a training day by the author for the Kalimantan Police, in Pontianak, June 8, 2010.

TT 2001. Chinese party to West Kalimantan conflict. Interviews, based on a questionnaire by the author, by S.I. Alqadrie.

Welles, J. 2006. Chinese Catholic student, lived in Pemangkat during the Sambas riots. Discussions in Bengkayang, Singkawang and Pontianak, March 22–25, 2006.

Widjaja K. 2003. UNTAN lecturer, PhD candidate at University of Malaysia, Sarawak. Discussions in Pontianak, March 6–8, 2003.

XX 2008. Public servant from Sanggau district, served in Sanggau Ledo during the conflict. Discussion in Pontianak, May 2, 2008.

YD 2001. Malay fighter. Interview, based on a questionnaire by the author, by S.I. Alqadrie.

YMD 2001. Dayak fighter. Interview, based on a questionnaire by the author, by S.I. Alqadrie.

YMT 2001. 23-year-old Dayak fighter. Interview, based on a questionnaire by the author, by S.I. Alqadrie.

Yon Gedean 2006. Sub-District Official (KasiKosos/SecDa), Sanggau Ledo. Interview by the author in Sanggau Ledo, March 22, 2006.

Yuyun Kurniawan 2003. Forestry activist. Interview in Pontianak, March 2, 2003.

Books and Articles

Acemoglu, D. and Robinson, J.A. 2006. *Economic Origins of Dictatorship and Democracy.* Cambridge: Cambridge University Press.

Acharya, A. 2009. *Constructing a Security Community in Southeast Asia: ASEAN and the Problem of Regional Order.* 2nd edition. London: Routledge.

Aditjondro, G.J. 1999. *Is Oil Thicker than Blood?: A Study of Oil Companies, Interests and Western Complicity in Indonesia's Annexation of East Timor.* Commack, NY: Nova Science Publishers.

Aditjondro, G.J. 2001. "Guns, Pamphlets and Handie-Talkies: How the Military Exploited Local Ethno-Religious Tensions in Maluku to Preserve their Political and Economic Privileges," in *Violence in Indonesia,* edited by W. Wessel and G. Wimhofer. Hamburg: Abera Verlag Markus Voss, 100–128.

Adler, E. 2002. "Constructivism and International Relations," in *Handbook of International Relation,* edited by W. Carsnæs, T. Risse and B. Simmons. Newbury Park, CA: Sage.

Agenzia Fides 2011. *ASIA/INDONESIA-Peace in the Moluccas through the social media, while the government closes 300 radical websites.* Blog published by the information service of the Pontifical Mission Societies, at October 7, 2011.

Alqadrie, S.I. 1987. *Cultural Differences and Social Life among Three Ethnic Groups in West Kalimantan, Indonesia.* M.Sc. Thesis. Lexington, KY: Department of Rural Sociology, College of Agriculture, University of Kentucky.

Alqadrie, S.I. 2002. *A Comparison of Conflict Patterns in Kalimantan.* Paper to the Indonesian Conflict Studies Network Conference, organized by the Universitas Katolik Parahyangan and Nordic Institute of Asian Studies, Bandung, September 27, 2002.

Alqadrie, S.I. 2009. "Seruan Pontianak," *Equator*, October 4, 2009.

Asia Times 1997. "Fight to the death for tribal rights," *Asia Times*, February 20, 1997.

Austin, A., Fischer M. and Wils, O. 2003. *Peace and Conflict Impact Assessment: Critical Views on Theory and Practice.* Berlin: Berghof Research Center for Constructive Conflict Management.

Bamba, J. 2000. "Land, Rivers, and Forests: Dayak Solidarity and Ecological Decline, Lessons from the Dayak of Indonesia," in *Indigenous Social Movements and Ecological Resilience*, edited by J.B. Alcorm and A.G. Royo. Washington, DC: Biodiversity Support Program, 5–15.

Bambang H.S. 2003. *Konflik Antara Kommunitas Etnis di Sambas 1999.* [Conflict between Commuities in Sambas 1999.] Pontianak: Romeo Grafika.

Bappenas, PSPK-UGM and UNDP. 2006. *Justice for All? An Assessment of Access to Justice in Five Provinces of Indonesia.* Available at www.undp.or.id/pubs/docs/Justice%20for%20All_.pdf (accessed July 17, 2012).

Barron, P. and Madden, D. 2003. *Violence and Conflict Resolution in Non-Conflict Regions: The Case of Lampung, Indonesia.* Jakarta: World Bank.

Bertrand, J. 2004. *Nationalism and Ethnic Conflict in Indonesia.* Cambridge: Cambridge University Press.

Blumer, H. 1962. "Society as Symbolic Interaction," in *Human Behavior and Social Process: An Interactionist Approach*, edited by A.M. Rose. Boston, MA: Houghton Mifflin, 179–92.

Booth, K. 1991. "Security and Emancipation," *Review of International Studies* 17(4), 313–26.

Booth, K. 1995. Human Wrongs and International Relations. *International Affairs* 71(1), 103–126.

Bouvier, H. and Smith, G. 2006. "Of Spontaneity and Conspiracy Theories: Explaining Violence in Central Kalimantan," *Asian Journal of Social Science* 34(3), 475–91.

Bouvier, H., de Jonge, H. and Smith, G. 2006. "Introduction," *Asian Journal of Social Sciences* 34(3), 357–9.

Brooks, S.G. 1997. "Duelling Realism," *International Organization* 51(3), 445–7.

Brown, D. 2001. *Why Might Constructed Nationalist and Ethnic Ideologies Come into Confrontation with Each Other?* Hong Kong: Southeast Asia Research Center, City University of Hong Kong.

Brown, J. and Isaacs, D. 2005. *The World Café: Shaping Our Futures through Conversations that Matter.* San Francisco: Berrett-Koehler Publishers.

Brown, M.E., Coté, Jr., O.R., Lynn-Jones, S.M. and Miller, S.E. 1997. *Nationalism and Ethnic Conflict: An International Security Reader.* Cambridge, MA: The MIT Press.

Burhanuddin, A.R.H. 2003. *Revitalisasi Sosial Pasca Rusuh Sosial Sambas* [Social Revitalization after the Sambas Conflict]. Paper to UNTAN/ICSN conference on Media and Conflict, Pontianak October 6–8, 2003.

Burton, J. 1990. *Conflict: Resolution and Prevention.* New York: St. Martin's Press.

Bush, K. 1998. *A Measure of Peace: Peace and Conflict Impact Assessment (PCIA) of Development Projects in Conflict Zones.* Ottawa, ON: International Development Research Centre.

Buzan, B. and Hansen, L. 2009. *The Evolution of International Security Studies.* Cambridge: Cambridge University Press.

Choy, L.K. 1999. *A Fragile Nation: The Indonesian Crisis.* Singapore: World Scientific.

Colapietro, V.M. 2005. "Charles Sanders Peirce," in *A Companion to Pragmatism*, edited by J.R. Shook and J. Margolis. Oxford: Blackwell Publishing.

Coleman, J.S. 1966. "Individual Interests and Collective Action," *Public Choice* 1(1), 49–62.

Coleman, J.S. 1990. *Foundations of Social Theory.* London and Cambridge, MA: Belknap Press.

Collier, P. 2000. "Ethnicity, Politics and Economic Performance," *Economics and Politics* 12(3) (November), 225–45.

Collier, P. and Hoeffler A. 1998. "On Economic Causes of Civil War," *Oxford Economic Papers* 50, 563–73.

Collier, P. and Hoeffler, A. 2000a. *Greed and Grievance in Civil War.* Available from World Bank homepage, www.worldbank.org (accessed: January 28, 2009).

Collier, P. and Hoeffler, A. 2000b. *Aid, Policy and Peace.* Available from World Bank homepage, www.worldbank.org (accessed: January 28, 2009).

Collier, P. and Hoeffler, A. 2004. "Greed and grievance in Civil War," *Oxford Economic Papers* 56(4), 563–95.

Collier, P.M., Elliott, V.L., Hegre, H., Hoeffler, A., Reynal-Querol, M. and Sambanis, N. 2003. *Breaking the Conflict Trap: Civil War and Development Policy.* Washington, DC: The World Bank.

Collins, R. 2008. *Violence: A Micro-Sociological Theory.* Princeton, NJ: Princeton University Press.

Connell, R.W. 2002. *Gender.* Cambridge: Polity.

Cribb, R. 2001. "Genocide in Indonesia, 1965–66," *Journal of Genocide Research* 3(2), 219–39.

Crouch, H. 1978. *The Army and Politics in Indonesia.* Ithaca, NY: Cornell University Press.

Curry, T.R. 2005. "Integrating Motivating and Constraining Forces in Deviance Causation: A Test of Causal Chain Hypotheses in Control Balance Theory," *Deviant Behavior* 26(6), 571–99.

Darwis 2009a. "Seruan Pontianak; jawab dari Sambas" [Pontianak Appeal: reaction from Sambas], *Equator*, October 1, 2009.

Davenport, C. 2007. *State Repression and the Domestic Democratic Peace.* New York: Cambridge University Press.

Davidson, J.S. 2003. "The Politics of Violence on an Indonesian Periphery," *South East Asia Research* 11(1), 59–89.

Davidson, J.S. 2007. "Culture and Rights in Ethnic Violence," in *The Revival of Tradition in Indonesian Politics,* edited by J.S. Davidson and D. Henley, 224–46.

Davidson, J.S. 2008. *From Rebellion to Riots: Collective Violence in Indonesian Borneo.* Madison, WI: University of Wisconsin Press.

Davidson, J.S. and Henley, D., eds. 2007. *The Revival of Tradition in Indonesian Politics.* London and New York: Routledge.

Davidson, J.S. and Kammen, D. 2002. "Indonesia's Unknown War and the Lineages of Violence in West Kalimantan," *Indonesia* 73(April), 53–87.

Davies, J.C. 1962. "Toward a Theory of Revolution," *American Sociological Review* 27, 429–69.

De Jonge, H. and Nooteboom, G. 2006. "Why the Madurese? Ethnic Conflicts in West and East Kalimantan Compared," *Asian Journal of Social Science* 34(2), 354–76.

Dewey, J. and Bentley, A. 1949. *Knowing and the Known.* Boston, MA: Beacon Press.

DFID (Department for International Development) 2002. *Conducting Conflict Assessments: Guidance Notes.* London: DFID.

Djalal, D. (Dini) 1997. "Fight to the Death for Tribal Rights," *Asia Times,* February 20, 1997.

Eck, K. and Hultman, L. 2007. "Violence Against Civilians in War," *Journal of Peace Research* 44(2), 623–34.

Eklöf, S. 1999. *Indonesian Politics in Crisis: The Long Fall of Suharto 1996–98.* Copenhagen: NIAS Press.

Elster, J. 1989. *Nuts and Bolts for the Social Sciences.* Cambridge: Cambridge University Press.

Fearon, J.D. 1995. "Rationalist Explanations for War," *International Organization* 49(3), 379–414.

Fearon, J.D. 2005. "Primary Commodities Exports and Civil War," *Journal of Conflict Resolution* 49(4), 483–507.

Fearon, J.D. and Laitin, D.D. 2011. "Sons of the Soil, Migrants, and Civil War," *World Development* 39(2), 199–211.

Feith, H. 1968. "Dayak Legacy," *Far Eastern Review,* January 25, 134.

Fisher, R.J. 1972. "Third Party Consultation: A Method for the Study and Resolution of Conflict," *Journal of Conflict Resolution* 16, 67–94.

Fisher, R.J. 1990. *The Social Psychology of Intergroup Conflict and International Conflict Resolution.* New York: Springer Verlag.

Fisher, S. 2000. *Working With Conflict: Skill and Strategies for Action.* New York: Zed Books.

Fisher, R. and Ury, W. 1981. *Getting to Yes: Negotiating Agreement Without Giving In.* Boston, MA: Houghton Mifflin.

FES (Friedrich Ebert Stiftung) 2004. *Peace and Conflict Impact Assessment: Methodological Guidelines* and *Annex.* Berlin: FES.

Frankl, V.E. 1966. "What is Meant by Meaning?" *Journal of Existentialism* 7(25), 21–8.

Fromm, E. 1941. *Escape from Freedom.* New York: Rinehart and Co.

Galtung, J. 1966. "Rank and Social Integration: A Multi-Dimensional Approach," in *Sociological Theories in Progress,* edited by J. Berger, M. Zelditch, Jr. and B. Anderson. Boston, MA: Houghton Mifflin.

Galtung, J. 1969. "Violence, Peace and Peace Research," *Journal of Peace Research* 6(3), 167–91.

Galtung, J. 1971. "A Structural Theory of Imperialism," *Journal of Peace Research* 8(2), 81–117.

Galtung, J. 1972. "Theory and Practice of Security," *Instant Research on Peace and Violence* 2(6), 109–12.

Galtung, J. and Höivik, T. 1971. "Structural and Direct Violence: A Note on Operationalization," *Journal of Peace Research* 8(1), 73–6.

Gerring, J. 2005. "Causation: A Unified Framework for the Social Science," *Journal of Theoretical Politics* 17(2), 163–98.

Glaser, C.L., 1995. "Realists as Optimists: Cooperation as Self-Help," *International Security* 19(3), 50–90.

Gleditsch, N.-P., Wallensteen, P., Eriksson, M., Sollenberg, M. and Strand, H. 2002. "Armed Conflict 1946–2001: A New Dataset," *Journal of Peace Research* 39(5), 615–37.

Gochman, C.S. 1990. "The Geography of Conflict: Militarized Interstate Disputes Since 1816," paper presented to the annual meeting of the International Studies Association, Washington, DC, April 10–14.

Goldsmith, B.E. 2006. "A Universal Proposition? Region, Conflict, War and the Robustness of the Kantian Peace," *European Journal of International Relations* 12(4), 533–63.

Goldsmith B.E. 2007. "A Liberal Peace in Asia?" *Journal of Peace Research* 44(1), 5–27.

Gurr, T.R. 1970. *Why Men Rebel.* Princeton, NJ: Princeton University Press.

Gurr, T.R. 1980. *Handbook of Political Conflict.* New York: Free Press.

Gurr, T.R. 1993. *Minorities at Risk: A Global View of Ethnopolitical Conflicts.* Washington, DC: US Institute for Peace.

Gurr, T.R. 1994. "Peoples against States: Ethnopolitical Conflict and the Changing World System—1994 Presidential Address," *International Studies Quarterly* 38(3), 347–77.

Gurr, T. R. 2000. "Ethnic Warfare on the Wane," *Foreign Affairs* 79(3)(May/June), 52–64.

Gurr, T.R. and Duvall, R. 1973. "Civil Conflict in the 1960s," *Comparative Political Studies* 6, 135–70.

Gurr, T.R. and Lichbach, M.I. 1986. "Forecasting Internal Conflicts," *Comparative Political Studies* 19(1), 3–38.

Habermas, J. 1971. *Towards a Rational Society.* London: Heinemann.

Hansen, L. 2006. *Security as Practice: Discourse Analysis and the Bosnian War.* London: Routledge.

Harbom, L. and Wallensteen, P. 2009. "Armed Conflict, 1946–2008," *Journal of Peace Research* 46(4), 577–87.

Harsanyi, J.C. 1961. "On the Rationality Postulates Underlying the Theory of Cooperative Games," *Journal of Conflict Resolution* 5(2), 178–96.

Harsono, A. et al. 2009. Seruan Pontianak, *Pontianak Pos*, September 28, 2009 available at http://andreasharsono.blogspot.com/2009/09/seruan-pontianak.html (accessed March 27, 2012).

Haseman, J. 1999. "Borneo Violence Overstretching Jakarta's Forces," *Jane's Defence Weekly*, April 14.

Heidegger, M. 1982. *The Basic Problem of Phenomenology.* Bloomington, IN: Indiana University Press.

Hempel, C. 1965. *Aspects of Scientific Explanation and Other Essays in the Philosophy of Science.* New York: Free Press.

Herriman, N. 2006. "The Killings of Alleged Sorcerers in South Malang: Conspiracy, Ninjas, or 'Community Justice'?" in *Violent Conflicts in Indonesia: Analysis, Representation and Resolution*, edited by C.A. Coppel. London: RoutledgeCurzon.

Hertz, J. 1950. "Idealist Internationalism and the Security Dilemma," *World Politics* 2(1), 157–80.

Hertz, J. 1951. *Political Realism and Political Idealism.* Chicago, IL: University of Chicago Press.

Hertz, J. 1959. *International Politics in the Atomic Age.* New York: Columbia University Press.

Hoadley, S. and Rüland, J. 2006. *Asian Security Reassessed.* Singapore: Institute of Southeast Asian Studies.

Horowitz, D.L. 2003. *The Deadly Ethnic Riot.* Berkeley, CA: California University Press.

HSRP (Human Security Research Project) 2006. *Human Security Brief 2006.* Vancouver, BC: University of British Colombia, Human Security Centre. Available at www.isn.ethz.ch/isn/Digital-Library/Publications/Detail/?ots591=0c54e3b3-1e9c-be1e-2c24-a6a8c7060233&lng=en&id=27140 (accessed July 23, 2012).

Human Rights Watch 1997. *West Kalimantan: Communal Violence in West Kalimantan.* www.hrw.org/reports/1997/12/01/communal-violence-west-kalimantan (accessed July 21, 2012).

Hume, D. 1777. *An Enquiry Concerning Human Understanding*, edited by P.N. Nidditch. 3rd edition. Oxford: Clarendon Press, 1975.

Husain, F. 2007. *To See the Unseen: Scenes Behind the Aceh Peace Treaty.* Jakarta: Health & Hospital Indonesia.

Huxley, T. 2002. *Disintegrating Indonesia? Implications for Regional Security*, Adelphi Paper 349. London: Oxford University Press for the International Institute for Strategic Studies.

IDRD (Institute of Dayakology Research and Development) 1999. "The Role of *Adat* in the Dayak and Madurese War," *Kalimantan Review*, English edition 2, 39–44.

International Crisis Group 2001. *Indonesia: The Aftermath of Mass Murder in Kalimantan*. Jakarta/Brussels: ICG, 27 June.

Jacobs, S., Jacobson, R. and Marchbank, J., eds 2000. *States of Conflict: Gender, Violence and Resistance*. London: Zed Books.

James, W. 1909. *The Meaning of Truth, A Sequel to "Pragmatism"*. New York: Longmans, Green.

James, W. 1912. *Works Essays in Radical Empiricism*. New York: Longmans, Green.

James, W. 1977. *The Writings of William James*, edited by John J. McDermott. New York: Random House.

Jönsson, C. 1979. "The Paradoxes of Superpowers: Omnipotence or Impotence," in *Power, Capacity and Interdependence*, edited by K. Goldmann and C. Jönsson. London and Beverly Hills, CA: Sage, 63–83.

Juleng, H. 2003a. Conflict in West Kalimantan. Paper to UNTAN/ICSN Conference, Media and Conflict, October 6–8, 2003, in Pontianak.

Juleng, H. 2003b. *Posisi Masyarakat Dayak Dalam Konflik di Sambas* [The Position of the Dayak Community in the Sambas Conflict]. Paper to UNTAN/ICSN Conference, Media and Conflict, Pontianak, October 6–8, 2003.

Kaufmann, C. 1997. "Possible and Impossible Solutions to Ethnic Civil Wars," in *Nationalism and Ethnic Conflict: An International Security Reader*, edited by M.E. Brown, O.R. Coté, Jr., S.M. LynnJones and S.E. Miller. Cambridge, MA: The MIT Press, 265–304.

Kelman, H.C. 1973. "Violence Without Moral Restraint: Reflections on the Dehumanization of Victims and Victimizers," *Journal of Social Issues* 29(4), 25–61.

Kelman, H.C. 1997. "Group Processes in the Resolution of International Conflicts: Experiences from the Israeli-Palestinian Case," *American Psychologist* 52, 212–20.

Kiernan, B. 2007. *Genocide and Resistance in Southeast Asia: Documentation, Denial, and Justice in Cambodia and East Timor*. Rudgers, NJ: Transaction Publishers.

Kingsbury, D. 2002. *The Politics of Indonesia*. Melbourne: Oxford University Press.

Kingsbury, D. and McCulloch, L. 2006. "Military Business in Aceh," in *Verandah of Violence: The Background to the Aceh Problem*, edited by A. Reid. Singapore: Singapore University Press, 199–224.

Kivimäki, T. 2001. "Long Peace of ASEAN," *Journal of Peace Research* 38(1), 5–25.

Kivimäki, T. 2005. Media's Contribution Towards Resolving Conflict: The Case of West Kalimantan, *Borneo Review*, 14(1), 76–91.

Kivimäki, T. 2006. *Initiating a Peace Process in Papua.* Policy Studies No. 25. Washington, DC: East West Center, www.eastwestcenter.org/publications/ initiating-peace-process-papua-actors-issues-process-and-role-international-community (accessed July 18, 2012).

Kivimäki, T. 2007. "Europe's Multilevel Challenge Of Conflict Management: The Case Of Aceh," in *Europe in Context: Insights to the Foreign Policy of the EU*, edited by T. Forsberg, T. Kivimäki and L. Laakso. Helsinki: Finnish International Studies Association.

Kivimäki, T. 2008. "Power, Interest or Culture: Is there a Paradigm that Explains ASEAN's Political Role Best?" *The Pacific Review* 21(4), 431–50.

Kivimäki, T. 2010a. "East Asian Relative Peace: Does It Exist? What Is It?" *The Pacific Review* 23(4), 503–26.

Kivimäki, T. 2010b. "The Jeju Process and the Relative Peace in East Asia," *Korean Journal of Defence Analysis* 22(3), 355–70.

Kivimäki, T. 2011. "East Asian Relative Peace and the ASEAN Way," *International Relations of the Asia Pacific* 11(1), 57–86.

Kivimäki T. and Gorman, D. 2008. *Non-governmental Actors in the Aceh Peace Process, in Non-Governmental Actors and Conflict Resolution*, edited by Anders Mellbourn and Peter Wallensteen. Stockholm: STINT.

Kivimäki, T. and Pasch P. 2009. *Peace and Conflict Impact Assessment: Burma/ Myanmar.* Bonn: Friedrich Ebert Stiftung.

Klinken, G. van 2002. "Indonesia's New Ethnic Elites," in *Indonesia: In Search of Transition*, edited by Henk Schulte Nordholt and Irwan Abdullah. Yogyakarta: Pustaka Pelajar, 67–105.

Klinken, G. van 2005. "New Actors, New Identities: Post-Suharto Ethnic Violence in Indonesia," in *Violent Internal Conflicts in Asia Pacific: Histories, Political Economies, and Policies*, edited by Dewi Fortuna Anwar. Jakarta: Yayasan Obor, 79–100.

Klinken, G. van 2007. *Communcal Violence and Democratization in Indonesia: Small Town Wars*. Routledge Contemporary Southeast Asia Series. Abingdon: Routledge.

Klinken, G. van 2008. "Blood, Timber and the State in West Kalimantan, Indonesia," *Asia Pacific Viewpoint* 49(1), 35–47.

Klotz, A. and Lynch, C. 2007. *Strategies for Research in Constructivist International Relations*. Armonk, NY: M.E. Sharpe.

Kratochwil, F.V. 1989. *Rules, Norms and Decisions*. Cambridge: Cambridge University Press.

Kreutz, J. 2006. "The Nexus of Democracy, Conflict, and the Targeting of Civilians," in *States in Armed Conflict*, edited by L. Harbom. Uppsala: Universitetstryckeriet.

Kriesberg, L. 1998. *Constructive Conflicts: From Escalation to Resolution.* Lanham, MD: Rowman and Littlefield.

Lacina, B. 2009. *Battle Deaths Dataset 1946–2008. Codebook for Version 3.0.* Available at www.prio.no/sptrans/973829835/PRIObd3.0_codebook.pdf (accessed August 26, 2011).

Lacina, B. and Gleditsch, N.P. 2005. "Monitoring Trends in Global Combat: A New Dataset of Battle Deaths," *European Journal of Population* 21(2–3), 145–66.

Lake, D.A. and Rothchild, D. 1997. "Containing Fear," in *Nationalism and Ethnic Conflict: An International Security Reader*, edited by Michael E. Brown, Owen R. Coté, Jr., Sean M. Lynn-Jones and Stephen E. Miller. Cambridge, MA: The MIT Press, 97–131.

Lederach, J.P. 1995. *Preparing for Peace: Conflict Transformation Across Cultures*, Syracuse, NY: Syracuse University Press.

Lederach, J.P. 2003. *The Little Book of Conflict Transformation.* Intercourse, PA: Good Books.

Lloyd Parry, R. 1998. What Young Men Do, *Granta* 62 (Summer), 83–123.

McAdam, A., Tarrow, S. and Tilly, C. 2001. *Dynamics of Contention.* Cambridge Studies in Contentious Politics. Cambridge: Cambridge University Press.

McBeth, J. and Cohen, M. 2002. "Murder and Mayhem," *Far Eastern Economic Review*, February 20, 26–7.

Margolis, J. 2005. "Introduction: Pragmatism, Retrospective, and Prospective," in *A Companion to Pragmatism*, edited by J.R. Shook and J. Margolis Oxford: Blackwell Publishing.

Mearsheimer, J.J. 2001. *The Tragedy Of Great Power Politics.* New York: W.W. Norton.

Messner, M.A. 1990. "When Bodies are Weapons: Masculinity and Violence in Sports," *International Review for the Sociology of Sport* 25(3), 203–220.

Messner, M.A. and Sabo, D.F. 1994. *Sex, Violence and Power in Sports: Rethinking Masculinity.* Freedom, CA: Crossing Press.

Mitchell, C.R. 2000. *Gestures of Conciliation.* Basingstoke: Macmillan.

Moravcsik, A. 2003. "Theory Synthesis in International Relations: Real Not Metaphysical," *International Studies Review* 5(1), 131–6.

Morgenthau, H.J. (revised by K.W. Thompson and W.D. Clinton), 2006 (1948). *Politics Among Nations: The Struggle For Power And Peace.* 7th edition. New York: McGraw-Hill/Irwin.

Munawar M.S. 2003. *The History of Conflict between Ethnic Groups in Sambas.* Pontianak: Kalimantan Persada Press.

Myrttinen, H. 2003. "Disarming Masculinities," *Disarmament Forum* 4(1), 37–46.

Nilan, P. 2009. "Contemporary Masculinities and Young Men in Indonesia," *Indonesia and the Malay World* 37(109), 327–44.

Nilan, P.B., Broom, A. Demartoto, A., Doron, A., Nayar, K. and Germov, J. 2008. "Masculinities and Violence in India and Indonesia: Identifying Themes and Constructs for Research," *Journal of Health and Development* 4(1), 209–228.

Onuf, N. 1989. *World of Our Making: Rules and Rule in Social Theory and International Relations.* Columbia, SC: University of South Carolina Press.

Owen, H. 2008. *Open Space Technology: A User's Guide*. 3rd edition. San Francisco, CA: Berrett-Koehler.

Parijs, P. van 1981. *Evaluationary Explanation in the Social Sciences: An Emerging Paradigm*. London and New York: Tavistock Publications.

Parsons, T. 1946. "The Science Legislation and the Role of Social Sciences," *American Sociological Review* (December), 653–66.

Patomäki, H. 2001 "The Challenge of Critical Theories: Peace Research at the Start of the New Century," *Journal of Peace Research* 38(6), 723–37.

Peluso, N.L. 2006. "Passing the Red Bowl: Creating Community Identity Through Violence in West Kalimantan, 1967–1997," in *Violent Conflict in Indonesia: Analysis, Representation, Resolution*, edited by Charles A. Coppel. Abingdon and New York: Routledge.

Peluso, N.L. 2008. "Political Ecology of Violence and Territory in West Kalimantan," *Pacific Viewpoint* 49(1), 48–67.

Peluso, N.L. and Watts, M. 2001. *Violent Environments*. Ithaca, NY and London: Cornell University Press.

Pines, C.L. 1993. *Ideology and False Consciousness: Marx and his Historical Progenitors*. Albany, NY: State University of New York Press.

Posen, B. 1993. "The Security Dilemma and Ethnic Conflict," in *Ethnic Conflict and International Security*, edited by Michael Brown. Princeton, MA: Princeton University Press, 103–124.

Pouliot, V. 2008. "The Logic of Practicality: A Theory of Practice of Security Communities," *International Organization* 62, 257–88.

Poulton, R.-E. and Youssouf, I. 1998. *A Peace of Timbuktu: Democratic Governance, Development and African Peacemaking*. Geneva: UNIDIR.

Prasojo, Z.H. 2009. *Riots on the News, West Borneo*. Pontianak: Stain Pontianak Press.

Pruitt, B. and Thomas, P. 2007. *Democratic Dialogue: A Handbook for Practitioners*. Washington, DC: GS/OAS.

Putnam, H.W. 1981. *Reason, Truth and History*, Cambridge: Cambridge University Press.

Rieber, R.W. 1991. *The Psychology of War and Peace: The Image of the Enemy*. New York: Plenum Press.

Rijoly-Matakupan, H. 2011. Provocateurs of Peace. Blog published on October 14, 2011 on the Uniting World Internet site, http://unitingworld.org.au/blogs/provocateurs-of-peace (accessed March 27, 2012).

Rios, D. 2004. "Mechanistic Explanations in the Social Sciences," *Current Sociology* 52(1), 75–89.

Robison, R. 1986. *Indonesia: The Rise of Capital*. Sydney: Allen and Unwin.

Rodan, K. and Hewison, R. 2004. *Neoliberalism and Conflict in Asia after 9/11*. Abingdon and New York: Routledge.

Rorty, R. 1991. *Objectivity, Relativism and Truth: Philosophical Papers I*. Cambridge: Cambridge University Press.

Ruggie, J.G. 1998 "Introduction: What Makes the World Hang Together," in *Constructing the World Polity*, edited by J.G. Ruggie. London: Routledge, 1–39.

Rüland, J. 2000. "ASEAN and the Asian Crisis: Theoretical Implications and Practical Consequences for Southeast Asian Regionalism," *Pacific Review* 13(3), 421–52.

Rummel, R.J. 1994. *Death by Government*. New Brunswick, NJ: Transaction Publishers.

Runciman, W.G. 1966. *Relative Deprivation and Social Justice: A Study of Attitudes to Social Inequality in Twentieth Century England.* Berkeley, CA and Los Angeles: University of California Press.

Russell, B. 1956. *Logic and Knowledge*. London: George Allen and Unwin.

Russell, B. 1984. *Theory of Knowledge: The 1913 Manuscript*. London: George Allen and Unwin.

Salancik, G.R. 1977. "Commitment and the Control of Organizational Behavior and Belief," in *New Directions in Organizational Behavior*, edited by B.M. Staw and G.R. Salancik. Clarkston, MI: St. Clair Press.

Schelling, T.C. 1980. *The Strategy of Conflict*. Reprint, illustrated and revised edition. Cambridge, MA: Harvard University Press.

Shaun, N. 2006. "Folk Intuitions on Free Will," *Journal of Cognition and Culture* 6(1–2), 57–86. Available at www.philosophy.utah.edu/faculty/nichols/Papers/JCCFinal.htm (accessed January 21, 2011).

Shook, J.R. and Margolis, J. 2005. *A Companion in Pragmatism*. Oxford: Blackwell Publishing.

Sil, R. and Katzenstein, P.J. 2010. "Beyond Paradigms: Analytic Eclecticism in the Study of World Politics: Reconfiguring Problems and Mechanisms across Research Traditions Perspectives on Politics," *Perspectives on Politics* 8(2), 411–31.

Simonsen, S.G. 2006. "Addressing Ethnic Divisions in Post-Conflict Institution-Building: Lessons from Recent Cases," *Security Dialogue* 36(3), 297–318.

Smith, G. 1997. "Carok Violence in Madura: From Historical Conditions to Contemporary Manifestations," *Folk: Journal of the Danish Ethnographic Society* 39, 57–75.

Smith, R. 2003. *Stories of Peoplehood: The Politics and Morals of Political Membership*. Cambridge: Cambridge University Press.

Snyder, G.H. 1984. "The Security Dilemma in Alliance Politics," *World Politics* 36, 461–95.

Snyder, G.H. 2002. "Mearsheimer's World: Offensive Realism and the Struggle for Security," *International Security* 27(1), 149–73.

Soysa, I. de and Neumayer, E. 2007. "Resource Wealth and the Risk of Civil War Onset: Results from a New Dataset on Natural Resource Rents, 1970–99," *Conflict Management and Peace Science* 24, 201–218.

Statement from Dayak Community Organizations Regarding the Pontianak Appeal, September 28, 2009. *Pontianak Pos.* September 30, 2009.

Staw, B.M., 1981. "The Escalation of Commitment to a Course of Action," *Academy of Management Review* 6(4), 577–87.

Stedman, S.J. 1997. "Spoiler Problems in Peace Processes," *International Security* 22(2), 151–62.

Stein, J.G. 1989. "Getting to the Table: Processes of International Prenegotiation," *International Journal* 44(2), 231–6.

Stein, J.G. 1996. "Image, Identity and Conflict Resolution", in *Managing Global Chaos: Sources of and Responses to International Conflict*, edited by C.A. Crocker, F.O. Hampson and P. Aall. Washington, DC: United States Institute of Peace Press.

Strawson, G. 1986a. *Freedom and Belief.* Oxford: Oxford University Press.

Strawson, G. 1986b. "Responsibility, Luck and Change: Reflections on Free Will and Indeterminism," *Journal of Philosophy* 96, 217–40.

Suckiel, E.K. 2005. "William James". In *A Companion to Pragmatism*, edited by John R. Shook and Joseph Margolis. Oxford: Blackwell Publishing.

Sugandi, Y. 2006. *Rural Safety Valve in Sambas Conflict, in Communal Conflicts In Kalimantan: Perspectives From The LIPI-CNRS Conflict Studies Program*, edited by G. Smith and H. Bouvier. Jakarta: LIPI-CNRS Conflict Studies Program.

Sukma, R. 2005. "Ethnic Conflicts in Indonesia: Causes and the Quest for Solution," in *Ethnic Conflicts in Southeast Asia*, edited by K. Snitwongse and W.S. Thompson. Singapore: ISEAS.

Suriansyah, G. 2004. Pengalima, Landak Malay community. Comment speech presented in ICSN Early Warning Workshop at Pontianak, January 20–21, 2004.

Svensson, I. 2011. "East Asian Peacemaking: Exploring the Patterns of Conflict Management and Conflict Settlement in East Asia," *Asian Perspective* 35(2), 163–85.

Syukur, A. 2003. *Conflict in West Kalimantan.* Paper to the ICSN Conference on Conflict Early Warning in Pontianak, March 6–8.

Taliaferro, J.W. 2001. "Security Seeking Under Anarchy: Defensive Realism Revisited," *International Security* 25(3), 128–61.

Taliaferro, J.W. 2006. "State Building for Future Wars: Neoclassical Realism and the Resource-Extractive State," *Security Studies* 15(3), 464–95.

Tangdililing, A.B. 2003. *Media and Conflict in Sambas*, presentation in an ICSN Conference, on Media and Conflict, Pontianak, October 6–8.

Tanter, R. 1998. *Rogue Regimes: Terrorism and Proliferation.* New York: St. Martin's Press.

Tilly, C. 1978. *From Mobilization to Revolution.* New York: Random House.

Turshen, M. and Twagiramariya, C., eds. 1998. *What Women Do in Wartime: Gender and Conflict in Africa.* London: Zed Books.

UNDP (United Nations Development Program) 1994. *Human Development Report 1994.* New York: UNDP.

Väyrynen, R. 1999. "From Conflict Resolution to Conflict Transformation: A Critical Review," in *The New Agenda for Peace Research*, edited by Ho-Wom Jeong. Aldershot: Ashgate, 135–60.

Vuokko, H. 2010. Yliopiston luentosalista yhteisön hyödyksi—rauhan vahvistamista Kalimantanilla [From university's lecture hall to the good of society—Building Peace in Kalimantan]. A news item at the Internet pages of the Finnish Embassy. Available at http://www.finland.or.id/public/default.asp x?contentid=197883&nodeid=31738&contentlan=1&culture=fi-FI (accessed August 1, 2012).

Wæver, O. 1995. "Securitization and Desecuritization," in *On Security*, edited by R.D. Lipschutz. New York: Columbia University Press.

Wallensteen, P. 2009. "The Strengths and Limits of Academic Diplomacy: The Case of Bouganville," in *Diplomacy in Theory and Practice*, edited by K. Aggestan and M. Jernek. Malmö: Liber, 258–81.

Waltz, K. 1979. *Theory of International Politics*, Reading, MA: Addison-Wesley.

Welsh, B. 2008. "Local and National: Keroyokan Mobbing in Indonesia," *Journal of East Asian Studies* 8(3), pp. 473–504.

Wendt, A.E. 1998. "On Constitution and Causation in International Relations," in *International Relations, 1919–1999*, edited by T. Dunne, M. Cox and K. Booth. Cambridge: Cambridge University Press, 101–118.

Wendt, A.E. 1999. *Social Theory of International Politics*. Cambridge International Relations, Vol. 67. Cambridge: Cambridge University Press.

White, A.R. 1959. *Philosopical Papers by George Edward Moore*. London: George Allen and Unwin.

Williams, L. 1996. "Bursting at the Seams: The Javanese Shove—Whether You Like It or Not," *International Herald Tribune*, December 21.

Wilson, I.D. 2006. "Continuity and Change: The Changing Contours of Organized Violence in Post-New Order Indonesia," *Critical Asian Studies* 38(2), pp. 265–97.

Wyn Jones, R. 1999. *Security, Strategy, and Critical Theory.* Boulder, CO: Lynne Rienner.

Zartman, I.W. 1989. "Prenegotiation: Phases and Functions," *International Journal* 44(2), 237–53.

Zartman, I.W. 1995. *Collapsed States: The Disintegration and Restoration of Legitimate Authority.* Boulder, CO: Lynne Rienner.

Zartman, I.W. and Kremenyuk, V. 2005. *Peace Versus Justice: Negotiating Forward- and Backward-Looking Outcomes.* Lanham, MA: Rowman and Littlefield.

Index

References to illustrations are in **bold.**